Marketing *Your* Business

AF652111

Marketing *Your* Business

A Guide to Developing a Strategic Marketing Plan

Ronald A. Nykiel

ATLANTIC®
PUBLISHERS & DISTRIBUTORS

Best Business Books®
New-York • London • Oxford

ATLANTIC®

PUBLISHERS & DISTRIBUTORS
7/22, Ansari Road, Darya Ganj
New Delhi – 110 002
Tel: 2327 3880, 2327 5880, 2328 0451
Fax: 91-11-2328 5873
E-mail: info@atlanticbooks.com
Website: www.atlanticbooks.com

Published in India by
Atlantic Publishers and Distributors, New Delhi
in association with
Best Business Books®, an imprint of The Haworth Press, Inc.
10 Alice Street, Binghamton, New York 13904-1580

First published 2003 by Best Business Books®
First Indian Reprint 2005

ISBN 81-269-0557-3

© 2003 by The Haworth Press, Inc. All rights reserved. No part of this work may be reproduced or utilized in any form or by any means, electronic or mechanical, including photocopying, microfilm, and recording, or by any information storage and retrieval system, without permission in writing from the publisher.

Printed in India by
Pushp Print Services, Delhi

Licensed for sale in India, Nepal, Sri Lanka, Maldives, Pakistan, Bhutan and Bangladesh only

CONTENTS

ABOUT THE AUTHOR

Ronald A. Nykiel, PhD, is the Conrad N. Hilton Distinguished Chair and Professor of Hotel and Restaurant Management at the Conrad N. Hilton College at the University of Houston. He is also Chairman of the Hospitality Industry Hall of Honor and the publisher of the Hospitality Business Review.

Dr. Nykiel began his business career with IBM in human resources. He has held managerial positions in market research and strategic/operational planning at Xerox and Marriott Corporation. He has been a senior officer of Holiday Corporation, serving in a development and strategic planning capacity. As a senior officer of Ramada Incorporated, Nestle's Stouffer Hotel Company, and Grand Met's Pearle Incorporated, he was responsible for all brand management and marketing functions worldwide.

Dr. Nykiel has addressed many corporate and association groups and has lectured at the Harvard Graduate School of Business and other prestigious universities on subjects including corporate strategy, marketing, consumer behavior, brand management, service excellence, and executive development topics. He has authored a number of books on business strategy, marketing, consumer behavior, and service excellence, has contributed to a variety of journals, magazines, and other publications, and has appeared on national television and radio in the United States.

Preface

Whether small or large, with a single brand or many, businesses should develop a strategic marketing plan to increase revenues, take market share, and promote new business. Revenue growth is the product of key marketing strategies that increase share, produce new customers, and extract incremental revenue from existing customers. These increased revenues allow for continued generation of growth through investment in additional marketing programs.

This book will provide businesses, new or old, with methods to enhance revenue growth through a step-by-step process or guide to preparing a strategic marketing plan. Guidelines for developing and selecting objectives, key strategies, and tactics to produce revenue and increase market share are included, as well as specific examples of each step in the strategic marketing planning process.

In addition to the step-by-step exhibits, specific marketing techniques and tools are delineated with actual examples. A sample promotional "calendar of events" shows a "how-to" example to plan and implement an ongoing series of promotions to fill every month of the year. An actual marketing plan model budget is provided, showing how to allocate expenditures to each of the marketing categories: advertising, promotions, public relations, etc., and tactical steps and ideas are presented. Appendix 1 has been designed to provide the reader with work forms that, when completed, result in a framework for a strategic marketing plan.

Irrespective of the size of your business, the strategic marketing planning process will provide a plan format that, if successfully completed, will help enhance revenue growth and generate increased demand. It will further serve to prioritize ideas into objectives and strategies that will produce measurable results—increased revenues.

Acknowledgments

I would like to thank the following individuals: Dr. Jim Myers, author of *Marketing Structure Analysis,* and Peter F. Drucker, Professor of Marketing Emeritus at The Claremont Graduate School, for sharing their knowledge on market positioning and brand preference. I would like to acknowledge Dr. Robert Buzzell, former Sabastian S. Kresge Professor of Marketing at the Harvard University Graduate School of Business, for helping me remain academically active in the field. To Eric Orkin, a sincere thanks for the healthy discussions on pricing and managing revenue. My special appreciation goes to Bill Marriott, Chairman of the Marriott Corporation; Kemmons Wilson, founder of Holiday Inns and Chairman of the Kemmons Wilson Companies; Mike Rose, former Chairman of the Promus Companies; Juergen Bartels, President and CEO of Meridien Hotels and Resorts; Bill Hulett, former President of Stouffer Hotels and Resorts; and Jim Biggar, former Chairman and CEO of Nestlé Enterprises, Inc., for the opportunities they provided me and the knowledge I gained from exposure to their leadership.

Some of my greatest marketing successes were due to the receptivity of my friends in the media, so special thanks to *USA Today*'s former president, Cathy Black, former publisher Carolyn Vespar Bivens, and Jacki Kelly, Senior Vice President, Advertising Sales. Thanks also to Steve Forbes, CEO of *Forbes* magazine.

Finally, a special acknowledgment to my father for sharing his wisdom that he gained during forty years in sales and marketing at Colgate-Palmolive, and to my son, Ron, for helping me master the computer and teaching me some new marketing tricks of his own, and to my wife Karen, for listening to both my good and bad promotional ideas during the course of my career.

Introduction

A strategic marketing plan is the basis for a win-win scenario for any size or type of business that desires to increase revenues. As greater sales and an increased number of customers are generated, higher revenues and profit are produced, which lead to more support for marketing. A strategic marketing plan is the road map to generating revenue. Frequently, this revenue is generated from incremental purchases by existing customers and creation of new demand. This is yet another win-win reason to have a strategic marketing plan for your business. Selecting the right objectives and key strategies can result in increased business, stronger revenues, and greater profits. Likewise, the lack of such a plan or even selecting the wrong strategies can result in displaced revenue, lost business, and may even increase costs. In fact, the use of a strategic marketing plan enables a business to make a better assessment of its future, thus making sound management decisions and putting itself in a position to influence its destiny.

Where should a business begin with its strategic plan; and what structure should it have? Utilizing a strategic marketing planning process will help to formulate objectives, select strategies, identify required resources, target action steps, and, yes, produce measurable results. This process also includes ways to improve the "packaging" of business by enhancing its image and appeal to existing, as well as potential customers.

This book will analyze strategic plans, their contents, and concepts that will help organize marketing ideas into productive action steps. Although the suggestions contained herein may not be applicable to every business or brand, the strategic marketing planning process has universal application as a tool to assist most organizations in developing objectives, selecting strategies, and targeting revenue-producing ideas.

The following describes a strategic marketing plan: *a broad structure that guides the process of determining the target market for your business, detailing the market's needs and wants, and then fulfilling these needs and wants better than competitive brands or businesses.*

To help simplify the planning process, the various steps that need to be addressed when developing a strategic marketing plan are outlined.

Before making a strategic marketing plan for any business, an overall strategy for the business and/or brands should be formulated.

PART A: THE STRATEGY SELECTION PROCESS

Prior to selecting marketing weapons or developing a strategic marketing plan, it is advisable to define (or redefine) your overall business strategy and positioning. In order to do this successfully, a number of focal points need to be assessed. These include, but are not limited to, your competition, industry and consumer trends, and everything else that can have an impact on your business. In Part A we will outline the tools needed to define your business strategy, assess both external and internal focal points, and help you select appropriate strategies to attain your goals.

Chapter 1

Defining Your Business Strategy

Prior to developing a strategic marketing plan, it is essential to take an objective view of your business. We are in a transitory and ever-changing period for both business firms and **marketing.** This applies to all businesses, be it a new e-commerce venture, a retail or service industry enterprise, a small firm, or a megacorporation. What worked in the past has no guarantee of working in the future as both external and internal change is taking place at a faster pace. New technologies, **new products** and services, new delivery systems, and new **competition** change the playing field on a regular and frequent basis. Any, or a combination, of these external and internal forces may suggest that it is time to redefine your business **strategy,** or, if you are managing a new brand or enterprise, define it for the first time. This process is essential prior to developing a **strategic marketing plan.**

If you were to analyze your market from a customer expectations and competitive perspective, you would likely discover that a great deal of change is taking place. You would likely see that internal changes are occurring such as: utilization of multidisciplinary management teams; managing up, down, and across; field-based management versus headquarters-based; etc., to name a few. You would see changes in how business is being conducted, such as more outsourcing, more collaborative efforts (alliances and networking), an accelerated development process, use of fewer but more responsive suppliers, etc. Businesses are seeking to develop new competitive advantages; be more market and customer oriented; improve by **benchmarking** (measuring themselves against others); and, where feasible, offer customized products or personalized services. Focal points are also changing such as looking globally versus locally, zeroing in on the value chain, and refining marketing targets. Customers are redefining value to include not just the traditional "quality at a fair price" but adding "speed and convenience" to the equation.[1]

All of these dynamics in the marketplace are not only changing how business is conducted, but also how it is defined. Before you begin the marketing planning process, take a while to reflect on your company's "core competencies" and **"driving forces."** Ask yourself these questions: (1) Where does our business make a significant contribution to the perceived customer's benefits with the end product(s) or service(s) offered? (2) What do we or can we do that is difficult for our competitors to imitate? and (3) Are we market or product/service driven and should we change? Then, record your new core values and driving forces.[2]

At this point, develop a new **mission statement.** To do so, you will need to: reexamine and record the philosophies of the firm, develop an overall **positioning** statement, and focus on your vision of the future—where you want the firm/business to go and what you want to achieve. The next sections will go into greater depth about how to prepare a positioning statement. One note of caution: take your time in drafting your mission statement and in defining your overall related business strategy. It may be very different than you originally conceived (preconceived more likely) and may also change as you go through the competitive and environmental assessment portion of the strategic marketing planning process.

Here are some hints to help you look for a potential winning business strategy. Ask yourself: can we supply something no one else does or that is in a short supply; can we do a better job than everyone else in our product or service category in supplying that product or service; can we offer a new product or service which is truly differentiated from existing products or services; and can we identify an entirely new market for product(s) or service(s)?

Once you have defined or redefined your overall business strategy and drafted your first cut at a mission statement, step back and assess all of the potential internal and external focal points impacting your business, assess your competitors, and examine external factors that may have a significant impact on your business strategy and/or how you go about marketing.

CASE EXAMPLE 1: ANOTHER PERSPECTIVE

A large waste management company recently went through the process of defining or redefining its business strategy and rethinking its mission statement as part of an overall strategic marketing planning process. For most of the history of the company, its mission statement and business strategy was focused on waste/garbage. The "old" mission statement and business strategy stated: "Our business is focused on waste removal and expansion of markets we serve, increasing volume and maintaining good community relations." Further, we seek to become number one (largest) in the regional market we serve." This was a traditional way of looking at their business. It was a product-focused and market-driven strategy.

After reexamining their business, focusing on how the business was conducted, analyzing the "value chain," thinking more broadly versus locally, and conducting a thorough review of their driving forces, the company discovered many things. First, its self-analysis revealed that its largest asset was not its trash hauling contracts, but rather its extensive land holdings—landfills throughout the **region** and country. Second, through its ownership of a rail line and extensive truck fleet, its second largest asset was its transportation system. Third, as it viewed its future, the company quickly realized that its potential was in real estate development and as a mover of solid materials. It also realized that it could capitalize on its extensive real estate and transportation capabilities to acquire new business, develop service agreements with smaller companies, and expand into other hauling businesses. The end product of this strategic marketing planning exercise to reexamine its business strategy/mission resulted in an entirely different perspective. The new mission statement and business strategy stated: "We seek to be the leader in land reclamation and related development, progressively grow our transportation business (hauling), and enhance our real estate assets through high-quality commercial and residential development."

A brief postscript of this case example is that the company not only redefined its overall business strategy, but went on to change its name and reorganize its entire managerial structure. It changed its focus and business strategy, name, and complete nature of the organization.

CASE EXAMPLE 2: PROVIDING VALUE AND REDUCING COSTS

Airline companies have long recognized the costs associated with obtaining and ticketing a customer. The old business strategy model called for extensive support of an **intermediary** system (travel agents) and a paper ticket that allowed for multiple copies for accounting and control purposes. In the old business strategy model, commissions were paid, incentives (including higher commissions) were offered, and even computer hardware and software were provided to agencies. Partly due to technology and partly due to the need to increase profitability, airline companies began to reexamine this key area of their business strategy. Driven by the financial side of the equation (lowering costs), they embarked on a multifold change in business strategy.

First, the airlines sought to lower costs through the introduction of electronic ticketing, in essence, replacing their labor with the customer's labor. The concept worked because it addressed the key words in the new definition of "value"—"speed and convenience." Incentives such as bonus miles/points, lower fares, and discounts, etc., were offered to end user(s) customers who used "e-tickets." Moreover, these customers were also bypassing the intermediary or travel agent, thus reducing the airlines' commissions costs.

Next, the airlines recognized that their flat percentage commission structure was lucrative to agents who were paid (for example purposes) 10 percent of all fares per ticket. Thus, for the same act of booking a client, an agent could receive $9.90 in commission for a $99.00 fare or $99.00 for a $990.00 fare. As airlines expanded their route systems and became more global in nature it became evident that commission payments overall were escalating. To address this cost-related item, airlines entered into a multifold new business strategy that involved reducing commissions, paying different commissions at different price/fare levels, and supporting the growth of direct customer bookings online or through their 800 numbers.

In summary, the new business strategy focused on value redefinition in a broad perspective. It focused on reducing labor and costs, while increasing customer convenience and speed of transactions. At first, there was customer resistance from both the end user and the intermediary travel agent. Today, we see the end user accepting and preferring e-tickets and fewer travel agencies.

Key Terms

benchmarking
core competencies
driving forces
mission statement
positioning
value

Chapter 2

Assessing Focal Points

At this juncture, a comprehensive assessment should be conducted which focuses on: (1) self-analysis (the business itself); (2) competition; and (3) environmental factors which can impact your business/strategy (see Exhibit 2.1).

Researching each of these areas is essential to developing the basis for a strategic marketing plan. In fact, before you can select a strategy or deploy marketing weaponry to execute those strategies you must know your product or service, your target markets and their needs, and your competition. You also need to know what the road ahead looks like with respect to the business environment in which you will be operating. In essence, your marketing strategies must be based on sound research.

In this section, a synopsis of basic types of research, selected marketing research techniques, and some analytical tools to help you categorize, prioritize, and present your research will be given.

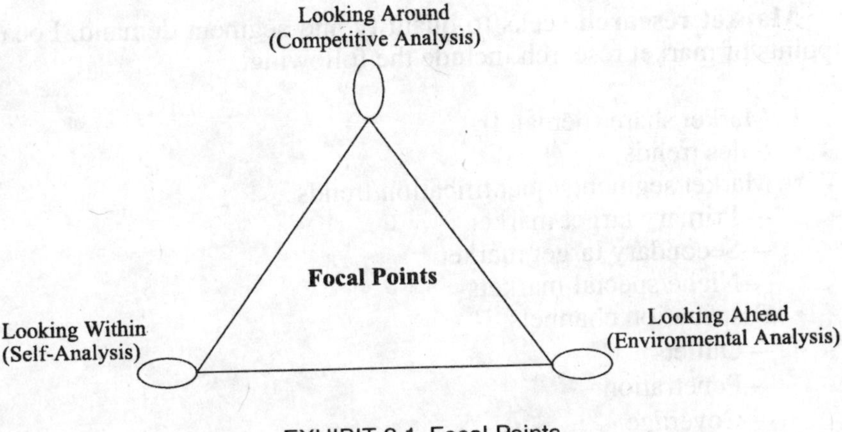

EXHIBIT 2.1. Focal Points

TYPES OF MARKETING RESEARCH

Broadly speaking, marketing research can be either quantitative or qualitative. Quantitative marketing research seeks to quantify data using numbers, projections, forecasts, etc. Qualitative marketing research seeks to identify, analyze, or profile consumers, looking at consumer attitudes, behaviors, etc. Both quantitative and qualitative marketing research can be either primary or secondary. Primary research is research you conduct yourself; secondary research is research that someone else has conducted.

Marketing research can also be categorized with respect to the following:

- Markets
- Products or services
- Consumers
- The competition
- The environment

In the following sections, each of these marketing research categories will be briefly examined.

Market Research

Market research seeks to quantify and segment demand. Focal points of market research include the following:

- Market share (demand)
- Sales trends
- Market segments/quantification/trends
  —Primary target market
  —Secondary target market
  —Niche/special markets
- Distribution channels
  —Outlets
  —Penetration
  —Coverage
- Geographic markets/trends

- Media markets
  - —Broadcast (television/radio)
  - —Print (newspaper/magazine)
  - —Electronic (Internet)
  - —Direct mail
  - —Outdoor
  - —Other

Product or Service Research

Product or service research usually focuses on your product's/service's strengths and weaknesses in relation to the products/services of competitors. This research focuses on these areas:

- Products/services
  - —Strengths
  - —Weakness
  - —Development
  - —Life cycle
- Positioning
- Branding
- Packaging
- Pricing strategies

Consumer Research

Consumer research takes many different forms and covers a very broad range of customer and potential customer-related issues. It may be quantitative or qualitative in nature. Consumer research may focus on these areas:

- Demographics
- Geographics
- Psychographics
- Behavioral patterns
- Social attitudes
- Habits
- Benefits and needs

Because marketing frequently relies on the media as one method to reach prospective customers, present and future customers can be categorized by DMAs (designated market areas—geographic areas reached by clusters of television stations, as defined by the AC Nielsen Co.) or ADIs (areas of dominant influence—geographic areas defined by the circulation zones of major newspapers, as categorized by Arbitron, an audience research firm).

In summary, consumer research seeks to identify the usage patterns of customers and their preferences. Consumer research also seeks to classify consumers by age, income, education, etc. (demographics), as well as discover their habits (psychographics) with respect to likes, dislikes, etc., always seeking to quantify wherever possible. Consumer research explores everything from the purchasing habits to the attitudes and behaviors of consumers.[1]

Competitive Research

One of the keys to successful marketing strategy is understanding how your product or service compares to your top competitors' products or services. **Competitive research** compares your product or service to the products or services of competitors and tries to discover how consumers perceive and experience your product/service offering in relation to the competitors' products/services. Focal points of competitive research include the following:

- Pricing
- Value
- Quality
- Convenience to purchase
- Customer satisfaction
- Delivery

Environmental Research

Marketing must take into account not only what consumers and competitors are doing, but also what is occurring within the total industry environment. **Environmental research** focuses on external forces—major issues which will have an impact on your business, such as these:

- Overall economic scenario
- Social issues
- Political issues
- Technological developments
- Legal implications
- Legislative issues

One key focus of environmental research is to look ahead at what form and shape opportunities and threats may take and how they will affect your activities. Frequently, competitive research and environmental research are linked. The output of these research assessments is often referred to with the acronym **SWOT,** which stands for strengths, weaknesses, opportunities, and threats. These strengths, weaknesses, opportunities, and threats can then be analyzed to provide support rationale for developing marketing strategies. Examples of focal points of a SWOT analysis include the following:

- Strengths
  —Company/brand
  —Value to the market
  —Product/service leadership
  —Brand awareness
  —Image
  —Technological
  —Operational
  —Marketing (distribution) share
  —Pricing
  —Financial
  —Customer loyalty/satisfaction
- Weaknesses
  —Consumption/sales trends
  —Product/service delivery
  —Technological
  —Operational
  —Marketing
    - Pricing
    - Distribution
    - Promotion

—Image
—Awareness
—Reputation
—Financial
—Obsolescence

- Opportunities
—Brand extensions
—New products/services
—New markets
—Incremental purchase
—Exploiting competitive weakness
—Excess demand (pricing)
—New distribution channels
—Technology
—New trends
- Threats
—Capacity to deliver
—Labor availability
—Cost to produce
—Superior new competitor
—Product/service obsolescence
—Regulatory
—Competitive pricing
—Declining demand

In summary, research focuses on both quantitative and qualitative trends. Quantitative trend research seeks to identify significant increases or declines in customer preferences, methods of purchase, usage/frequency, and other factors impacting future demand. Qualitative trend research seeks to identify changes in consumer attitudes, interests, tastes, benefits sought, and so on. Trend research findings help marketers make strategic marketing decisions.

MARKETING RESEARCH TECHNIQUES

Many types of marketing research techniques can be used to make sound marketing decisions. Which technique works best for a company depends on many factors, such as the product/service offering, nature of the problem or opportunity, amount of resources available, time or urgency, budget, etc. Basic marketing research techniques widely used include surveys, questionnaires, and focus groups. Of course, there are many other quantitative and qualitative research techniques, but the purpose of this section is to familiarize you with these basic techniques. Regardless of the research technique selected, the goal remains the same—to gain information and apply the findings to improve the marketing and/or marketability of a product or service.

Surveys

A **survey** seeks to elicit consumer opinion, uncover facts, and gain insights on potential trends. Surveys may be conducted in a variety of ways, at various locations, among customers or potential customers, or even among competitors' customers. Surveys may be conducted in person, by phone, electronically, or by mail.

A survey is a structured document, usually seeking to quantify its findings in terms of percentages of those who agree or disagree with particular statements. It also seeks to measure the depth of agreement or disagreement, often employing a point scale—for example, "Circle 1 if you strongly agree, 5 if you strongly disagree." Five-, seven-, and ten-point scales are commonly used. Surveys are also used to seek qualitative information, especially when open-ended questions are asked—i.e., "What else would you like to see or have," etc. Surveys may be conducted only once or may be periodically scheduled, such as an annual frequent-flier program preference survey. Multiple-period (semiannual, monthly, etc.) surveys often seek to spot improvements or declines in such areas as service levels or consumer preferences, thus providing a rationale for a marketing, operational, or development decision.

Questionnaires

Perhaps the most widely used research technique is **questionnaires.** These come in all types of forms and are used for multiple purposes. As data collection vehicles, questionnaires seek both factual information and opinion. Data that questionnaires are designed to collect include customer comments, customer profiles, product and service information, demographic and psychographic data, attitudinal information, consumer usage patterns and preferences, etc. The data collected may be used to measure performance, improve products or services, qualify prospects, build leads, create **mailing lists,** determine consumer price sensitivity, and analyze menus. For additional analysis, focus groups may be recorded or observed via one-way mirrors. Focus group members may volunteer their time or be compensated.

Focus groups can range from single-area focus groups to regional/market-area focus groups to multiple focus groups. Single-area focus groups are drawn from one market; regional/market-area focus groups are single focus groups held in one or more regions of the country; multiple focus groups are more than one focus group held in multiple regions of the country. Also, there are product/service-user groups and nonuser focus groups. Focus groups may be made up of your customers, your competitors' customers, prospective customers, or any combination thereof.

Like surveys, questionnaires can be conducted in person, by phone, by mail, or electronically. Questionnaires are often ongoing, such as customer satisfaction comment questionnaires, new customer/purchaser questionnaires, etc. Also, like surveys, questionnaires can use scales or point systems to yield quantifiable data or rank items in order of importance.

Frequently, the terms "survey" and "questionnaire" are used interchangeably. However, questionnaires tend to be briefer than surveys and are usually less complex in content.

Focus Groups

A **focus group** is a marketing research technique that combines personal opinion solicitation in the form of group discussion with a structured set of questions. During a focus group session, a moderator conducts or facilitates the discussion using a script designed to elicit opinions from focus group members.

Focus groups, by nature, are more time-consuming for marketers to conduct and follow through on than surveys or questionnaires. Focus groups involve script writing, hiring a professional group leader, holding the focus group session itself, and then analyzing the focus group and its responses. In general, focus groups provide more in-depth qualitative findings related to attitudes and behavior than do questionnaires or surveys. Sometimes focus groups come up with useful questions that can be placed on subsequent questionnaires or surveys.

Five Essential Marketing Intelligence Tools

As indicated at the outset of this section, prior to developing your strategic marketing plan you need to "look within," "look around," and "look ahead." The following suggested five marketing intelligence tools provide key research findings or a "fail-safe" plan for any business:

1. *SWOT Analysis*—Recording and analyzing your capabilities or resources can improve your competitive position and performance. You can develop this intelligence by looking within at your internal company data. Looking within and analyzing any capability or resource that may cause your organization to underperform or lose market share (weaknesses) may also be identified from this intelligence tool. Your external focus—looking around at competition and looking ahead at environmental trends—provides you with the marketing intelligence to spot opportunities, justify new marketing strategy, and may help to identify trends which require changes to marketing strategy.
2. *CSI*—Consistently measuring **customer satisfaction** is essential to marketing strategy. Developing a methodical marketing intelligence tool such as a customer satisfaction index (CSI) can provide you with an ongoing, periodic scorecard on how your business is performing. Wherever possible, your CSI should be closely linked to performance evaluation and reward systems throughout every level of your organization.
3. *CPA*—**Customer perceptions** audits are marketing intelligence tools which provide objective (external) evaluations of how your business is performing and delivering throughout the entire prepurchase to postpurchase experience. A CPA is a step-by-step walk-through of all "point of encounters" with the customer from the customer's perspective—prepurchase through postpurchase. Often, "mystery shoppers" or external firms are used to perform the audit.
4. *GAP Analysis*—A "GAP" analysis as a marketing intelligence tool seeks to identify the difference between management's per-

spective of how the business is performing with respect to customer satisfaction and how the customer evaluates that performance. The difference is referred to as the "GAP." A good GAP analysis can be quantified/measured using an index. For example, on a 100-point index, management rates unit customer satisfaction at 85 percent and the customer rates their experience at 65 percent—thus a 20 percent "GAP" between management's perspective and the customers.

5. *OPD*—Not every business can afford to conduct extensive marketing research with their limited resources. One solution is to employ the marketing intelligence tool called "OPD" or other people's data. OPD is secondary research that is conducted or compiled by someone other than yourself, face-to-face with customers or potential customers. It may be industry or product category information. Many people (agencies, competitors, the U.S. government, etc.) are constantly conducting research (primary research) and reporting or sharing the findings with the public. Take advantage of this free or very inexpensive marketing intelligence tool.

MARKETING RESEARCH PRESENTATION TOOLS

Marketers can use many presentation tools to help individuals understand and analyze research findings. Some of these presentation tools are simple graphics such as triangles or pyramids, circles or maps, linear diagrams, boxes or rectangles, and grids or matrices.[2] Granted, some may view this as an oversimplification of the presentation process. However, the majority of research findings and models are visually presented using these simple forms. Following are a few research presentation tools that you may find helpful in presenting data/findings.

Pyramids

Pyramids are often used to depict the size of markets, service levels, rates/prices, and product/brand positioning. Exhibit 2.2 presents a pyramid that profiles three brands by service levels and prices. This same presentation tool can be used to structure a profile of market and price strategies.

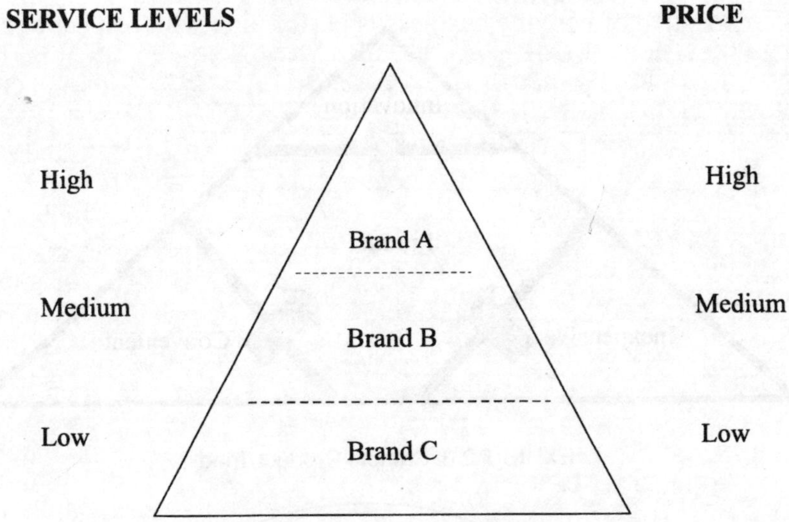

EXHIBIT 2.2. Sample Pyramid

Other uses of the pyramid include: **segmentation,** problem resolution, prioritizing, categorizing, targeting, and importance/weighting. Also, subdividing the pyramid allows for benefits prioritization, strategy selection, positioning, cost/quality equations, etc. In these instances, the pyramid is referred to as a "product triad" (see Exhibit 2.3).

Circles

Circles are frequently used for **mapping** purposes, to compare your product/service to the expressed needs and wants of consumers and/or in relation to the products/services of competitors (see Exhibit 2.4). A "perceptual map" will help you focus on how well your product or service is doing in comparison to others in terms of quality and value, as perceived by your customers. In Exhibit 2.4, "quality" is plotted along the horizontal axis, "value" along the vertical axis. How your product/service is perceived by consumers is what locates you on the map. A perceptual map can help identify your problems and opportunities in relation to the market and your competition. A positioning map can also be of great value in creating advertising or

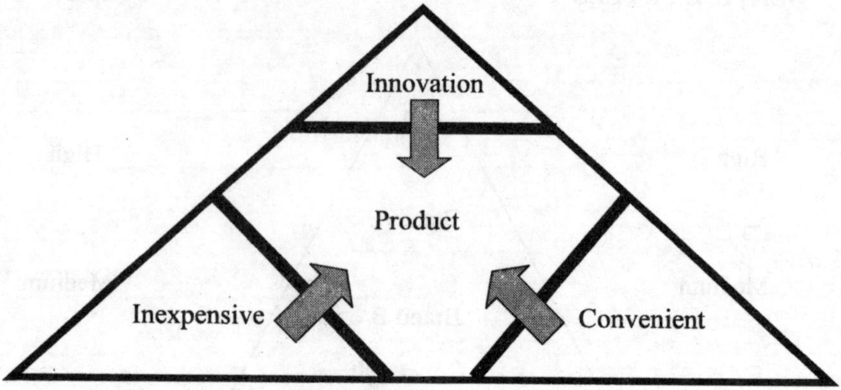

EXHIBIT 2.3. Sample Product Triad

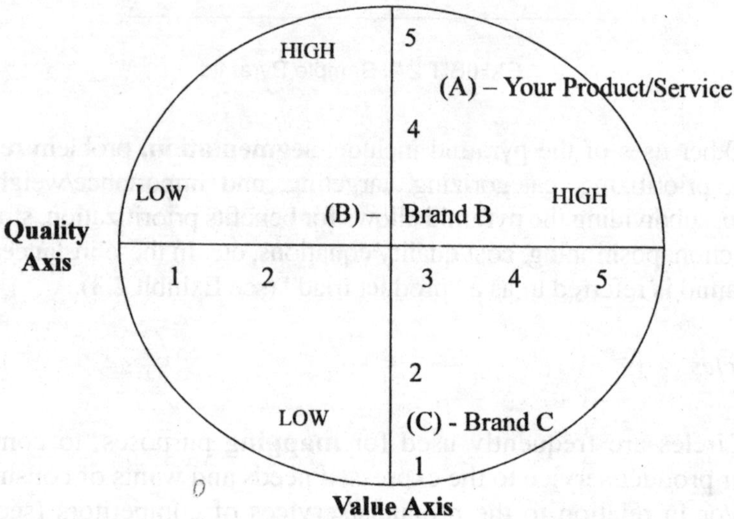

EXHIBIT 2.4. Sample Circle—Positioning Map

pricing strategies, or determining the necessity for product or service-level enhancements.

Other uses of the circle include mapping of product/brand attributes, competitive relationships, inclusion and exclusion of services/benefits, needs assessment, and price/value relationships. In these instances, axis definitions and scales may be customized. In an inclusion/exclusion application, the focus is on what is inside the circle, i.e., within the scope of the business strategy, or what is outside the circle or excluded from the current business strategy.

Linear Diagrams

Linear diagrams are frequently used to show pathways to targets, to look at alternative strategies, develop networks and alliances, and aid in the decision-making process. One of the most popular linear diagrams is the "decision tree" (see Exhibit 2.5). It is most often used to view product/service extensions and expansions, market segment alternatives, **product/service hybrids,** etc. Decision trees show various possible "branches" that you might take to reach an objective or outcome. Decision trees have applicability in the product or service development process, operations, and marketing. Their benefit is to clearly show alternative or multiple routes to achieve goals and objectives.

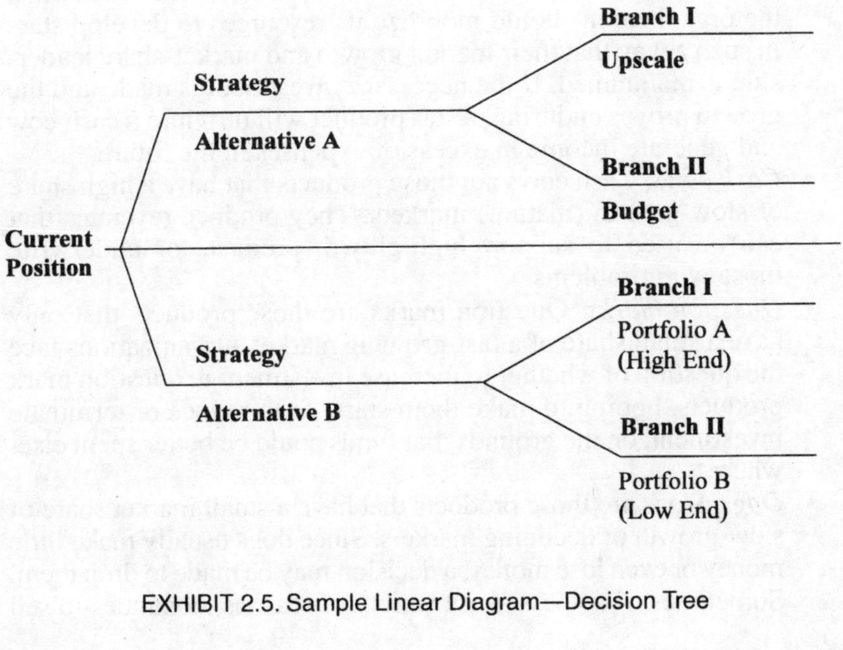

EXHIBIT 2.5. Sample Linear Diagram—Decision Tree

Boxes/Rectangles

For many years, box and rectangle graphics have been useful presentation tools for marketers. One of the most well-known "box" creations is attributed to the Boston Consulting Group and is referred to as the "portfolio approach to strategy formulation." This leading management consulting firm recommended that organizations appraise each of their products on the basis of market growth rate (annual growth rate of the market in which the product is sold) and the organization's share of the market relative to its largest competitor. Each product is then placed in the corresponding quadrant of the Boston Consulting Group Portfolio Box (see Exhibit 2.6). By dividing product-market growth into high growth and low growth, and **market share** into high share and low share, four categories of products can be identified: stars, cash cows, question marks, and dogs. These categories can be summarized as follows:

- *Stars.* Stars are those products which have a high share of fast-growing (new) markets. Star products grow rapidly and typically require heavy investment of resources. In such instances, the organization should mobilize its resources to develop stars in such a way that their market growth and market-share leadership is maintained. If the necessary investment is made and the growth proves enduring, a star product will turn into a cash cow and generate income in excess of expenses in the future.
- *Cash cows.* Cash cows are those products that have a high share of slow-growth (mature) markets. They produce revenues that can be used to support high-growth products or underwrite those with problems.
- *Question marks.* Question marks are those products that only have a small share of a fast-growing market. Organizations face the question of whether to increase investment in question mark products, hoping to make them stars, or to reduce or terminate investment, on the grounds that funds could be better spent elsewhere.
- *Dogs.* Dogs are those products that have a small market share of slow-growth or declining markets. Since dogs usually make little money or even lose money, a decision may be made to drop them. Sometimes a business, for a variety of reasons, continues to sell

dogs even though they are unprofitable. However, managers must remember that the resources that go into maintaining dogs are resources that business can't use for other opportunities.

The Boston Consulting Group Portfolio Box can also be used to analyze companies, brands, or markets.

Grids

An extension of the box concept is the grid concept. Grids are excellent tools that help businesses formulate marketing strategies and plans. The **marketing strategy grid,** for example, is a dynamic tool that usually views both present and future market and competitive conditions (see Exhibit 2.7).[3] It allows you to gain perspective on your own product or service through an honest and frank evaluation. To objectively select the appropriate marketing strategies, you must understand the conditions (present and future) of the market you are in, where the market is going, and how your product relates to both the current and future conditions as well as the competition's products.

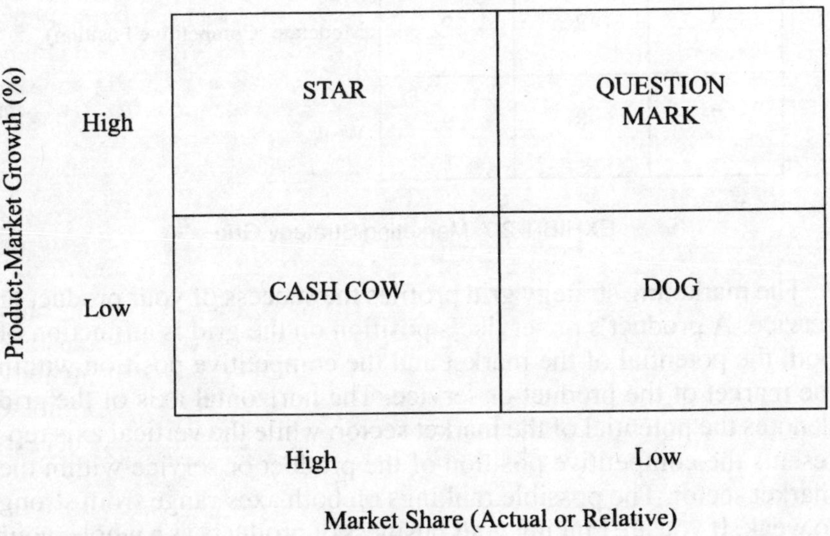

EXHIBIT 2.6. The Boston Consulting Group Portfolio Box

Present Time
(Market Potential)

Strong	Moderate	Weak	
1	2	3	Strong
4	5	6	Moderate (Competitive Position)
7	8	9	Weak

Future Time
(Market Potential)

Strong	Moderate	Weak	
1	2	3	Strong
4	5	6	Moderate (Competitive Position)
7	8	9	Weak

EXHIBIT 2.7. Marketing Strategy Grid

The marketing strategy grid profiles the success of your product or service. A product's or service's position on the grid is a function of both the potential of the market and the competitive position within the market of the product or service. The horizontal axis of the grid denotes the potential of the market sector, while the vertical axis represents the competitive position of the product or service within the market sector. The possible rankings on both axes range from strong to weak. If you are ranking your business or products as a whole, your competitive position is a function of both quantitative and qualitative considerations. This includes the amount and quality of competition;

your competitive advantages as to amount and quality of competition; your competitive advantages as to distribution, **share,** image, pricing, and so on; and your ability to meet the needs of target market segments. It is a good practice to develop two grids—one on your present competitive position, the second on your projected competitive position two to five years into the future. This will help you focus on the dynamics of your marketplace and competition.

Obviously, there is a meaning to the position on the grid in which a particular product or service is placed:

- Boxes 1, 2, and 4 denote a favorable, advantageous, or "go" situation. This situation occurs when both factors—market potential and competitive position—are either strong or moderate.
- Boxes 3, 5, and 7 denote a less favorable, less advantageous, or "caution" situation. A "caution" situation occurs when one factor is weak and one is strong, or both factors are moderate.
- Boxes 6, 8, and 9 denote an unfavorable, disadvantageous, or "no-go" situation. This situation occurs when one or both factors are weak and neither factor is above the moderate level.

Given these definitions, the optimum position on the grid is the upper-left corner (the "1" box), where a strong **market potential** combines with a strong competitive position within the market. The worst position on the grid is the bottom-right corner (the "9" box), where a weak market potential combines with a weak competitive position within the market.

Because both factors being evaluated (market potential and competitive position) are dynamic, movement can take place within the grid framework—that is, the position of a particular product or service can vary over time. Horizontal movement involves changes in the potential of a market. Such changes are due to pressures in both the overall and local external economic and social forces. Vertical movement on the grid is possible from the lower six positions. These positions can be considered "action squares," because anyone with a product or service in these squares would want to take action to move up. Such vertical movement denotes changes in the product's/service's competitive position within the market and can be accomplished through strategies, product development, technological improvements, etc.

The use of the grid concept is based on two key assumptions:

1. To best meet the needs of each market segment as well as maintain a strong image and market share, we can assume that business and products/services will always seek the 1, 2, and 4 positions (favorable positions) on the grid whenever possible.
2. The position on the grid in which you place yourself assumes that no major improvement programs or other strategy changes will be undertaken soon, and few, if any, major changes will be made in marketing. As previously stated, you may wish to use two grids—one for the present and one for the future (usually within the next five years).

In the next section we will provide examples of potentially appropriate marketing strategies based on the nine different grid positions.

Hopefully, some of the assessment processes outlined in this section will lead you to prepare a list of the key strategic issues that could change your overall business strategy. At this juncture, it is usually a good idea to take another look at your mission statement and prepare another draft. Also, you should make a list of any major marketing issues that emerged from the assessment. Issues such as: new competitors; changes (declines) in customer loyalty (CSI scores); new delivery or channels of distribution (e.g., Internet); changes in buying habits; technological breakthroughs; and increased niche attacks, to name a few.

In the next section, we will look at "selecting strategies."

CASE EXAMPLE 1: LOOKING WITHIN

At the North American headquarters of a major global food corporation, there was a formal process of ongoing research on everything from new formulas to new packaging. The market research committee would meet at a different company facility across the country on a regular basis to exchange ideas, findings, etc. There was an extensive, formalized research budget. Competitive moves were monitored and monthly competitive/environmental reports, along with periodic "flash" reports were issued. A great deal of "looking around" and "looking ahead" research was going on at all times. However, not many were "looking within" to see if there were any key focal points of interest.

One of the organization's marketing managers (the one with the smallest research budget) decided to look within utilizing an inexpensive technique called observation. The marketer observed that the employees were provided complimentary coffee, soft drinks, and certain snack and candy products, which were made by the company. Focusing on the employees' habits, the marketer observed that most employees would drink regular coffee with their first fill-up in the morning. However, the second, third, and sometimes even the first fill-up was different. Employees (eight out of ten) would pour one-half cup of regular coffee and one-half cup of decaffeinated coffee most of the time. This observation was followed up with a simple questionnaire seeking the reasons for this mixing. The results/answers were twofold. One group stated that they wanted to cut down on caffeine. The other group stated that they just didn't like the taste of the decaffeinated coffee and rather than switch they would improve its taste with a little regular coffee.

The marketer soon discovered that the mix/blend process was pretty much a standard procedure at many coffee stations around the company. This observational research led to a formal recommendation to the new products group to develop a reduced caffeine product with the taste of regular coffee. It seemed that half regular and half decaffeinated would do the job from observation. After formal lab work and field testing, it turned out that the formula was pretty close and the "market" would respond. The new 50 percent less caffeine product with the taste of regular coffee was launched. First-year sales surpassed $100 million dollars!

CASE EXAMPLE 2: MAILING LESS AND MAKING MORE

A New England-based publishing company offered educational products from preschool to college market level. Products were sold primarily through direct mail. As postal rates began to escalate, the company faced dramatically rising mailing costs. This was coupled with two new competitors entering the market. A meeting was called to ascertain what could be done to reduce costs yet retain volumes/market share. Traditionally, the company analyzed its sales of certain product lines by titles and by distribution warehouse volumes. The latter was tied to a state-by-state, city-by-city report. It seemed that one of its most profitable product lines was its preschool through grade six children's book clubs. It was also the area the competitors had zeroed in on for their business. Mailings to the customer lists were escalated both in terms of number and intervals between mailings (from four mailings to six and from four weeks apart down to two-week intervals). The results were the same—same sales trends, only an even higher cost.

Market research suggested that the answer might be found in a more refined approach to customer analysis. Management listened and decided to invest in new software and external research services. The new software would analyze sales by zip code for each mailing and the external research services would profile the demographics and psychographics of the customer base. The results were eye opening. Over 80 percent of the sales were coming from less than 30 percent of the **zip codes.** Moreover, the demographic and psychographic profiles suggested that 20 percent of the zip codes would buy incremental products at even higher prices (quality-driven perceptions related to price and customers who wanted the "best" for their children). Moreover, these 20 percent of the zip codes were responding to the first three mailings. Needless to say, the company reduced its mailing costs (number of mailings and zip codes mailed to) and introduced a new line of books at a higher price point in selected markets. The results were increased revenues and reduced costs.

Key Terms

ADIs (areas of dominant influence)
Boston Consulting Group Portfolio box
competitive and environmental research
consumer research
CPA (customer perceptions audit)
CSI (customer satisfaction index)
GAP Analysis
marketing research
marketing strategy grid
qualitative
quantitative
SWOT (strengths, weaknesses, opportunities, threats)

Chapter 3

Selecting Strategies

Whether you are in an existing business or a new start-up, it is now time to reexamine or develop your major strategies. In this section, we will examine overall business strategies and positioning options, look at brand/product-related strategies, and then focus on marketing strategies and tactics. Now that you have completed the comprehensive assessment process outlined in the previous chapter, you are ready to either reaffirm your existing positioning, clarify your positioning strategy, or select a new positioning strategy.

POSITIONING STRATEGIES

Your overall positioning strategy should take into account the consumer's perspective. This should include the data collected with respect to your attributes, your relationship to competition with respect to value, quality, price, and convenience to purchase (speed).[1] This information is derived from the maps your research produced with respect to quality/price positioning and attributes. You may wish to combine your findings by using an attributes and competitive ranking scale (see Exhibit 3.1). Completing this exercise will provide a guide and parameters for your positioning choices/options. From this graphic tool you should draft your overall positioning strategy noting qualifiers and rationale.

Given this data plus all other research findings, it is time to examine your positioning options. A good question to ask yourself at this point is: What strategic descriptor will be best associated with or will best describe the foundation upon which your business strategy will stand?

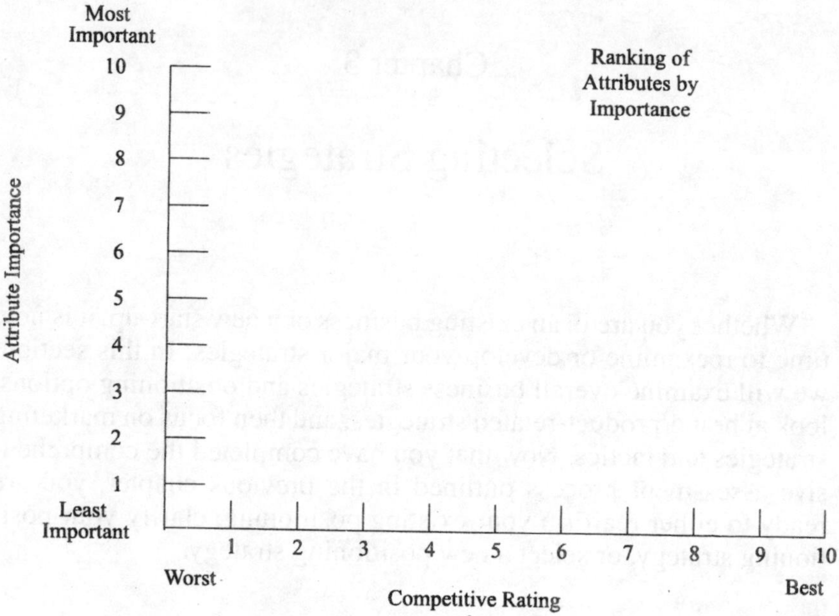

EXHIBIT 3.1. Positioning: Attributes and Competitive Ranking

The following are some sample strategic descriptors or positioning options.

Ten Positioning Options

1. *Highest quality*—your business/product(s)/brand(s) represent the very best on the market with respect to quality.
2. *Least expensive*—your business/product(s)/brand(s) are the most affordable on the market.
3. *Best value*—your product attributes, pricing, and convenience of purchase add up to the best value for the money on the market.
4. *Design or style leadership*—your product(s)/brand(s) represent the newest and most advanced in design and style on the market—you are the leader in innovation.
5. *Most prestigious*—your product(s)/brand(s) are presented to appeal to the ego, to the "only the best will do" consumer.

6. *Performance leader*—there are a number of ways to position your product(s)/brand(s) as the performance leader. These include:
   - *Best performance*—usually based on independent (external/objective survey or poll)
   - *Most durable*—holds up the longest
   - *Most reliable*—breaks down the least
   - *Easiest to work with*—most flexible and consistent to wholesalers, retailers, or public
7. *Most convenient*—we are everywhere/locations desirable.
8. *Fastest/speed*—we get it there first, we are there when you need us.
9. *Safest*—our product(s), service(s), brand(s) are the safety leader.
10. *Simplicity*—we or our product(s)/service(s) are the easiest to use.

Other positioning tactics may work well for your business, product(s), service(s), or brand(s). Perhaps you offer "more for less" and are therefore the quantity/value leader. Or, perhaps you're offering "more for more" and are therefore providing a higher level of service or greater amount of product than anyone else in your field.[2] The key to positioning strategy is to develop one that gives you the competitive advantage and translates into powerful marketing strategies. Some words of caution: don't "overposition," which is akin to overpromising. Likewise, don't underposition. Be careful not to complicate your positioning with the irrelevant (to the consumer), too descriptive, or nonsupportable claims. Focus, clarity, simplicity, and truth make positioning statements powerful and easily understood.

Brand Strategies

Your product(s)/**brand**(s) positioning should reflect your overall business positioning strategy. This can involve the actual naming of the brand(s), associations used in conjunction with the brand message, slogans, symbols, and **logos,** etc. In choosing a brand name, seek a name/word(s) that suggests something about the product's/service's positioning, benefits, qualities, or major attributes. Be distinctive, but keep the name easy to pronounce, recognize, and remember. Also, consider the translation factor in a global marketplace. Be sure that the brand name selected does not convey a distasteful or poor meaning in another language. Anything associated with the brand should reflect the positioning of the brand. Seek to develop rich associations related to specific attributes, benefits, values (company), personality, users, etc. Look for outstanding word associations, a slogan, colors (look/logo/design). Should your brand be fortunate enough to lend itself to a legend or famous story, capitalize on the association, as long as it is a positive one.[3] Two final comments on brand-related strategies. First, if you're in a co-op, be sure your product(s)/brand(s)/ partner(s) are of an equal or higher quality/reputation than your brand. Second, manage all customers' brand contacts so that they meet or exceed customer expectations associated with your brands' "perceived" positioning.

Marketing Strategies

Once you formulate a well-defined overall business and brand positioning strategy, it is time to focus on marketing strategies. At the outset, you should recognize that your marketing strategies are the visible communications links to all constituencies (see Exhibit 3.2).

The perceptions your marketing strategies convey while directed at one focal point can very well influence other constituencies. Likewise, if a consumer marketing strategy is found to be distasteful or

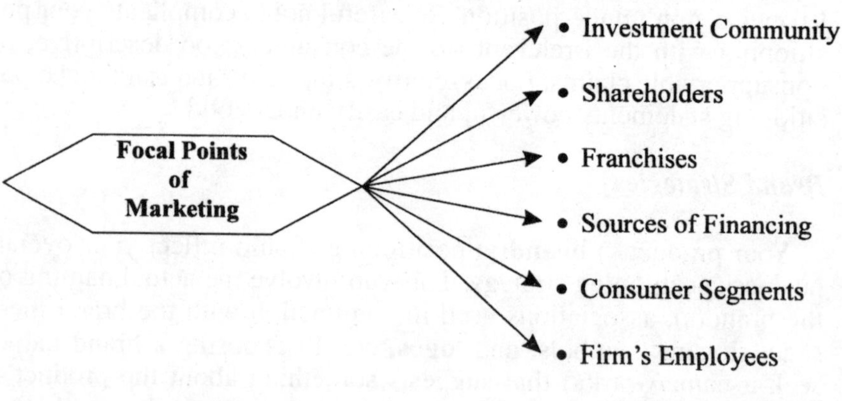

EXHIBIT 3.2. Overall Marketing Strategy Constituencies (Focal Points)

controversial there could be major ramifications from shareholders, franchisees, etc.

We will now examine the specific direct targets for marketing strategies related to actual consumption of the product or service (see Exhibit 3.3).

You will need to tailor your marketing strategies to each direct target you wish to influence. Always keep in mind your overall business and brand positioning.[4] There are many different perspectives on marketing and marketing strategy, especially in our ever-changing environment. For nearly thirty years, and still today, marketers have focused on the Four Ps identified by McCarthy and Kotler.[5]

- Product
- Price
- Place
- Promotion

In the 1990s, as we transitioned to a predominantly service-oriented economy and marketing environment, marketing strategies shifted to focus on the Four Cs as delineated by Lauterborn.[6]

- Consumer wants and needs
- Cost to satisfy (wants and needs)
- Convenience to buy
- Communication (creating a dialogue)

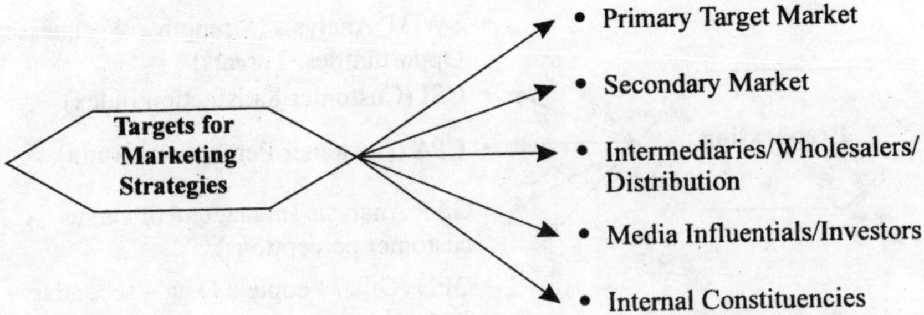

EXHIBIT 3.3. Specific Direct Targets for Marketing Strategies

In the current decade, although marketing must still focus on the four Ps and four Cs, marketing strategies appear to have shifted and are now more and more based on the New Five Ps (see Exhibit 3.4).

The first New P, preparation, translates to assessing your focal points or looking within, looking around, and looking ahead. It involves all the research steps and analyses described in the previous section including deployment of the five essential marketing intelligence tools (see Exhibit 3.5).

The output of this assessment should provide a clear, concise, and a most likely advantageous positioning strategy (the next New P) (see Exhibit 3.6).

The next three Ps of the New Five Ps, perception, proclamation, and power thrusts, are what marketing strategy is all about. Successful businesses and brands today are those who succeed in creating winning perceptions for their products/services. We are living in a marketing environment that is perception-driven. Consumers want to "ride the wave," "have the latest," "go counter to the masses," "want it all now," "seek the newest," etc. These are all perceptions that your marketing

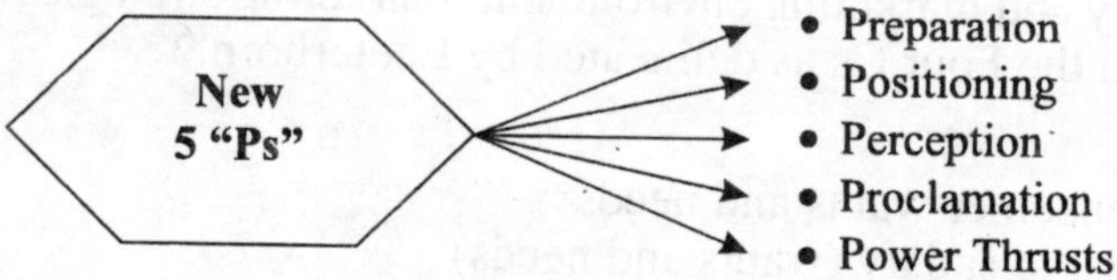

EXHIBIT 3.4. The "New" 5 Ps

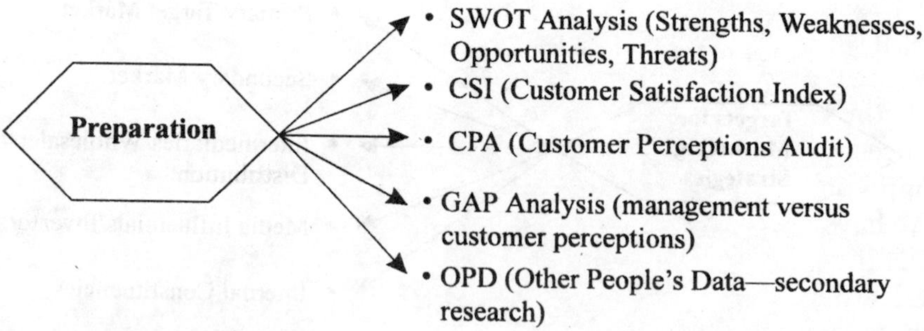

EXHIBIT 3.5. The Five Essential Marketing Intelligence Tools

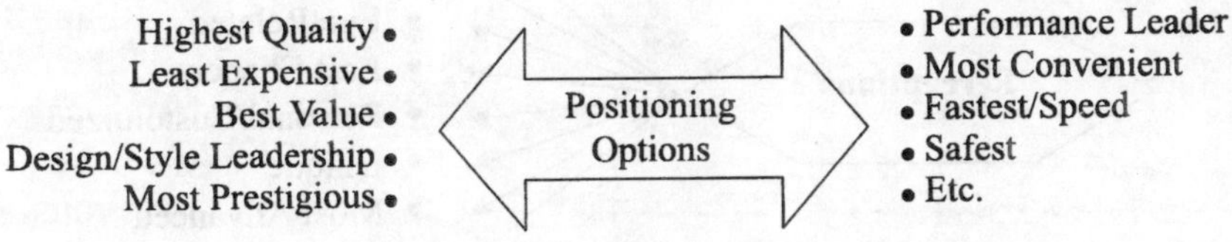

EXHIBIT 3.6. Positioning Options

strategy must convey from a message/creative perspective. Creating a perception in tune with your target market is essential for successful marketing strategy. Perception can be directly linked to positioning; however, it must be perceived as a "driver" or creator of a compelling call to purchase. In other words, the positioning strategy is the base and the perception message is the call to action. Perception options are dynamic; they move with the pulse and mind-set of consumers. For some, the message is "new," and for others, it is "retro." Exhibit 3.7 (Perceptions) outlines some perception strategies. However, these are always changing with today's consumers.

Linking your positioning and your perception message requires reading the current and near-term future pulse of the market. Assuming that your reading of the pulse of the market is correct and you have formulated your perceptions strategy, you now need to deploy the fourth P—"proclamation." Proclamation is a declaration that your product/service/brand is worth looking at, trying, buying, or repurchasing. Proclamation may take on a different meaning depending upon where your product/service/brand is in its life cycle. For example, if your brand is new or unique, you can immediately proclaim "we are the newest" or "we have the only," etc. This is a great position to be in, but most products/brands are not so fortunate. In some instances, you may only be able to declare: "Look—we are changing, improving, etc.," or perhaps you're at the stage of telling the market: "We have changed, we are like new" (improved). Hopefully, you will be at the point where you're ready to declare: "We are . . . new, the leader, the best . . ." or whatever your positioning and brand strategy support as a proclamation or declaration to the marketplace. Exhibit 3.8 shows the phases and thrust (expenditure) levels usually associated with the fourth P—"proclamation."

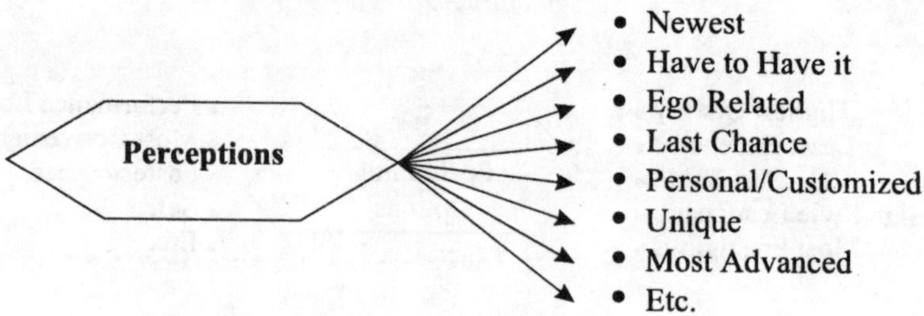

EXHIBIT 3.7. Perceptions

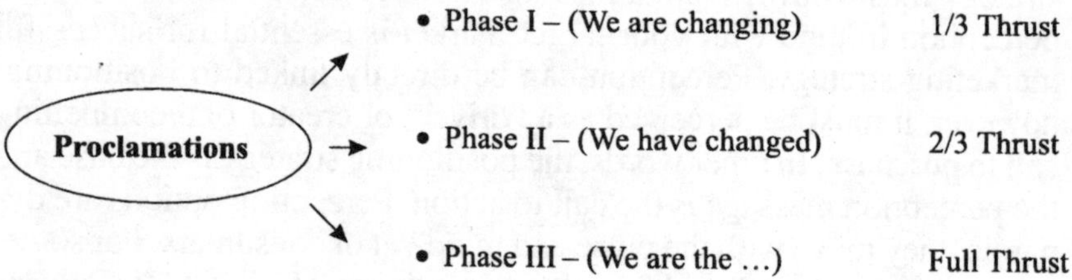

EXHIBIT 3.8. Proclamations

Now your marketing strategy has moved to the active or launched phase. This is the time to deploy the fifth P—"power thrusts." Even though you have proclaimed you're on the move doesn't mean that the consumer world will listen automatically. You will need to focus on a "breakthrough" or "unique" message and delivery to be successful. Let's assume you have a very creative, unique, and on-target proclamation/message. This is still no guarantee that you will be successful as the marketing channels are very crowded with many other messages. To be heard or seen you will have to have a multiple-pronged approach, which should involve as many marketing weapons as possible, i.e., advertising, promotions, public relations, etc. These weapons will require synchronization to work most efficiently and effectively. Power thrusts are created from a variety of techniques such as "heavy up-front" and/or "waves" of advertising; overlapping direct mail and direct sales efforts, carrying your promotional offers in your advertising, and hyping the offers with public relations, etc. In essence, you are synergistically and methodically using your expenditures and marketing weaponry to create "waves" or "power thrusts" for your product/service/brand offering (see Exhibit 3.9).

Not every situation calls for deployment of all of your weaponry in concentrated periods of time or up-front advertising. If you have strong brand awareness or are in a market leadership position (box 1 on the marketing strategy grid) you may be better off selecting "maintenance level" advertising or reminder messages and/or utilizing public relations to consistently trumpet your position. Selecting strategies often depends on your market's relative strength (overall consumer demand) and your competitive position. To illustrate examples of marketing strategies, we return to the marketing strategy grids. In each exhibit which follows, a product/brand is depicted in a different position on the grid (1-9). Some potential accompanying marketing strategies that could be appropriate are also provided (see Exhibits 3.10-3.18).

The marketing strategies accompanying these nine sample grids are only suggestions. There are many variables to consider and each product or service may have a uniqueness that needs to be taken into consideration prior to selecting a strategy. The marketing strategy grid is a tool designed to help you think about how to maximize your marketing strategies for the most productive results. In the final analysis, it is your judgment that will dictate the strategy selected; the marketing strategy grid only helps sharpen that judgment.

Following are some key points about selecting strategies. A marketing strategy that sells products and services is created by understanding the **consumer's perspective.** The marketing process must be thorough in its research and analysis of the consumer. Product development or changes to services offered should be in line with what consumers express as their needs. Marketing cannot succeed if the product or service is not in line with its consumers' needs.

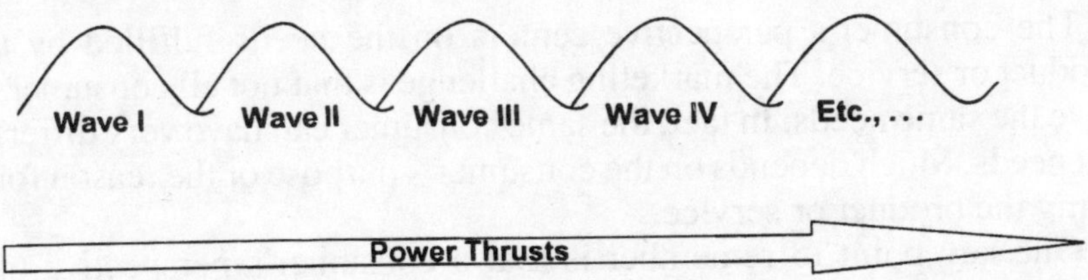

EXHIBIT 3.9. Power Thrusts

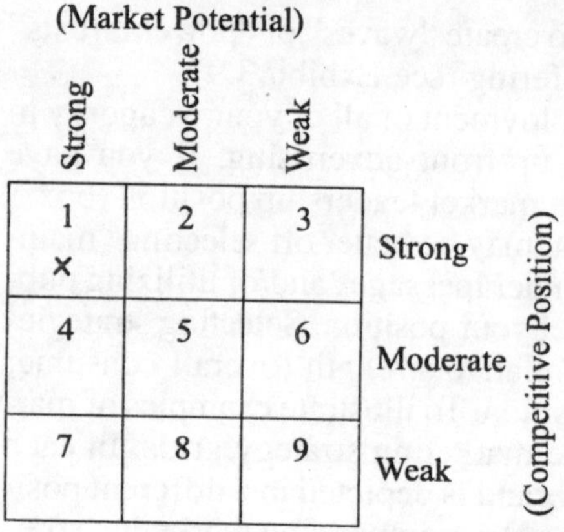

1. Maintain position.
2. Cultivate core customers.
3. Maximize profits through pricing.
4. Keep competitively ahead by adding services or upgrading product.
5. Expand your product or service offerings or extend your brand.

EXHIBIT 3.10. Position #1: Strong Market—Strong/Best Product or Service

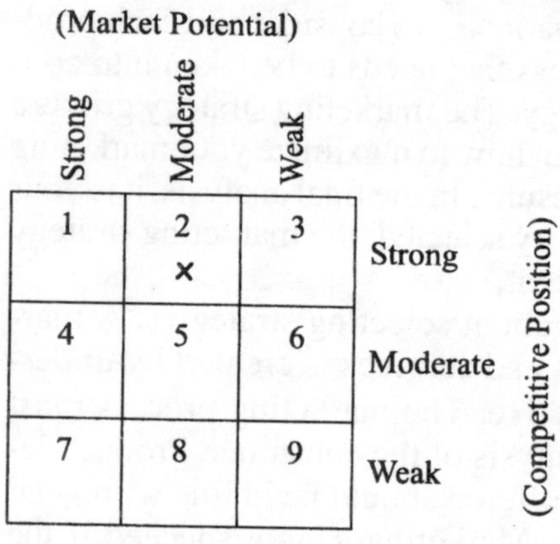

1. Go for market share via competitive pricing.
2. If the market movement tends to be strong in future years, improve to a #1 position.
3. If the market movement tends to be weak, go after traditional marketing segments (for example, build core market, consider alternate pricing strategy, etc.).
4. Create and capitalize on perceptions, i.e., the "only," "ego related," etc.

EXHIBIT 3.11. Position #2: Moderate Market—Strong Product or Service

The consumer's perspective centers on the needs fulfilled by a product or service. The marketing challenge is that not all consumers have the same needs. In fact, the same consumer can have very different needs. Much depends on the consumer's purpose or the reason for using the product or service.

One key point to remember is that a consumer's perspective of products and services may and does change based on the perception created by marketing.

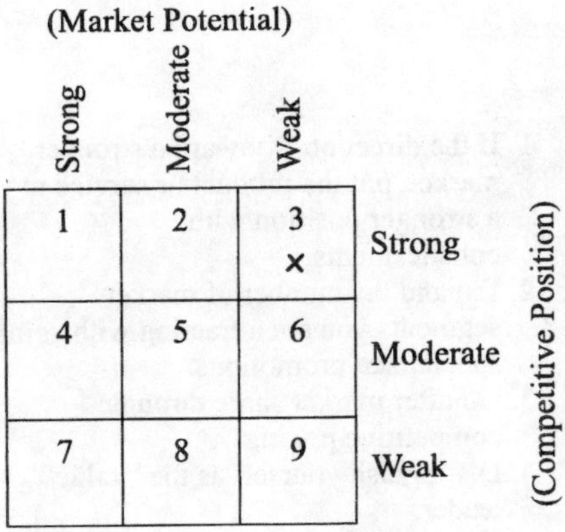

1. If the market is moving toward becoming moderate or strong, build market core now and retain loyalty of consumers.
2. Go after all market segments with multiple pricing strategies and/or product and service offerings.
3. Strongly emphasize cost control and targeted promotions.
4. Develop new "trial" business with promotional offers to build the customer base.

EXHIBIT 3.12. Position #3: Strong Product—Weak Market

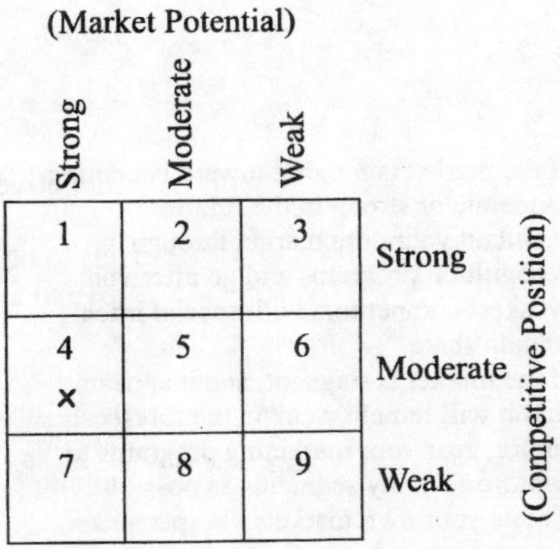

1. Maximize profits through pricing slightly below the #1 competitor.
2. Consider strengthening or upgrading your product or service to move closer to or into the #1 position if the future markets look strong.
3. Go after the "value-oriented" market segments.
4. Distinguish your product or service as an acceptable replacement for the #1 competitor.

EXHIBIT 3.13. Position #4: Strong Market—Moderate/Average Product or Service

The nurture, care, and conveying of what the brand stands for and how it meets the needs of the consumer is what marketing strategy is all about. The nurture and care of the brand creates a perception. This perception translates into action and to purchases. The perception created by packaging the brand helps to dictate the price consumers are willing to pay for the brand. Conveying how the brand meets the specific needs of buyers is one role of marketing strategies and promotional techniques.

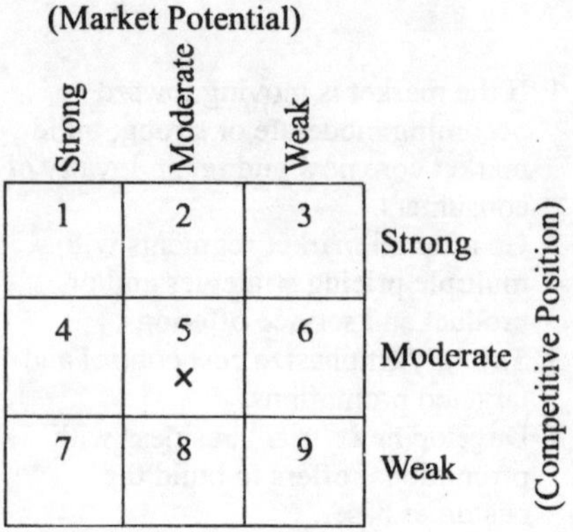

1. If the direction is toward a stronger market, put the product or service in a stronger position with enhancements.
2. Expand the number of market segments you are attracting with specialized promotions.
3. Go after market share through competitive pricing.
4. Distinguish yourself as the "value" leader.

EXHIBIT 3.14. Position #5: Moderate Market—Moderate/Average Product or Service

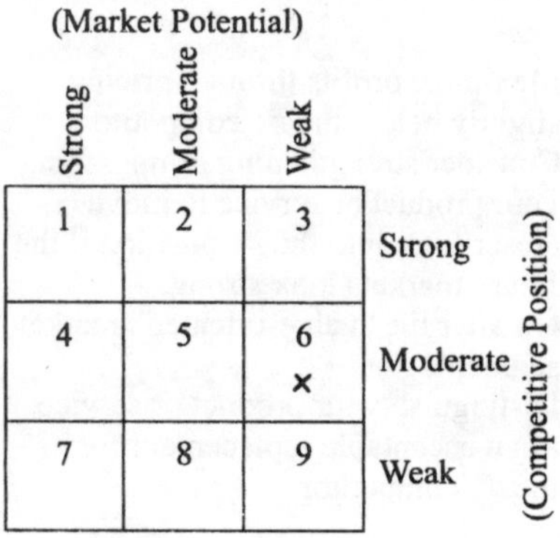

1. If the market is moving toward becoming moderate or strong in the future, maintain your core market through recognition programs and go after your weakest competitors with special pricing to gain share.
2. If the market is stagnant, and it appears that it will remain weak in the foreseeable future, gear your marketing programs to capture as many segments as possible.
3. Create your own markets via specialized promotions and co-op programs.

EXHIBIT 3.15. Position #6: Weak Market—Moderate/Average Product or Service

Strategy selection is dependent upon the overall strength of your market (demand) and your product's/service's competitive position. Sound strategy is premised on responding appropriately based on your positioning, anticipating the movement of the market (demand), and shaping your message to capitalize on the needs of the market in relationship to your attributes. Marketing strategies need to be constantly revisited in response to a dynamic and ever-changing market.

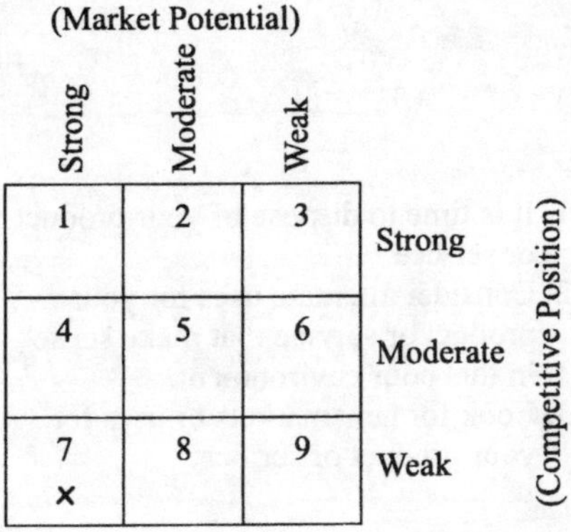

1. Repackage, improve, or upgrade the most visible aspects of your product or service.
2. Once this process is completed, increase your prices to take advantage of strong demand periods.
3. Become the best at servicing the market segments your stronger competitors are not paying attention to.
4. Theme your promotions toward special or unique concepts and go for volume.

EXHIBIT 3.16. Position #7: Strong Market—Weak Product or Service

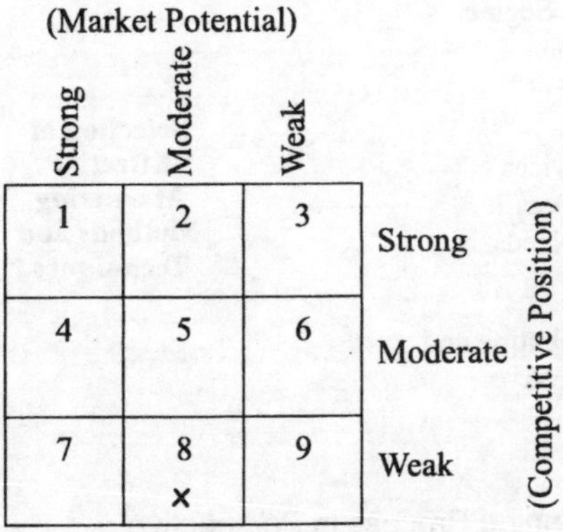

1. If the market is not moving toward being strong, look at special price schemes to build share.
2. If the market is moving toward being strong, make every effort to upgrade the product or service offering to move along with the market.
3. If this is true, work promotions, sales, and advertising to convey your product's or service's availability and value orientation.
4. Consider marketing your product or service around a theme.

EXHIBIT 3.17. Position #8: Moderate Market—Weak Product or Service

Your most valuable customers will quickly lose their loyalty to your products/services if you do not keep up with their evolving needs. Marketing strategies may also be different based upon the market target selected or stage of customer development.

In Exhibit 3.19, an outline of the marketing planning process is shown. In the next section we will discuss the types of marketing weapons and their applications.

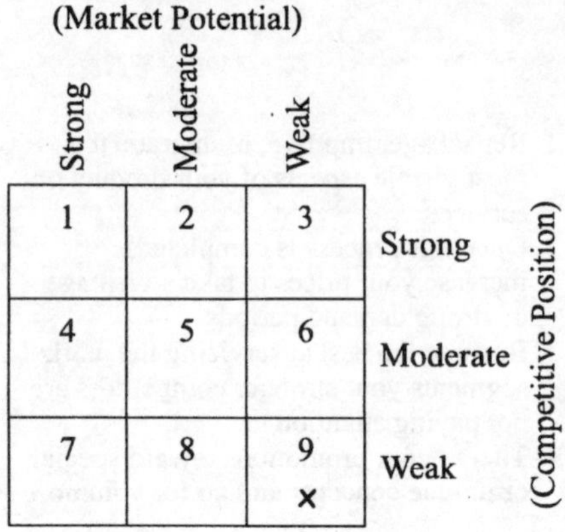

1. It is time to dispose of your product or service.
2. Consider alternate uses for your product or service that make sense in this poor environment.
3. Look for new markets or uses for your product or service.

EXHIBIT 3.18. Position #9: Weak Market—Weak Product or Service

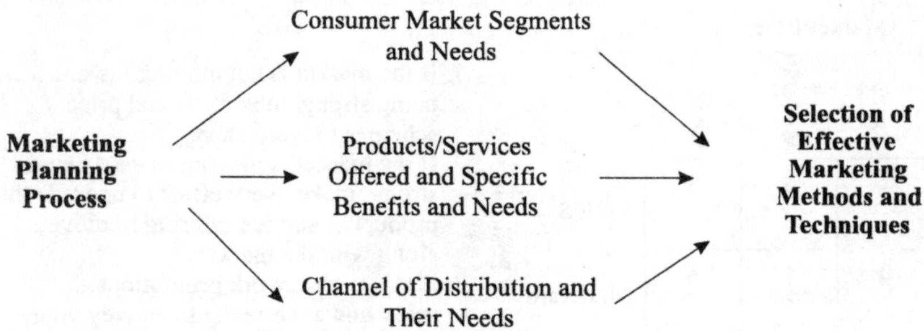

EXHIBIT 3.19. The Marketing Planning Process in Perspective

CASE EXAMPLE 1: POSITIONING TO PERFECTION

Launching a new brand to be in position at a price and quality level substantially above a company's other brands is difficult. It requires in-depth thought and the ability to practice the Five Ps to perfection. Following is an example of how one company did just that—positioning to perfection.

When the Toyota Motor Corporation introduced the Lexus, they did so in an extraordinary manner. They knew that they had a problem. They recognized that in the U.S. market, and others, Toyota did not have a reputation for building larger cars, luxury cars, or cars in a high price range. But they knew they had one thing going for them: the Toyota car brand was widely associated with value and quality. Clearly, they had to take that reputation and convince customers that they could deliver on a whole new type of product.

To begin with, Toyota spent countless hours on consumer market research. The results allowed them to conclude which specific steps they would need to take to break into this new market of upscale automobile owners and leasees.

Research showed that what people disliked most was the auto service establishment (the dealership) and related servicing. Research also showed that people don't strongly associate the name Lexus with Toyota. So Toyota made the extraordinary investment of building all new state-of-the-art dealerships and service shops just for the Lexus. It built these facilities with the customers' desires in mind. But the facilities would only be perceived to be as good as the service personnel and service experience itself. So Toyota provided training for all employees from receptionists to sales executives, from service managers to mechanics. The common denominator in this extensive training was the customer experience. The focus—make it pleasant and, if possible, eliminate all frictional points of encounter.

Lexus keeps all of their showrooms and repair facilities clean enough to eat off the floor. They offer pick up and delivery for even routine maintenance. There are new (or like new) loaner cars for those who desire a car while theirs is in for repair. Lexus goes one step further with follow-up phone calls, sporadic calls to see "how you like the car," and an 800 number for twenty-four-hour road service just in case it is ever needed.

For years, customers had learned to accept less from car dealers. Research showed that Lexus could not only achieve a 100 percent satisfaction level, they could exceed it without going overboard. Their definition of a perfect car experience was actually higher than the consumers'. As a result, Lexus aimed to deliver 110 percent while the consumer expected 85 percent. The result—extraordinary customer satisfaction. Of course, it helps when your product is a state-of-the-art, very low maintenance, extraordinarily high quality automobile. It was this high quality that allowed extraordinary promises to be made through advertising, promotion, and publicity when the car was first introduced.

Here is another example of Lexus' 110 percent effort. A dealer phoned a customer shortly after the purchase to ask if anything was wrong. The customer was greatly pleased and reported that the only thing wrong was "the wind noise from the phone antenna." When the customer went to get his car after the next maintenance visit (the car was brought to the curb next to the door), he said, "That's not my car!" The service manager looked puzzled. The customer said, "It's the same color and model, but the phone antenna is different and my car was coated with mud." The service manager smiled and said, "We contacted our technicians about that wind noise you referred to and they designed a new windless antenna. It's on us and we really appreciate your calling it to our attention. Also, it is our standard procedure to clean and vacuum your car before returning it to you." There are many more such stories from many other very satisfied customers.

Did this passion for customer service excellence pay off? You bet. Lexus was rated number one for customer satisfaction the very first year it was measured, scoring the highest in the index of any car in history. Lexus sales soared in a down market. The luxury car category was experiencing a severe downtrend. Lexus sales increased nearly 30 percent in its second year while its two primary established competitors experienced declines of as much as 34 and 27 percent. That's taking market share. Granted, some of the gain was due to value (quality at a fair, and in this instance, lesser price), but a lot of it was due to customer satisfaction.

Lexus understands the keys to winning new customers and is building a loyal base for repeat business with a highly fickle consumer group, and in a highly competitive industry. Lexus is succeeding with sales and marketing savvy closely integrated with a never-before-offered level of customer service. Expect Lexus to remain rated the very best for a long time.

CASE EXAMPLE 2: SPEED, RELIABILITY, AND CONVENIENCE

Speed, reliability, and convenience are the successful ingredients for a winning business strategy in the new millennium. These three positioning attributes were also the winning combination for Federal

Express over twenty-five years ago when it launched a remarkable business strategy—overnight guaranteed delivery nationwide. They "absolutely, positively do get it there overnight" (original advertising campaign). This proposition of guaranteed overnight delivery was coupled with a unique "hub" concept and state-of-the-art design for a customer-friendly tracking system.

Moreover, Federal Express developed a ready-to-use and easy-to-use system from the customer's perspective. From the distinctive envelopes and boxes to the pick up, delivery, or drop off systems, the customer has always been foremost on FedEx's mind. This ideal-for-the-procrastinator service is also blessed with thoroughly trained personnel who are supported with state-of-the-art technology.

Virtually no stone was left unturned when it came to positioning the FedEx company/brand. Its "branding," including the paint and colors on the airplanes and packages, is distinct and memorable. Its name selection conveyed a national and reliable message coupled with a synonym for speed. Think about all the positioning strengths associated with FedEx—quality service, performance leader, most reliable, easy to work with, fast, safe, and simple. No wonder Federal Express exemplified a winning business strategy in most everyone's opinion.

Key Terms

brand strategies
consumer's perspective
five Ps
four Cs
four Ps
perception
positioning strategies
power thrusts

PART B: SELECTING WEAPONRY

As discussed in the previous section, one of the five new Ps, "power thrusts," is the deployment of multiple marketing weapons in overlapping "waves." For any business, product/service, or brand, understanding what each weapon in your marketing arsenal is capable of doing and how and when to use it is yet another key component for marketing strategy. This section focuses on your weapons and your choices/options for development.

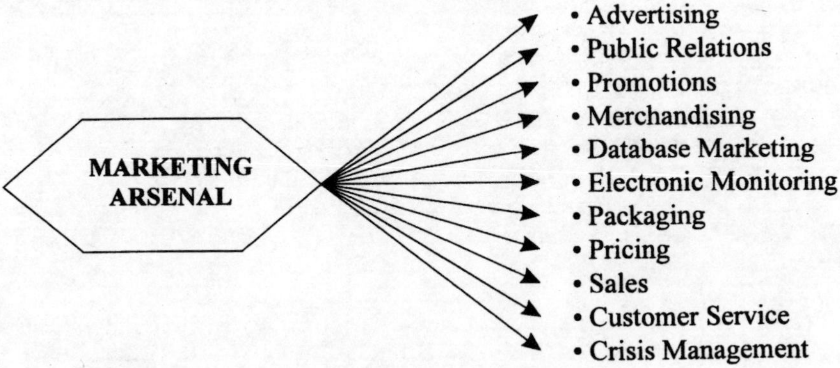

Marketing Arsenal Weaponry

Chapter 4

Advertising

The strength of **advertising** is its usefulness in creating and/or maintaining brand awareness. It helps position a brand, demonstrates **product attributes,** and is cost efficient for mass-marketed products.[1] In general, advertising is very useful in controlling message content and timing. Its weaknesses include low credibility, the potential for a high percentage of reach to be wasted, message clutter, and its perception as being intrusive. Advertising is ideally used to: (1) establish awareness, (2) create image(s), and (3) create lifestyle associations. Advertising builds awareness and can positively affect attitudes and initiate behavior. Selection of the appropriate media and knowing where and when to place your ad are essential to effective advertising.[2]

Advertising includes both the "creative" strategy and the "media strategy." Creative strategy focuses on the key **target market,** the promise (why, what, etc.), the proposition (support for the promise) and tone (feeling/personality). Media strategy focuses on the delivery vehicles and the planning and execution. Media's goal is to deliver the target audience at the lowest cost within the most appropriate environment for the message.

There are many lists of do's and don'ts for advertising, yet few of them acknowledge the product or service itself and the role that advertising plays in the overall marketing of that product or service. However, there are some advertising guidelines that can help you acknowledge both your product or service and your total marketing plan.

ADVERTISING GUIDELINES

The following list of advertising guidelines can help you put together successful advertising campaigns.

1. Know your product or service
2. Advertise as part of the total marketing strategy
3. Develop a proposition
4. Create a platform
5. Be realistic about the level of expectation
6. Review for **customer needs**

Know Your Product or Service

What do you know about the product or service you want to advertise? What consumer needs does it fulfill? Do you understand how consumers currently perceive your product or service in terms of price, quality, relationship to competition, consistency, and inconsistency? Knowing the role your product plays in the market and how the product is perceived by consumers is essential to creating effective advertising. Without these basic facts, you cannot get a clear, realistic picture of where your product stands in the market and where you want it to be.

Advertise As Part of the Total Marketing Strategy

What role do you anticipate advertising will play in your total marketing strategy? Do you even need to use advertising as a marketing tool? If so, should you use advertising with a narrow range but direct aim, or do you want to target a large region with more general advertising tools?

Develop a Proposition

Have you developed a general **proposition** to be conveyed in your advertising message? A proposition is the strongest truthful statement you can make to the consumer on behalf of your product or service. Your proposition should agree with and support your overall marketing strategy, and meet the purpose of your advertising. For example, if you are trying to persuade people to use your product or service, does your advertising include a toll-free telephone number that consumers can call to order your product or service or get further information?

Create a Platform

Once you understand your product or service, the consumer's perspective of it, the role your advertising will play as part of your total marketing strategy, and you have developed your proposition, you can then focus on the advertising **platform.** The platform is an item-by-item list of facts that support your proposition. Platform statements illustrate the strength of your proposition.

Be Realistic About the Level of Expectation

Regardless of your advertising purpose and its strategic role in your overall marketing plan, there is one key principle that you should remember when advertising products and services. *Never promise more than your product or service can deliver.*[3] The **"level of expectation"** principle is graphically presented in Exhibit 4.1.

Keep this idea in mind whenever you plan advertising. Many companies/brands have made the mistake of promising more than they could deliver. The result was customer dissatisfaction.

Review for Customer Needs

Does your advertising strategy relate to your customers' needs? Your customers' needs should be the focal points of your advertising strategy. Are you reinforcing your product/service/brand attributes?

Once you understand the six guidelines just described, you can begin developing an actual advertising campaign.

Advertising Promotion and Platform → **Promise** → **80 to 95% of What Is Actually Deliverable** → **Result** → **Customer Satisfaction**

Advertising Promotion and Platform → **Promise** → **100% or More of What Is Actually Deliverable** → **Result** → **Customer Dissatisfaction**

EXHIBIT 4.1. Level of Expectation

THE SIX-STEP ADVERTISING PROCESS

The following is a six-step advertising process that can help you develop a successful advertising campaign.

Step 1: Identify Your Purpose

Clearly identify *one* purpose that you expect your advertising to serve. What do you want your advertising to do for you? Advertising is usually used to:

- Inform customers that your product or service is available and tells them how to get it
- Persuade consumers that your product or service is better than your competitors'
- Remind consumers to use your product or service

Identify the purpose for advertising your product or service and then make sure that the ads you create fulfill that purpose. For example, if you want to inform consumers that you are offering a new service, your ads should not focus on reminding consumers that you're still in business.

Step 2: Target Your Audience

Assuming that you know what you want to say and why you want to say it (your purpose), the next step is to precisely *identify to whom you want to say it.* You want to advertise to people who will buy your product or use your service. "Who are these people?" and "How do I reach them?" become the next critical questions to answer. Market research can tell you who and where your target consumers are, and proper selection of **advertising media** can help you reach them.

Step 3: Select a Medium

You want to reach as many potential customers as possible with the most effective, efficient, and affordable **medium** you can select for advertising. Depending on your product or service, and your target consumers, it may be television, radio, or magazine advertising; in other situations, it may be **direct mail,** directories, outdoor advertising, or the yellow pages. Your choice of **media** also depends on how much money you have to spend and the role advertising is to play in your total marketing plan.

Step 4: Create the Ad

The advertising you develop largely depends on all of the other steps and guidelines previously cited. Despite wide interest in great creative advertising, your product or service, purpose, and budget are the practical parameters of what you can and cannot do with your creative strategy. Make sure your ad is appropriate for your audience, product, service, and budget.

Step 5: Place and Time the Ad

Thanks to your (or your ad agency's) creativity, you have a great ad ready for the market. Don't blow it now! The proper selection of *where* your advertising goes and *when* it is aired is critical to the success of your advertising campaign. When you select where to place your ad, consider:

- Markets
- Media selection
- **Placement** (where and when your ad runs)

To determine when to run the ad, think about:

- Time of year
- Month
- Week
- Day of the week
- Hour of the day

Step 6: Fulfill Expectations

You ran a great ad at the right time and place, and now the phone is ringing off the hook. Is there *anyone* there to answer it? Make sure you can fulfill your ad promises after you have motivated the consumer to purchase. Meeting the expectations generated by your advertising should always be considered within the total context of your advertising strategy.

DO IT YOURSELF OR SELECT AN AGENCY?

Depending on your skills and the size of your budget, you may want to do an advertising campaign yourself or contract with an advertising agency to handle the campaign for you. For example, the scope and breadth of hospitality industry advertising is immense, ranging from local newspaper ads to national television campaigns. If you cannot afford the luxury of hiring an agency, here are a few suggestions to help you handle your own campaign.

First, start your own master notebook. This notebook should contain examples of clean ads that you have developed and used. The notebook will help you review the effectiveness of your ads and should include such information as how and where your ad came together. Include a section in the notebook labeled "Monitor" to record the history of your advertising and a statement of results. For example, it could read as follows:

> Tues., February 20. Print Ad "A-1"—*Telegraph,* Entertainment Page
> Wed., February 21. Print Ad "A-1"—*News,* Sports Page
> Thurs., February 22. Print Ad "A-1"—*Telegraph,* Lifestyle Page
>
> *Results:* Business up by 25% over same period last year and/or week.
>
> *or*
>
> Revenue up 16% February 22 and 28% February 23 compared with same period last year and/or last week.

This simple procedure will give you a history of which ads were run, where they were run, and the results.

Also, consider including in your master notebook examples of your competition's best advertising. Analyze the file to determine what advertising strategies your chief competitors are using, trends they're following, and what you can do to combat your competitors' moves. For example, let's say your competitor has advertised **"two-for-**

one" sales. Analyze their ads to determine if you can offer a similar or better sale. Look for patterns as to when these sales are run. For example, you might discover that your competitor runs a two-for-one ad the fourth week of every month. You might counteract this strategy by advertising your two-for-one sale during the third week of the month.

Selecting an Agency

If you can afford to hire an ad agency, you should probably do so, even if you believe you have the capability of running your own advertising campaigns. Why? Because advertising professionals are best equipped to navigate through today's complex and sophisticated marketing arena.

Selecting an agency is more like selecting a business partner than selecting just another supplier of services, so ask a lot of questions before forming this vital partnership. Agencies will provide you with their credentials in terms of work they have performed, awards they have won, current and past clients, and so on. Look closely at these credentials and talk to the agency's former and current clients to get a balanced perspective of the agency's strengths and weaknesses. Evaluate an agency's strengths and weaknesses in relation to your own. Where do you or your company need more help—for example, in creativity? in media planning? etc. The following is a list of the major functional areas within ad agencies; keep in mind that not every agency can be outstanding in every area:

- *Account management/account executive area*—the staff members in this area have the overall management responsibility for a brand, product, or client company; they are the primary contact persons with clients ("accounts") and manage the "account teams" (the persons who do the work for the clients)
- *Research*—provides quantitative and qualitative data on the market, needs, benefits, competition, customers, etc., using an array of services and techniques
- *Creative* (the imagination function)—generates ideas to link the brand or product to consumers' needs
- *Casting*—identifies people, voices, actors: the ingredients that make an ad or commercial work

- *Media*—looks for the best reach and frequency to reach your target audience, given your budget
- *Production*—pulls together creative, media, and other agency areas and delivers the final product

Perhaps the most important question to ask is: Who will actually work on your account—an experienced creative team or new hires?

Make sure that the agency you select knows something about your market and your customers. Good research, either conducted within the agency itself or contracted out to another research supplier, can increase your knowledge of target markets. If an agency immediately wants to discuss creative strategy, media, or contract, take another look. A good agency will listen and learn as much as possible about your product or service, markets or consumers, and about you and your overall marketing philosophies before moving on to actual strategies.

One way to choose an agency is to place your business out to bid or out for proposal. An amazing amount of good work done absolutely free of charge can come from bid presentations. Consider more than one agency in the proposal stage so that you will have a basis for comparison.

Only you can judge how long to stay with an agency or how often to switch. Make changes only when your objective measurements indicate that it is time for a change. Objective measurements include declining sales, lower levels of brand awareness among customers and potential customers, negative customer feedback about your advertising, excessive errors in the advertising copy, missed deadlines, and so on.

Trade-Outs, Barter, and Co-Oping

One way to reduce your advertising costs is to exchange your product or service for advertising space or broadcast exposure. An infinite variety of **trade-outs** or **barter** agreements exist which you can negotiate with advertising suppliers, ranging from a "one-for-one" trade to a "five-for-one" or even greater trade. A one-for-one trade means that you will provide a set dollar amount of products or services for an equal dollar value of space or air time, for example, $1,000 worth of your product or service for $2,000 worth of air time or space, and so on. If negotiated properly, trade-outs can be an effective way to stretch your advertising dollars and increase your business.

Another way to stretch advertising dollars is to **co-op,** or join with other companies to advertise, thereby sharing the costs. Resort areas frequently run cooperative advertising campaigns that promote the region or area and also list or mention specific products or services. A more popular use of co-oping is when two or more firms advertise each other's services or products, either individually or collectively, in the same advertising campaign.

ADVERTISING TYPES AND THEMES

An ad is not just the product of an idea. Effective advertising begins long before the "great idea" stage. As previously discussed, you need to answer some key questions regarding the purpose of the advertising, the platform, and the proposition. Even a great idea must have a purpose, or the ad campaign will be ineffective. Later in the chapter we will look at some examples of great advertising ideas. As you will see, great ideas can backfire if the consumer's reaction to an ad differs from the reaction the advertisers were trying to evoke. Different types of ads are described as follows.

Reputation Builders

These ads feature *testimonials,* self-claims, or other-party claims, or cite leadership or professionalism as a way to enhance the reputation of the product or service advertised. One common reputation-building technique is to have a recognized celebrity speak on behalf of the product or service, or lend his or her photo or signature as an implied **endorsement** of the product or service. A slightly different version of the celebrity testimonial is the self-testimonial ad, in which the CEO, president, or chairperson of the company speaks on behalf of the company's product or service. (This is also sometimes referred to as the "ego trip.")

Another form of the reputation builder is the *professional trust ad* in which the platform itself is self-implied professionalism. The ad features the entire property of company staff in uniform standing at attention, just waiting to professionally serve guests.

Finally, we have the "image" form of a reputation builder, in which one or more images are used to represent your product or service.

Product/Service Touters

A product or service touter ad can have a number of looks. The *direct* look features the product or service and boldly states the reasons for its greatness. Touting the actual elements of the platform produces results similar to those of the reputation-builder ads—they both enhance the product or service. Another form of touter ad is the *comparative research.* Here, the ad compares your product or service with a competitor's product or service to demonstrate that your product or service has more to offer than the competitor's.

A touter ad may feature an unusual product element or characteristic. For example, an amenity of unusually high quality may be the ad's focal point. Sometimes a touter ad will feature a scene such as an elegant-looking couple or a luxury setting as the positioning statement for the product or service. Product/service touter ads can have multiple elements, such as "we were rated highest by an independent survey, our service is extraordinary, and our facilities are world class."

Brand Identifiers

In today's crowded marketplace, getting your brand known—also known as achieving *brand awareness*—is not an easy job. What may be even more difficult is to effectively convey what your brand stands for, or your *brand identity.* To achieve brand awareness and brand identity:

- Include statements that boldly feature the brand.
- Develop a *brand identifier*—a *character, voice,* image, phrase, etc., that becomes synonymous with the brand.
- Make an introduction or announcement about the brand.
- Develop a niche by providing a unique service.

Offers

In an offer ad, the platform becomes part of the proposition. One common type of offer is the straight *price offer:* "Newark $99 Round Trip." In a price offer, the actual price, not necessarily the product or service itself, is featured and highlighted as the key motivation for consumers to buy. Another variation of the straight price offer is the price offer plus—something additional is included with the product at no additional cost.

Today, one of the strongest-hitting offer ads focuses on *repeat* or *build* promotions such as frequent traveler or frequent guest promotions. These ads feature offers or benefits for customers who repeatedly use one product or service.

Human Scenarios

A long-standing type of advertising is the *human scenario*. A person or group is the focal point of the ad, either directly or by an identifiable event or circumstance. For example, an employee or group of employees is featured, accompanied by a gratuitous statement or slogan, or an exceptional employee is portrayed as representing the norm.

On a more sophisticated level (and more risky if it doesn't work well) is a "situation identification." Here, a "wrong-way" scene is shown and a statement is made that this situation won't occur with your product or service. These often humorous ads should be carefully considered, because they can backfire.

Last, but certainly not least, is the age-old "suggestive" approach featuring or implying the promise of romance or sex to the consumer. This type of ad features an attractive person or implies how people who use the product or service become more attractive, successful, etc. The "hook" is a consumer's imagination.

Benefit

The benefit ad reflects the advertising platform in that it states, item-for-item, why consumers should purchase your product or service. Sometimes the ad will focus only on a primary benefit and at other times the benefit becomes engulfed in an overall umbrella of a more complex benefit and/or multiple benefits.

Series

Perhaps one of the most famous series ads to run in print was for Porsche. Actually numbered 1, 2, and so on, these bold ads stated the "numerous" reasons that Porsche was a superior automobile.

Line Art and Silhouettes

More of a technique or production treatment than ad type or theme, line art and silhouettes have become more and more popular in advertising. Their popularity stems largely from their effectiveness in a newspaper or other black-and-white setting.

Trade

A trade ad is aimed at intermediaries who are between your products/services and the consumer. These may be agents, distributors, wholesalers, retailers, etc. Trade ads should focus on the needs of the intermediary, i.e., new product information, commissions, etc.

Remember when selecting a type of advertisement to keep in mind your target market, their needs, the benefits they seek in your product/service and your own product/service attributes. Select an ad type that is compatible with the psychographics of your market and place it in an appropriate media vehicle.

MARKET COVERAGE

The next step is to think about where to expose your product or service to the consumer. Look at each case individually. There are no real golden rules for determining how and where to cover your market. You don't always have to stick to the same media or technique. In the following sections, we will discuss some definitions to help you understand different techniques for reaching your markets through advertising.

Nationwide Campaigns

Simply stated, nationwide campaigns give you coast-to-coast coverage or **exposure** of your product or service. If your market is nationwide or if you are trying to develop a national market presence, it might make sense to look at this type of total market exposure. Nationwide campaigns are particularly useful for large chains seeking to increase their brand awareness levels or provide an "image" for their brand. Also, nationwide campaigns can be used to introduce a national product simultaneously in all markets.

Major Markets

Based on research or because of budget constraints, you might want to advertise only in those major markets you want to penetrate with your campaign.

Regional Markets

Advertising can be purchased or selected on a regional basis also. There are many ways to identify marketing regions for your product or service. For example, one large chain of cafeterias selects only the southwestern United States for advertising exposure, since this is the primary market for its locations and customers.

Population Markets

Population markets are major **concentrations** of population that can be categorized according to size, such as standard **metropolitan areas** with populations of over 1,000,000, over 750,000, over 500,000, and so on. Populations may be measured in terms of viewers, readers, listeners, exposures, etc., depending on the type of media you are considering.

Viewer/Reader/Listener/Subscriber Market Areas

Television stations, radio stations, magazines, and newspapers can provide detailed descriptions of the number of people within their range or on their circulation lists. In addition, they can provide you with various *buyer characteristics* that will help you choose the best match of media to your product or service consumer. Using this advertising method allows you to better define a market area for your advertising message.

Feeder Markets

Feeder markets are geographical areas (markets) from which your customers originate and are usually likely targets for your advertising.

Cities

Advertising can be placed in individual cities or even in areas within an individual city. Local market research can be a valuable aid to selecting the proper media for each city.

MEDIA SELECTION

Carefully evaluate media selection before creating your advertising. *Broadcast media,* which include television and radio, provide one type of exposure for your product or service. *Print media,* which include magazines, newspapers, supplements, catalogs, directories, yellow pages, brochures, flyers, and so on, provide other types of exposure for your product or service.

Before you select media for delivering your advertising message, carefully analyze the various media to determine the number of potential customers they can reach, your expected return on investment, and the best, most cost-effective method to convey your advertising strategy. Again, consider your needs, purpose, and budget as part of your media analysis.

Media Strategies

Media strategies can be viewed or subdivided into planning, executing/buying, and measuring delivery. The overall goal is to deliver the target audience at the lowest cost in the most suitable environment for the message. Media "planning" simply involves selecting and sorting the various media in combinations and support levels that produce the most efficient and effective plan to achieve the marketing

objectives. Media "execution" is the actual process of negotiating/buying and placing the media after the plan and budget have been determined. "Measuring delivery" is the process that determines if types and weights of media have performed to deliver the target audiences initially calculated. The "target audience" is the target market simplified by listing key strategic and demographic descriptors.

An advertising media plan, like any plan, should contain a media objective, media strategies, a media plan calendar, and budget. Your plan should address: (1) to whom the advertising is aimed (target audience description); (2) where the advertising will go (market coverage desired expressed geographically); (3) when the advertising is to appear; and (4) how much advertising is needed for optimum communication (weight/impact).

Selecting media involves both qualitative and quantitative decisions. Key questions to consider include: (1) what are your target market's media behaviors and patterns (what do they watch, read, listen to, etc., and where); (2) what are their buying behaviors and patterns (when do they purchase your product/service); (3) when and where are the best times and places to reach your target market (i.e., direct mail to the home, drive-time radio, late news on television, etc.); and (4) what alternative media do they use (i.e., special interest cable channels, trade magazines, etc.).

Strategic decisions will have to be made with respect to **media mix**—the different types of media to be used (i.e., television, magazines, radio, etc.) that produce the most efficient and effective plan/results. Furthermore, **medium use** must be addressed, which includes the ad sizes, part of the day (day part), length of the commercial, type of faces, etc. Also, calculations will need to be made to determine the cost per thousand (CPM or cost per mil) to reach your audience. Finally, determinations will have to be made with respect to: geographic weighing (distribution of your advertising geographically); seasonality (purchasing patterns); relationship of media selected to product/market distribution; and the overall right time and right place to run/place your advertising.

To facilitate decision making, advertising agencies subscribe to services/organizations, which provide data on audiences, readership, etc., and on costs. Some agencies develop models based on the data of your product/service market characteristics. These models then provide various choice options. Table 4.1 provides a listing of some of the major data sources.

TABLE 4.1. Major Data Sources

Medium	Audience Data	Cost Data
Direct Mail	Direct Mail SRDS Dun's Marketing Services	Direct Mail SRDS Dun's Marketing Services
Magazines	Audit Bureau of Circulation (ABC) Simmons Market Research Bureau (SMRB) Mediamark Research Inc. (MRI) Individual Magazine Representative	Magazines SRDS Magazine representatives (Ad position is usually negotiable, but cost usually is not)
Newspapers	Simmons/Scarborough Report Newspaper Association of America Local newspaper representative	Newspaper SRDS (space costs national products) Local rate cards via newspaper representatives (lower cost for local business advertising than national products)
Outdoor	Traffic Audit Bureau (TAB) Local representative	Outdoor SRDS Outdoor representatives (costs are sometimes negotiable and board position is usually negotiable depending on availability)
Radio	RADAR—Network Arbitron Research—Spot	Network/station representatives Media Market Guide Radio SRDS (costs are negotiable)
Television	Nielsen Research Services (NTI, NSI)	Network/station representatives Media Market Guide Spot Quotations and Data, Inc. (costs are negotiable)

Source: Adapted from Hiebing, Roman G., and Cooper, Scott W. (1996). *The Successful Marketing Plan*, Second Edition (p. 313). Lincolnwood, IL: NTC Business Books.

Media Scheduling

When reviewing media **scheduling** it is a good idea to first determine how much "frequency" you need for your specific product/service/brand. The following lists provide an overview for frequency determination.

More Frequency	**Less Frequency**
New campaign	Established leader/brand/ product service
New product service	Strong market/strong competitive position
New brand introduction	Simple message
Trial offer	Established campaign
Promotion or sales event	Reminder messages
Complex message	Low or less crowded
Short product purchase cycles	Competitive advertising levels
Crowded/highly competitive advertising market	Longer purchase cycles

Once your overall frequency is identified, a number of options for advertising media scheduling are available:

- *Continuity Schedules*—continuous run at a relatively fixed level—nonseasonal—nonpromotional levels
- *Flighting in Scheduling*—generally three to six weeks of continuous advertising followed by hiatus periods or periods of no advertising
- ***Front Loading***—running heavier weight levels with the commencement of a media schedule—kickoff
- *Heavy-Up Schedules*—incorporate incremental media weight to support periods of higher market activity
- *Pulsing Schedules*—run in continuous on/off patterns

Media Measurement and Terminology

Not every media selection is evaluated or measured in the same way. "Rating points" for broadcast media are usually determined by a formula involving percent of "reach" and of frequency. Rating points may be expressed as GRPs **(gross rating points),** or TRPs (target rating points). A rating point is defined as 1 percent of the universe being measured. GRPs provide a common term of measurement to help assess how much weight is going into a specific marketplace and allows for comparisons between media selections. To determine total GRPs, reach (which is defined as how many homes/persons your message has reached, expressed in an absolute percentage) is multiplied by **frequency** (which is defined as how often the homes/persons have been reached on an average basis). The total GRP formula follows:

Percent Reach × Frequency = Total GRPs
(i.e., Reach 75 × Frequency 10 = 750 GRPs)

As previously discussed, there are different methods to measure specific types of advertising media. These are summarized as follows:

- *Broadcast* (TV, radio, etc.)—uses gross rating points to assess viewership/listeners in a defined marketplace. Percentage of reach multiplied by frequency equates to GRPs.
- *Direct Mail*—uses percent coverage for reach (number mailed/total market, target households, or target persons); number of mailings for frequency.
- *Magazine*—uses percent coverage for reach (circulation/total market households or total readers/target persons); number of insertions for frequency.
- *Newspaper*—uses percent coverage for reach (circulation/total market households or total readers/target persons); number of insertions for frequency.
- *Outdoor*—uses a standard four-week showing time frame, reach and "showing" (i.e., 50 showing = 85 reach and 15 frequency). Many view "traffic counts" as another key indicator of outdoor value.

Other evaluation and measurement techniques exist to help quantify overall media goals. These include what is referred to as the macro method wherein advertising is used as a percentage of sales based on an industry (specific to your product/service category) average. Here share of media voice (SOV) is compared to share of market (SOM). In the micro target method, the amount of GRP media weight that is necessary to effectively reach or communicate with large portions of your target market to assure that they understand your message to a degree to support a sale of the product or service offering is determined. Two other overall indicators frequently referred to are the BDI **(brand development index)** and CDI **(category development index).** BDI is determined by the relationship between the percent of product sales divided by the percent of households in a given market. CDI is the percent of category (product category) sales divided by the percent of households in a given market.[4]

Summary

Developing your advertising message requires detailed planning, establishing objectives, strategy, and execution. Objectives should be established for increasing awareness levels and changing attitudes/behaviors. Advertising strategy must address the overall "promise," "proposition" (support for the promise), and "tone" of the message. Advertising execution is based on key research information (data) and takes into consideration specific creative requirements, legal considerations (claims/disclaimers), etc.

An advertising checklist can help you determine if your advertising is organized and effective. The following checklist can be adapted to your own advertising efforts, and may prove to be a useful tool for your organization. A checklist can do more than save you money; it can provide a cross-check to ensure that advertising, sales, and public relations personnel are all working together to execute your marketing plan.

Advertising Audit/Checklist

___ Do your advertising plans support the objectives and strategies of the current marketing plan?

___ Does your chief marketing officer understand the responsibilities of everyone involved in executing the advertising strategy for your product or service?

___ Is the sales manager or director involved in the planning and execution of the advertising strategy and program? To what extent?

___ Do your key marketing and advertising people have good rapport with the media? Are they capable of executing trade-outs or barter agreements?

___ Do you have a master notebook containing up-to-date examples of your advertising?

___ Do you have a monitoring and results-measurement system in place to determine the outcome or effectiveness of your advertising expenditures?

___ Do you have a clippings file? Is someone specifically assigned to analyze what the competition is doing?

___ Are request forms, exceptions reports, insertion orders, sample copy, and sample ads readily accessible?

___ Is there a master file for all media and trade-out contracts?

___ Have you prepared advance advertising schedules?

___ Are advertising work request forms used? Are they sent in with sufficient lead time? Are copies on file?

___ How is the advertising production budget managed? Have all ads and expenditures received proper approvals?

___ Are insertion orders submitted to the media on time? Are copies of completed orders properly distributed?

___ Do all key marketing personnel understand the conditions of all media contracts—print, broadcast, outdoor, airport display, and trade-outs?

___ What is the condition of outdoor signs? When were they last checked? When are they scheduled for reprint?

___ Is an advertising verification process in place? Are all ad invoices from the media supported by tear sheets or affidavits? Are copies of invoices and tear sheets on file? Are they checked for accuracy against insertion orders?

___ Are rates and discounts verified? By whom? Are rate changes supported by new rate cards?

___ Have there been any major changes in the approved advertising schedules? Is everyone aware of these changes?

___ Have all deficiencies from the previous audit been corrected?

Developing your media plan requires establishing media objectives related to your target audience, geography, seasonality, advertising levels and placement, and overall qualitative judgment. Media strategies must address media mix, specific medium usage, and scheduling. A media plan checklist will assure that you are addressing key concerns and questions with respect to your media plan.

Media Plan Checklist

___ Will your plan provide a competitive advantage?
___ Is the media plan based on a factual assessment of your market and competition?
___ Is the media plan in sync with the overall marketing strategy?
___ Is the advertising media plan interlinked with all other marketing weaponry plans and strategies?
___ Is the media plan appropriate for the creative message that was developed?
___ Will the media plan support the promotional objectives and is it interlinked with the promotions calendar?
___ Is the media plan in sync with the geographic and seasonality patterns?
___ Is the type of scheduling appropriate to the objectives and overall expenditure levels?
___ Is the media plan delivering more (i.e., GRPs) than in previous years based on the level of expenditures?
___ Are evaluation and measurement processes in place to assess performance?
___ Are alternatives developed and ready for implementation?
___ Have all of the organizational functions been completely informed about the media plan?

Before we transition to the next major marketing weapon, public relations, two case examples of advertising strategies will be discussed.

CASE EXAMPLE 1: EXTREME TARGET MARKET EXECUTION

A small, upscale hotel and resort company trying to compete with much larger chains such as Hyatt, Hilton, and Westin needed to employ an advertising media/strategy we will call extreme target market execution.[5] The small chain's marketing budget was one-fifth to one-tenth of competitors' budgets. Its brand awareness on an unaided basis was less than 1 percent compared to its competitors' whose **unaided awareness** levels were in the 70, 80, and 90 percent levels.

With a very limited research budget, the small chain discovered, by "looking within" at its core customer base, that over 85 percent of all customers arrived by air. Furthermore, through some cooperative research with American Express, it discovered that over 75 percent of these core customers used the American Express credit card. These cardholders were then profiled and the results indicated demographic, psychographic, and benefits/needs findings. In essence, these core customers displayed a consistent habit of reading and viewing very specific media. Most of their reading was done while traveling, either on a plane or in their hotel room at night. Most of their television viewing during the week was limited to CNN Headline News or The Weather Channel. In fact, they were very consistent about the weather. They indicated that they checked the weather for their home location and the cities they were traveling to on a daily basis and sometimes up to three times a day. They also indicated that they carried a pocket edition of the airline timetables (pocket-sized official airline guide, or the American Express Skyguide). They almost all belonged to the airline VIP clubs. When questioned about their specific reading habits, nearly all indicated that they read *USA TODAY* and *The Wall Street Journal* daily, and when on planes would read or scan the major business publications such as *Forbes, Business Week,* etc.

Given this base of information, the hotel chain decided to drastically modify its media plan. It reduced and eventually eliminated all television advertising, except for a heavy schedule on CNN Headline News (time slots at the weather forecast) and an even heavier schedule on The Weather Channel. It also dramatically changed its print media plan by eliminating almost all sports/golf/tennis publications, almost all ads in travel magazines, and all ads in consumer magazines except for *Forbes* and *Fortune*. With these now available dollars, the hotel chain made the decision to seek to dominate media related to air travelers and weather watchers.

In the course of the next twelve months, the hotel had signed agreements providing it exclusive advertising rights with the following print media:

1. *USA TODAY,* where it created a new advertising space called the "weather band" (a 4 ½ inch horizontal bar at the bottom of the weather page).
2. *The Wall Street Journal,* where it provided a special weather forecast (through an agreement with The Weather Channel) on a daily basis in the upper right hand corner of page three of the paper.
3. It signed contracts for the back cover ad space of the pocket edition of the Official Airline Guide and the American Express Skyguide.
4. It purchased the inside front cover ad space and additional space in *Frequent Flyer* magazine providing monthly weather data.
5. It contracted with the company that supplied all of the consumer magazines (forty-five titles in all, including the business magazines) to all of the airlines with rights to the back cover and inside back cover advertising spaces, as well as the cardboard "wraps" or binders placed on the magazines.
6. It supplied these same magazines to all of the VIP clubs.
7. It secured the on-board video advertising rights in the hotel category with ABC Video, who supplied video programming to most of the major airlines at the time.
8. It also purchased ad space including inside front, back covers, and center spreads in the East-West network and other major airlines' on-board airline magazines.
9. On occasion, it purchased the rights to insert a miniversion of its directory in the plastic bags holding the personal headphones on the major airlines.

This concentrated target market media plan cost the same as the hotel's previous plan and was still one-fifth to one-tenth of what its major competitors were spending. With this advertising spending plan, the hotel was able to reach its target market customers and potential customers. In fact, their advertising was on all the televisions and in the newspapers at their competition's hotels. This resulted in: (1) a dramatic increase in brand awareness on par with competition on an **aided awareness** basis and to within 10 to 20 percent points on an unaided basis; (2) strong gains in market share, average rate, and occupancy increases; and (3) a perception that this hotel chain was five times its actual size (as perceived by the target market).

CASE EXAMPLE 2: ICON POWER

Icons can take many different shapes, forms, and personalities. Think of Mr. Clean, Colonel Sanders, the Energizer Bunny, and Ronald McDonald to name a few. One of the most successful advertising icons is "Jack" of the Jack in the Box fast-food chain. This icon changed not only its personality/character, but also rescued a fatally wounded fast-food chain. The original Jack was a wise guy radical character who had his swan song in a television spot where he attempted to blow up the boardroom. Shortly thereafter, disaster struck in the form of *e. coli* bacteria infections (which was linked to hamburger meat eaten at a Jack in the Box), that resulted in four deaths. Sales plummeted and the first Jack was shelved.

Resurrecting the brand was going to be a very difficult task. After all, they didn't want to talk about their hamburgers and remind everyone of the previous problem. It was inappropriate to bring back the old Jack, as his character related to a younger, youth-orientated market. Research indicated that the hamburger business had changed and so too would the character or the new Jack, if he were to come back and be on target/successful. According to the research, the market was now more complex and older. Distinct categories of burger eaters had evolved. These included what were referred to as the "cravers" or individuals that had to have their burger every day. There were the "dealers," those who wanted the most food for the dollar, and there were the "quality seekers."[6] How would the "new" Jack come back and how would he relate to these distinct types or segments?

The world-renowned Chiat/Day ad agency recreated Jack (the new Jack) as a new breed of executive clearly in charge and with a wonderful new personality as a smart-talking, no-nonsense executive/CEO. The new character, with its Ping-Pong ball head and yellow hat is recognized and easily distributed as a give-away and as a fixture for auto aerials across America. The new Jack has become an icon with the personality power to bring back the brand. His character allowed for over 100 different advertising spots each aimed at the three market segments and/or newly emerging segments. The results have been a remarkable turnaround for a brand many wrote off as deceased. The power of (Jack) the icon is a very tough ad concept to beat.

Key Terms

advertising
awareness
barter
BDI (brand development index)
CDI (category development index)
co-op
creative strategy
feeder market
GRPs (gross rating points)
icon
level of expectation
media
platform
proposition
scheduling
SOM (share of market)
SOV (share of media voice)
trade-out
TRPs (target rating points)

Chapter 5

Public Relations

The purpose of this chapter is to help you to understand how public relations can help improve sales and boost employee morale. Internal, or "within-the-house" public relations applications will be reviewed as well as the full range of external public relations techniques and methods. In addition, different types of public relations opportunities that have proven their worth will be examined. Finally, we will discuss how to tie your public relations effort to your marketing strategy and how to measure the results.

Public relations is a marketing weapon. It is a communications vehicle that connects your marketing message to a variety of audiences. Public relations must include the *total audience,* which includes the investment community, shareholders, and franchisees, among others, as well as intermediaries and individual consumers of your products and services. Public relations can effectively reach and affect everyone in this broad external audience. Furthermore, public relations can prove to be a very effective internal marketing device to communicate and motivate employees.

Publicity is only one facet of public relations. Publicity can be free, but it can also be negative as well as positive.[1] We will discuss publicity in more detail later in the chapter.

Many fallacies about public relations abound: "PR is BS"; "Public relations is undefinable—it doesn't do anything and can't be measured"; "It's a waste of time and money"; "Anyone can do PR work." People who make these comments either do not understand public relations or have only been exposed to disorganized public relations efforts. It's true, public relations does not directly make sales; however, it can be very influential in seeing that sales are made. In this chapter we'll look at some ground rules for various aspects of public relations, and explore what public relations is, how it can be applied, and how it can be measured.

WHAT PUBLIC RELATIONS IS

Public relations is a powerful marketing tool that is capable of reaching all marketing audiences. In positive applications, public relations is on the offensive; in negative situations, public relations can provide a strong defensive strategy.

Public relations involves dealing with all of the public, including individual consumers and potential consumers, the financial community, the local community, the media, and even your own employees. Effective public relations can provide a competitive advantage within your own business area—be it manufacturing, services, retail, or distribution. This competitive advantage is frequently overlooked, even by public relations personnel. In essence, a well-executed public relations program can provide a good image within your industry segment. That image pays dividends in consumer preference for your product or service, and it may also result in attracting and retaining good employees.

Public relations can create a favorable environment for your company, product, or service. It creates this favorable environment most effectively if it is part of the firm's overall marketing plan. Objectives, strategies, target markets, expected results, timetables, and measurement can and should be established for all public relations programs. Of equal importance in a formal plan for public relations is the selection of the trained professionals to create and execute the plan. It is an absolute fallacy to believe "anyone can do public relations."

The resources that can be used in public relations are unlimited. Following is a brief list of some of the vehicles public relations personnel use to reach various audiences:

- Announcements
- Broadcast media (TV and radio)
- Print media (newspapers, magazines, etc.)
- News conferences
- News releases
- Civic, social, and community involvement
- Employee relations
- Speeches
- Interviews
- Photographs

In addition, there are many different public relations techniques that can be employed to obtain media exposures. Numerous articles and books provide list after list of ideas and suggestions for generating positive publicity, but many authors forget one basic thing—the planned purpose or strategy for achieving such exposure. Even if your relationship with the media is superb, the use and placement of publicity must support your overall marketing strategies. The caution is simply stated: "Make your PR count." Some ideas for making your PR count are included in the following list. Each of the ideas listed should be placed within the context of an overall marketing strategy.

Public Relations Opportunities

- Accomplishments of employees or firm
- Activities involving your company employees
- Anniversary dates
- Appointments of key people
- Awards received by firm or employees
- Celebrities who use your products/services
- Community awards
- Contributions to charities and the local community by the firm or employees
- Displays of all types
- Events
- Events of special interest—humorous or creative
- Grand openings of all types
- Industry-related events
- Interviews
- New management, ownership, employees, etc.
- Openings of all kinds
- Organizational and/or operating changes of major significance to the public
- Public service events/activities
- Receipt of certificates, awards, etc.
- Recognition of people, places, things, etc.
- Special displays, features introduced, etc.
- Special events of all types
- Speeches of employees

How Public Relations Can Be Applied

Once the ideas and objectives for your public relations plan have been established and tied into the overall marketing plan, it is time to consider how to apply or execute those ideas. You must first answer some questions: (1) What medium can best execute this strategy? (2) Who are the key contacts for this task? (3) Is it necessary to establish or resolidify any personal relationships with the media before executing the strategy? (4) Do we have a delivery package ready for the media?

The **delivery package**—a package for the press containing news items, names of contact persons and their phone numbers, property information, photographs, brochures, and so on—is essential. Although there is no guarantee that your copy or materials will be used, it is much more likely that your public relations message will correspond to your intentions if you make a delivery package available. The list of delivery package requirements will aid you in compiling a package that will be useful to the media.

Delivery Package Requirements

- Addresses and phone numbers of key media contacts
- Addresses and phone numbers of key corporation personnel
- Approval procedures and required forms
- Biographies of key personnel
- Briefing sheets on individuals, company, product, etc.
- Brochures, if applicable
- Product/service procedures and policy
- "Canned" formats, releases, letterheads, logos, symbols, etc.
- Confidentiality statements/procedures
- Contacts list and phone numbers/procedures
- Ad copy samples and actual copy
- Displays, podiums with logos, etc.
- News conference procedures list
- Photo inventory of product, people, etc.
- Photo library and selection ready for press
- Previous problems files and checklist
- Previous questions files and checklist
- Price/information

- Procedures for distribution
- Promotional package on firm or product
- Request forms—data, photo, product information, etc.
- Scrapbook or clippings files
- Speech copies for distribution

Some public relations opportunities—speeches, press conferences, meetings, interviews, and so on—involve personal contact with media personnel and others. If you are going to employ one of these direct-contact PR methods, you need to prepare the individual(s) who will be making the direct contact with the media. *Thorough preparation is essential for successful direct-contact public relations.* Ground rules and suggestions abound as to how to prepare a speech or other public presentation. Assuming your spokesperson follows the rules and makes a good presentation, there is still one critical mistake that can be made—using the wrong person. Simply stated, be sure you put the right speaker in front of the media. If the talk is on technical matters, be certain that the speaker has total command of the technical terms. If the talk is on corporate strategy, be sure the individual has enough authority within the corporation to be credible. If the talk is on your own product or service, make sure the speaker can relate it to the audience's perspective. The following is a brief list of public speaking do's and don'ts:

Do's

- Carefully organize and allow yourself enough time to prepare.
- Be prepared—write out the talk, memorize it, and keep notes.
- Rewrite, review, and rewrite again.
- Create an outline or plan for your speech and follow it.
- Use pauses for emphasis.
- Check and double-check the visuals, equipment, room, visibility, etc.
- Speak out clearly and deliver smoothly.

Don'ts

- Don't speak on subjects about which you are not qualified.
- Don't ad lib.

- Don't guess or estimate numbers.
- Don't read in a monotone.
- Don't use excessive pauses, either in number or length of time.
- Don't prepare unreadable visuals.
- Don't mumble, slur, laugh to yourself, etc.
- Don't wait to read what you are going to say until the plane ride or cab ride to the location for your speech.

Dealing with the Press

Dealing with the press is one of the most difficult tasks marketing and public relations personnel undertake. It is difficult for many reasons, but most of all because the press is *powerful.* It reaches many consumers with a message in writing, so you must be absolutely certain that the press has your facts correct.

Again, many good articles have been written on public relations and the press, many golden rules have been laid down, and many do's and don'ts have been listed. The recognition factors that follow represent a composite of a number of such lists. These are not all-inclusive, nor are they intended to be golden rules. They are factors that may keep your public relations efforts on a positive note—on the offensive rather than in a defensive position.

Recognition Factors

1. *Identify your purpose.* What is your purpose or reason for seeking the public relations exposure? If your purpose is to make others aware of your new product/service, be sure that is exactly what you convey—don't let it be lost in a story about your production process. Be precise and be sure your intent is communicated.
2. *Identify your target and objectives.* Who is your target? Is it prospective consumers of your product? Is it the local financial community? Is it your employees? What are your objectives? Do you want to boost employee morale? Do you want to increase sales or brand awareness, support a new promotion, etc.? Think it out and identify how and where in the media you will best achieve your objectives.

3. *Understand the press's perspective.* You know your purpose and your target; that is your perspective. What is the press's perspective? Identify and understand the press's interests. Determine how you can place your purpose and target within a package that directly meets the interest of the press or other media. Think about what will help increase their circulation.
4. *Tailor your preparation.* Having identified your purpose, your target, and the media's perspective, tailor your preparation to include all three. Be sure to include everything that the press will need to convey the story—photos, names, and releases. Be sure your story is typed, double-spaced, and in the style the medium is currently using. *Follow the editorial style of your selected medium at all times.*
5. *Know the transmission channels.* Knowing where to send your material means knowing the difference between a news and a feature story. News should be directed to the city desk and feature stories should go to the appropriate editor. Better yet, get to know the editors who can be of most help to you and cultivate those relationships (but don't wear them out).
6. *Deal with the human element.* People do not like extra work or being pressured, and most cannot afford the time to tell you the ground rules. People basically want the easy way out. This sounds cruel, but it should help you understand how to deal with the human element. Find out the media's deadlines in advance. Do not waste your time or the valuable time of media contacts. Do as much of their work as you can. Remember, if your material is well prepared and you do most of the work for them, your material may be used. If you do not do the work, you can expect nothing to appear. Also, remember to be available to respond to any media questions or requests for clarification. If you are unavailable, your material may be scrapped or come out wrong.

You will also need some guidelines for answering questions from media representatives. The keys that follow are not all-inclusive, nor are they original, but they are very practical:

1. *Tell the truth.* The message you want to convey should be pure fact. The media want credible, straightforward, and truthful material and relationships. This simply means that your materials

should be thorough and honest. It does not mean that you need to reveal confidential data or private sources, nor does it mean you should violate confidentiality.

2. *Be responsive.* You may not have all the answers at your fingertips for every question or inquiry. Do not lie or guess; say, "I do not have that information with me; however, I will call you and provide it today." Then get the information fast and provide it accurately.
3. *Provide the facts and follow up.* Supply the key facts in print to lessen the chance of being misquoted on key data. If at all possible, follow up with media personnel by going over the facts or key numbers with them to ensure accuracy. If you do not have a requested statistic, get it and call or send a note to the person who requested it. Be sure accurate numbers reach the media.
4. *Be concise.* People usually get into trouble with the media for what they say, not for what they do not say. Provide the facts in a concise, uneditorialized, and unexaggerated manner. Be precise and accurate. Ranges may be okay, but pulling numbers out of the sky is a disaster.
5. *Build the relationship.* If you follow steps 1 through 4 by being truthful, responsive, factual, and concise, you are on your way to achieving the fifth practical key—building good relationships with media personnel. Hostile attitudes, reactionary statements to sensitive questions, aloofness, or a combative position damage relationships with the press. Work hard at being in control of yourself and your responses, no matter what you think of the media or a particular media representative. After all, someone who dislikes you is not going to be eager to give you space or air time.

TOOLS OF PUBLIC RELATIONS

A **press kit** is usually a two-sided folder of high quality, often customized with the firm's logo or other identification markings. Background materials are normally placed in the left side pocket, timely news items in the right. Examples of background information might include biographies of key property personnel, property fact sheets, and photographs. Timely news items include the actual **press release(s).**

The cover of the kit should not only convey your firm's image, but also be of a practical weight, size, and nature to protect photos. Photos should be clearly labeled on the reverse side. Few things are more embarrassing to marketers than to have the wrong photo get picked up with a press release.

Press releases may sometimes be picked up verbatim. Therefore, all releases should be "in form" and grammatically flawless. In form means that the release should be exactly in the form you would want a publication to present your story. More often, the press release will be used as background or a resource from which the magazine or newspaper editor or reporter will work to mold an actual story. Seven keys to creating a press release with the proper form follow:

Key 1: The top right or left corner of the press release is almost always used for the name of the "contact" person(s); sometimes the contact person(s) appear at the end of the release. These contacts are the people who are readily available to provide more information. This means that they should be knowledgeable enough to speak to the press. Under the names should appear their phone numbers, fax numbers, and addresses.

Key 2: A specific release date should be noted at the top of the page, slightly below the contact information. If the information is for a feature story that can appear at any time or is otherwise not date sensitive, the words "FOR IMMEDIATE RELEASE" should appear there, usually in capital letters and sometimes underlined.

Key 3: The headline should be presented in capital letters and underlined (if desired) about one-quarter to one-third of the way down the first page. Considerable effort should go into developing the headline, because it is the "hook" that might catch the editor's eye or make your release stand out from others seeking the same precious space.

Key 4: The "dateline"—city and state in capital letters followed by the month and day—should be the lead into the actual text of the release. Datelines are important because they tell the reader where and when an event is occurring.

Key 5: The "body" or main part of the release should always be double-spaced. Paragraphs should be short, journalistic, and to the point. Like the headline, the first few sentences or lead is a hook that must grab the attention of the reader and address the key questions (who, what, where, when, and why—the five Ws).

Key 6: Including a few quotes is almost standard procedure with a press release. Whether the quote is from an internal source (someone employed by the organization issuing the release) or an external source, it is imperative that the individual quoted is aware of and approves of the quote. It is best to also let the individuals being quoted know of the date and time of the release so that there are no surprises. When multiple quotes are used, it is usually best to alternate direct quotes (those in quotation marks) and factual nonquoted information.

Key 7: Photographs almost always enhance a story. You cannot always read the minds of those picking up your releases/stories; therefore, if you do not know the specifications, it is usually better to provide black and white photos as well as color photos. Color slides or negatives (assuming the publication uses color) are generally better, but send the actual photo to help the editor see what is on the slide or negative.

Internal Public Relations

The jobs of many people are challenging and require long hours. Keeping employees motivated and proud of their jobs is a difficult task. One of the most effective devices for combating these problems is a well-organized internal public relations effort. It can take many shapes and forms. An especially effective technique is to promote or provide special recognition of employees, their efforts, or even their interests. "Employee of the Month" awards, posters, photos, and so forth, all work well. Special incentive awards, and related public relations also are a valuable motivational tool. Giving cash, **prizes,** or even novelty awards or plaques to deserving employees will help boost morale. Activities and events that employees and managers do together—a bowling club or a joggers' group, for example—will help build a team spirit. A common goal, such as companywide support of a selected charity, is another type of internal PR device for building unity. Perhaps most important of all is the continual recognition of human dignity, pride, and desire for respect. Make internal public relations one of your key strategies for helping your employees be productive and happy.

How Can Public Relations Be Measured?

You frequently hear this comment: "PR is useless because you can't measure it." This is absolutely false! If a public relations program is well organized, it can be measured in many ways. One way is to measure the number and type of media exposures received. Keep a scrapbook of clippings and a current log of exposures—newspaper stories, magazine articles, mentions on the local television news, and so on. Set goals for the number and type of exposures, then measure actual performance versus target.

A second measurement method is geared to evaluating the effectiveness of internal PR efforts. Look at questionnaires that assess employee morale, as well as employee turnover rates, breakage, pilferage, etc. If your internal PR is working, certain quantifiable trends should emerge. Do not, however, ignore a more subjective yardstick of your efforts: have you improved the esprit de corps in your organization? Are employees busy and enthusiastic?

Specific public relations activities may be measured by increases in sales. For example, if a major event or product is promoted through PR, and sales volume directly increases as a result of additional customers coming in for the event or for the product, you will know that public relations is working for you.

The following is a short checklist to assist in managing the public relations function.

Public Relations Checklist

___ Does a PR plan exist and does it support the current priority areas of marketing?

___ Do the director of marketing and all staff members understand their responsibilities with respect to the press, PR firm, and other outsiders?

___ Do key managers have good relations with the local media?

___ Are press release mailing lists up to date, accurate, and readily available?
___ Are *fact sheets* readily accessible to all and near the phones?
___ Are *photo files* up to date and fully stocked? Is there an up-to-date black-and-white photo file?
___ Are brochures and other collateral materials accessible?
___ Are there definite plans, budgets, reviews, and measurement procedures in place for PR?
___ Is there a property or product press kit? Is it up to date?
___ What is the quality of photos and stories, and how are they to be used?
___ Are all key employees briefed and knowledgeable about the value of public relations? Do they know the procedures to follow for press inquires?
___ Are PR network memos kept on file? Where? How often are they looked at or discussed?
___ When was the last PR audit? What were the results, and were all follow-up steps completed?

Publications and Trade Media

Most industry sectors have publications dedicated to the types of firms, products, and services within the industry sector. These are referred to as trade publications. They are often widely read by those who have an interest in your industry such as wholesalers, distributors, agents, and other intermediaries. These are excellent sources in which to publicize a new product, explain a change in policy or change in management personnel, etc. In general, it is also usually less expensive to advertise in the trades and easier to obtain coverage for your releases, stories, etc.

Should your product or service lend itself to advertising in consumer-related publications, be sure that your ad agency and public relations department/agency work together. Frequently, in order to secure your advertising, consumer publications will provide "advertorial" type space or agree to include your product/service in a story or article. The synergy of advertising and public relations working together is a win-win scenario.

Many different types of PR can be pitched in publications. These include new releases, announcements for an event, feature stories, concept articles, opinion pieces, and public service announcements (PSAs). Remember that publicity is a non-paid media communication that helps build target market awareness and positively affects attitudes for your product/services, brand(s), and/or firm. Just like all other marketing weapons, public relations should be planned and work in concert with your total marketing strategy. Public relations is your best marketing weapon for establishing creditability and building trust. Exhibit 5.1 shows a simple way to help you remember six tools or focal points for public relations.

CASE EXAMPLE 1: SOURCES AND EXPERTS

One goal of public relations is to extend your brand awareness and work in conjunction with your overall marketing strategies. Achieving press/media coverage is no easy task as there is limited space or air time and unlimited demand for that space or air time. One major medical clinic became a master at garnering space in local, national, and international media. It developed a multifaceted plan for its public relations program with a goal to enhance its reputation and achieve the highest top-of-the-mind awareness. The plans were interlinked with other marketing weaponry such as research and advertising. The medical clinic capitalized on its research capabilities by conducting a series of surveys and questionnaires on a variety of topics. Each time a newsworthy finding was discovered, a series of steps was taken to assure broad distribution and related name awareness for the medical

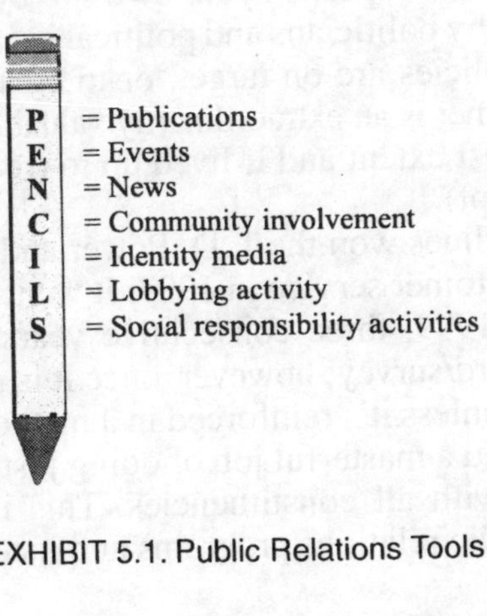

EXHIBIT 5.1. Public Relations Tools

clinic. This strategy relied on both primary research and secondary research to create items (findings) that would generate media attention. For example, "a recent study by the XYZ Clinic revealed that 75 percent of American children are overweight." This is the type of finding that has broad appeal and will get the media's attention. Other releases dealt with findings on heart attacks, smoking, the elderly, cancer, etc. The planned and systematic approach soon began to convey the positioning message that this was one of the best-informed medical clinics (a "source of expertise") as well as build its brand/ name awareness.

The medical clinic went one step further by providing an "experts" call line for the media. If the media had a health or disease-related question, all they needed to do was dial a 1-800 number and they would receive an answer from one of the medical clinic's experts in the field. This proactive approach to the media resulted in not only awareness building, but also in creating the perception of being the medical clinic with a vast resource of expertise. It helped build the medical clinic's reputation to one of the best in the country.

CASE EXAMPLE 2: THE POWER OF THE SURVEY AND AWARD

There are two ways to use the power of the survey or award. One is to be fortunate enough to be ranked number one in an external objective consumer survey of products or services in your category. The other is to conduct and report on your own survey. This latter practice is frequently used by politicians and political parties to create perceptions that their policies are on target, or to create momentum for a candidate. The former is an extraordinarily valuable marketing weapon if used to the fullest extent and if lived up to (remember the level of expectation concept).

Continental Airlines won the J. D. Power and Associates number one ranking in customer service in 1997. It went on to win this ranking in 1998 and 1999, three consecutive years. Granted, this is a highly visible award/survey; however, once it is released, it could be yesterday's news unless it's reinforced in a methodical manner. Continental Airlines did a masterful job of doing just that, reinforcing its accomplishment with all constituencies. This included employee-based internal public relations programs and incentives, external advertising campaigns, and constant reminders in its promotional literature, timetables, frequent traveler programs, etc. In fact, Continental's CEO, Gordon Bethune, even wrote a book *From Worst to Best* that further publicized the achievement. In a business where service is the business and a major competitive advantage, Continental has the edge as a result of reinforcing its achievement through an aggressive internal and external public relations program that is also interlinked to its other marketing weapons.

Key Terms

delivery package
exposures
news releases
press
press kit
public relations
publicity
trade media
transmission channels

Chapter 6

Promotions

Promotions have been used widely in many industries for a long time and are powerful and effective marketing tools. Promotions should support the overall marketing effort and be linked to the strategic marketing plan and other marketing weaponry whenever possible. Promotions can be defined as an activity offering added incentives to stimulate incremental purchase or **trial** purchase for a product or service. They may be aimed at target market consumers and/or trade intermediaries. Incentives to purchase include price, incremental products/ services, merchandise or gifts, experiences and allowances (cash, **credit,** etc.). Promotions may be "immediate" or on the spot, "chance" driven, and of the instant or delayed payoff nature. They are measured in terms of incremental volume (sales, units, revenue, profit, etc.) or desired behavioral outcomes. Promotions may be delivered via the media, through sales personnel, or in or near the package/unit/ outlet, etc.[1]

Parameters for promotions are time specific and include causing incremental consumer behavior over what was normally anticipated. Promotions usually have a specific, singular, identifiable goal, which can be measured quantitatively or qualitatively. They may also be limited by geographic focus. Promotions are usually designed to affect target market behavior through bringing back current users, increasing trial from new users, increasing purchases from current users, and/or obtaining repeat usage after trial. There are two general categories of promotions, open and closed. An open promotion is one in which the business offers an added incentive to purchase with no specific behavior required to take advantage of the offer, e.g., a 40 percent-off sale in a store. A closed promotion is one in which an added incentive to purchase is offered to consumers, but they are required to do something in order to take advantage of the offer, e.g., clip and present a voucher or **coupon.**

An infinite number of different promotions abound, and their diversity is limited only by the boundaries of people's imaginations. However, the one element common to all promotions is that they are designed to fulfill marketing needs. These needs may include building new business, gaining a greater share of existing business, keeping business, or gaining repeat business. Regardless of the type of promotion, the objective is to support the overall marketing effort and it should be linked to the overall plan and other marketing weapons when possible.

Just as there are many reasons for promotions, there are many keys to making promotions successful, which are discussed in the following section.

KEYS TO SUCCESSFUL PROMOTIONS

There are ten keys to successful promotions:

1. *Purpose.* Why is the promotion needed? Answering this fundamental question is the start of executing a good promotion. Is the promotion necessary to create new business? To stimulate demand in a down period? To take business from a competitor?
2. *Target identification.* Who is the promotion aimed at? Be specific in identifying your target. Is the promotion geared toward potential first-time users of your product or service? Is it geared toward previous users? Are they young or old, male or female, upscale income or low income?
3. *Type matchup.* What is the best type of promotion for the purpose and target identified? There are many types of promotions, and not every one will be compatible with your creative idea, or, more important, with your marketing objective. Some key questions to ask are: What is it I want to promote, and to whom? What is the demographic and psychographic profile of my target?
4. *Execution determination.* Once you know the purpose of the promotion, its target, and the type of promotion required, it's time to determine how to carry out the promotion. To do so,

you must answer these questions: What is the best method to reach the target? When is the best time to promote? Where is the best place to promote?

5. *Fulfillment.* Anticipate the needs that the promotion will create and be sure you can fulfill them. Ask yourself this critical question: If this promotion works as planned, will I have enough available products or services to meet the demand? Otherwise, you may well lose that sale or customer for good.
6. *Fallback.* No one is ever completely correct in predicting the response to every promotion. If your promotion is a greater success than expected, you may not be able to fulfill the expectations created by the promotion. To avoid customer dissatisfaction in this situation, plan a fallback or substitution. An important key when planning a fallback is to ensure that it is of like or better value than the promoted item. Even if you use the "rain check" fallback, consider adding some extra value to that rain check to offset the customer's inconvenience.
7. *Real expectation.* Promote only what you intend to deliver. Never lie, exaggerate, or make false promises. Always remember that the level of expectation your promotion creates *must* be fulfilled for the customer to be satisfied.
8. *Communication.* Don't forget to tell everyone at your company exactly what you promoted and how it is to be fulfilled. Be sure you clearly communicate in writing such key items as price, quantity, acceptance procedures for the promotion, dates, times, and other key details. Nothing is more irritating to a consumer than responding to a promotion only to find that no one at your company knows about it.
9. *Measurement.* Why did you go through the entire promotion effort? Establish a goal or goals and measure the results of your effort. Did the promotion do what you wanted it to do? Did it accomplish more or less than expected? If more, will it work as well again? If less, what went wrong?
10. *Record keeping.* Write down what you did for the promotion and how it worked. Don't be forced to reinvent the wheel next time. How often have you heard, "What was that promotion we ran so successfully a few years ago?"

TYPES OF PROMOTIONS

Many different promotions have been used in various industry sectors. Most of these can be grouped according to the following types or classifications:

1. ***Price.*** This is a promotion in which the incentive to purchase is based on price. The price is the main attraction and is featured prominently in the promotional message.
2. *Trial.* This is a promotion designed to get your target to try your product or service. Price is one method that is frequently used to motivate customers to try something. Sampling is yet another technique.
3. *Share.* This is a promotion geared toward taking market share away from the competition through some form of incentive. Lower price, an upgraded product, or an advantage clearly established over the competition is the focus of the promotion.
4. ***Introductory.*** This is a promotion designed to introduce a new product or service to the market. An introductory promotion may also be designed to build repeat purchases.
5. *Build.* This is a promotion designed to build repeat business through an increase in the reward or payoff for multiple purchases. Frequent flier programs are forms of build promotions.
6. ***Giveaway/sweepstakes.*** This is a promotion geared toward getting people to buy your product or service by offering the chance of a monetary award or a giveaway item. Giveaway item promotions are referred to as premium promotions.
7. *Ego/recognition.* This is a promotion designed to appeal to an individual's desire to be valued. These promotions may offer customers special recognition in the forms of upgrades, special product customizations, or complimentary services.
8. ***Tie-ins.*** This is a promotion of a product or service that ties into another company's product or service. Usually a tie-in is undertaken when there is a clear benefit to both parties.
9. ***Refunds/rebates.*** This is a promotion designed to provide a cash incentive (equivalent to a discount) to purchase. These

are most often used to stimulate sales or clear out items, e.g., automobile rebates.

10. *Trade allowances (commissions/discounts).* These promotions provide a monetary incentive to the trade or intermediaries.
11. *Events.* This is a promotion built around a specific event, e.g., the appearance of an entertainer, concert, designer, etc.
12. ***Cooperative.*** This is a promotion similar to a tie-in in which two firms cooperatively promote a product or service for a mutual benefit. The cooperative promotion may be undertaken because of the limited budget of each firm, or because the products or services are of more value promoted together.

There are many other types of promotions or variations of the promotions listed. Some promotions may be intended to build good will, others are designed as paybacks for the use of your product or service, and still others are designed to expand the awareness of your product or service into new **market areas** or expose new **market segments** to your product. Always keep in mind your purpose for entering into a promotion and the *benefit* you will receive from the promotion.[2]

A word of caution is appropriate at this point. Do not enter into a tie-in, cooperative, or other **joint promotion** without determining the impact that the promotion will have on your base business, your image, or your overall market. Although it is enticing to be offered a low-cost tie-in to someone else's package or promotion, it may not always be beneficial. In fact, it could be detrimental. Look closely at your own image and reputation and make it your rule of thumb not to enter into a joint promotion unless the other parties have an equal or better overall reputation.

Methods for Executing Promotions

One of the key reasons promotions fail is because the wrong method of execution is used. Take the time to determine the best promotion method for reaching your target and achieving your purpose. These methods include advertising (outdoor, displays, TV, radio, and print), direct mail, **tent cards,** publicity, personal selling, handouts, telephone sales, a special benefit to loyal customers or club members in monthly billings, online offers, and so forth.

You may promote your purpose and reach your target by directly appealing to the end users of your product or service, or you may reach your target through appropriate intermediaries such as **agents,** retailers, wholesalers, suppliers, organizations, associations, bureaus, **franchise** affiliates, and distributorships. You may use credit card mailing stuffers, mailing lists, someone else's outlets, and posters and flyers of all types. Just make sure you select the methods that most efficiently and effectively reach your target and accomplish your purpose.

Internal Promotions

Frequently, a major way to increase the revenue and profit yield from your existing customers is to promote to them once they are inside your door. This can be achieved in many ways, but should be done selectively and with a specific purpose or goal in mind. Internal promotions should be created and executed with the same care that is given to external promotions. In fact, there are additional considerations to take into account when promoting internally. Assuming all the keys to successful promotions have been followed, consider these additional items:

- *Compatibility.* Is your internal promotion compatible with how your customers perceive your product or service? Never cheapen the image that your loyal customers have of you by using a slapped-together, poorly thought out, poorly executed promotion.
- *Benefit.* Will your internal promotion not only meet your purpose, but also offer a perceivable benefit to the customer? Will it keep the customer as a friend, or will the customer be offended?
- *Value.* Does the internal promotion provide your customers with a perceived value for their money? Value means quality at a fair price—not cheapness.
- *Clutter avoidance.* Will your internal promotion piece clutter or detract from your environment where it is presented? Be sure your overall product quality is not cheapened as a result of the physical promotion piece or content of the promotion.

These considerations should be thought out prior to doing any internal promotions of your own or allowing anyone else's promotions to be viewed by your customers.

Cost/Payback

When developing a promotion, it is essential to preplan your costs and try to ascertain the desired payback. This requires identifying all of your "redemption costs," such as: the "value" of the discount (e.g., coupon), the number of coupons distributed, the estimated redemption rate, the number redeemed, and the dollar value or offer (number redeemed × value of coupon). In addition, advertising and media costs need to be factored into the equation. These costs include the printing, mailing, envelopes, and any design or legal costs. After arriving at the total cost of the promotion, a "payback" calculation can be determined. Included in this calculation are estimated sales with and without the promotion (to arrive at the promotional impact on sales in dollars or units), estimated gross margin dollars for the period with and without the promotion, and estimated net margin dollar increase with the promotion. The same rationale of calculating with and without advertising and media costs should be applied. Also, any incremental advertising and media costs attributable to the promotion should be factored into the calculation. The **payout** factors also need to include incremental margin sales, incremental advertising and media expenditures, and contribution to fixed overhead.[3]

The promotions checklist that follows provides some key questions that should be addressed before undertaking a promotion.

Promotions Checklist

___ Are your promotions part of your total marketing effort/plan?
___ Are your promotions scheduled at the optimum times to produce the desired results?
___ Are your promotions in sync with your other marketing weapons?
___ Do your promotions support your image and positioning?
___ Is the promotion appropriate or matched to the objective/strategy or purpose?

___ Can your competitors readily match or "one up" your promotional offer?
___ What are the quantifiable expectations (results)?
___ How much will the promotion cost and how much return do you expect/desire?
___ Is the promotional incentive strong enough to evoke the behavior change/incremental purchase desired?
___ How will the promotion be delivered in the most effective and efficient way?
___ Do you have a fallback planned and ready to go?
___ Is everyone posted/communicated with and/or trained who needs to be?
___ When will the promotion begin and how long will it remain in effect?
___ Have you checked with your legal department with respect to the promotional offer?
___ How can you maximize the distribution of the promotional offer?
___ Is there anywhere (geographic area) you do not desire the promotion to be run?
___ Can you fulfill the promotional offer if it succeeds beyond your response estimate?
___ How will the promotion be communicated to the sales force, distributors, agents, etc.?
___ How will you actually measure the promotional results?
___ If the promotion does not work, do you have a cut-off plan?
___ Is the promotion consistent with your overall positioning for the product, service, or brand?
___ Have you reviewed the history of the specific offer or similar offers?
___ Is there a logical partner to co-op with to give you a stronger promotion or extend your reach?

Here is a recap of some types of promotions.

Promotions—Types/Tools

- Contests
- Coupons
- Bonus offers

- Build promotions
- Events
- Sweepstakes
- Refunds/rebates
- **On pack**/in pack
- Premiums
- Sampling
- Trial offers
- Price
- Introductory
- Share
- Tie-ins
- Cooperative
- Ego/recognition
- Giveaways

CASE EXAMPLE 1: MORE THAN A PROMOTION

Although one objective of a promotion is to build short-term business, some promotions can achieve that and much more. In the 1990s, Pearle Vision ran one such promotion. Their concept was quite simple. They provided a percent discount that equated to the consumer's age bracket, e.g., 40 years of age got 40 percent off, 50 years of age got 50 percent, etc., and 100 years of age got 100 percent off or free glasses. Pearle knew that it would lose money on those 100-year-olds; however, it recognized the immense value of the public relations this promotion could generate. Needless to say, every time a 100-year-old person received free glasses there was a photo opportunity and a feeling of goodwill toward the company brand. The media (newspapers and local television stations) just loved the concept.

Pearle also solicited that "800-pound gorilla" everyone wants for a partner—the partner with both the size and reputation to provide instant success. In this case, AARP (American Association of Retired Persons) was selected as a partner. The ads describing the discounts were placed in AARP's magazine/newspaper. The AARP members simply had to show their membership card for the discount. You can imagine the sales impact of some 30 million-plus target market consumers getting that offer! Again, the awareness created by the public relations in local markets reinforced the national promotion from

Florida to California and from Texas to Minnesota. This was much more than a promotion, it was a brand builder and a public relations bonanza.

CASE EXAMPLE 2: LEFT BRAIN/RIGHT BRAIN

One frequently used generalization is that people who are financially and analytically oriented are dominated by the left side of their brain while those who are more marketing and creatively oriented are driven by the right side of the brain. One hotel chain discovered that its customer base was equally divided between "left brainers" and "right brainers." This posed a dilemma in terms of what the awards should be in its promotional offer. The solution was to view this information as a research and marketing opportunity. Focus groups with each group revealed contrasting perspectives. Left brainers categorically preferred the lowest rates and right brainers consistently wanted payoff-type rewards, either upgrades to suites, executive levels, or other ego-driven recognition. Left brainers wanted to "beat the system" and right brainers wanted to "break the rules." As the focus groups evolved, a few common perspectives emerged. Both wanted to be appreciated for their patronage. Both wanted to pay corporate or preferred rates for their volume. Both wanted to be treated differently than other guests. Both wanted to be recognized by some sort of club or membership program.

Based on this research and focus groups, a new, frequent-guest program was developed to appeal to both the left and right brainers. The club membership was provided to both groups at no cost by waiving the initial fee "compliments of a co-op partner" (airline, credit card company, rental car company, etc.). This established a perceived value to the membership. To the left brainer it was "paid for by someone else." To the right brainer it was "they recognize my importance."

The rewards structure presented a real challenge. Awards would have to appeal to both groups and would have to be perceived on a corporate and/or preferred rate. The solution was found in the research which indicated that the left brainers responded to the "beat the system" concept and the right brainers to the "break the rules" notion. Each group was offered an automatic upgrade to the executive/club level or a suite, if available, at the corporate or preferred rate for a regular room. In fact, although never indicated or promised, each group could receive the Presidential Suite under certain circumstances. For example, if it was a CEO or a key corporate or group meetings account, the hotels had the option to place them in the (usually unoccupied) Presidential Suite. Now, you can imagine what that did for brand loyalty. The left brainer, who was paying a corporate rate of $89.00, would look on the door and see that he or she was staying in the $1,200.00 per night Presidential Suite—that is beating the system. The right brainer would be "ego satisfied" and would think that his or her weight/clout helped to break the rules. Both groups were highly satisfied.

As for "awards," the ultimate for a left brainer was free cash or as close to it as one can get. For the right brainer, it was a prestige-oriented gift that they could use for themselves. The club members had their choice, either U.S. Savings Bonds or American Express gift certificates. It didn't surprise the company that the left brainers went for the U.S. Savings Bonds (more than 85 percent of the time) and the right brainers went for the American Express gift certificates (more than 95 percent of the time). The promotional concept was successful primarily because it was based on sound research, research that looked into the psyche and motivations of the guest/customer and then responded by directly meeting their needs and providing the benefits they sought.

Key Terms

allowances
build
chance
closed
cooperative
cost/payback
fallback
fulfillment
giveaway/sweepstakes
introductory
open
price
refunds/rebates
share
trial

Chapter 7

Merchandising

If your product or service offering lends itself to visual display, the **merchandising** marketing weapon is appropriate to utilize. Merchandising is used to reinforce the advertising message, communicate product/service information and/or promotions through specific visible (on site) techniques. Merchandising can be delivered at the point of purchase (POP), through personal sales presentations, and via events. Merchandising, like any other marketing weapon, should be planned as part of the overall marketing effort and in conjunction with the other marketing weapons (e.g., advertising and promotions). Merchandising is the support material that helps market your product or service. It is important to approach the preparation of your merchandising efforts with the same care that you would give your best advertisement or most important sales call. Your merchandising efforts are always being viewed by the potential market and customers. Some key points to keep in mind when preparing and presenting merchandising materials are presented as follows.

- *Identification of purpose.* What is the primary purpose of the merchandise effort and who is the intended audience?
- *Compatibility.* Your merchandise materials should reinforce the image you are trying to establish or maintain regarding your product or service. They shouldn't contradict that image. At times, you might try to improve your image by improving the merchandising materials. An example might be creating a new brochure that portrays a better image than the one currently being portrayed. A word of caution, however: if you allow a new brochure to build a level of expectation beyond what the product can deliver, you could be doing yourself more harm than good.
- *Consistency.* The single greatest fault with most merchandise material is its lack of consistency. Is your material consistent

with your other marketing and image-related visual aids? Simple things such as the use of a logo, certain colors, print styles, and so on will help build consistency. You may want your materials to stand out, and they should, but not by detracting from your image.

- *Practical detail.* Does the merchandising material accomplish the marketing purpose it was designed to meet? Too often, issues such as picture selection take precedence over clear directions. The result may be great photos, but customers may be confused. Remember to review the materials and be sure that every detail is accurate and useful.
- *Visibility.* If you want customers to pick up and respond to your merchandising materials, don't hide them! Check often to see that these materials are where they belong—somewhere that the customer or potential customer can clearly see them and pick them up.
- *Clutter avoidance.* Be sure you are not a victim of "the-more-the-better" syndrome. Yes, it's great to have good merchandise/displays for your customers, but too much material in one place results in clutter.
- *Keep it clear.* Make sure that the purpose of each merchandise effort and piece of material is clear. Do not overload it with too much copy or detail or it will lose its purpose as a marketing vehicle. A customer or potential customer view merchandise to get a message. Don't bury that message in fine print or, worse, too much print.

TYPES OF MERCHANDISING

There are many ways to merchandise your product or services. A few of the more widely used techniques follow.

Brochures/catalogs—A brochure is a highly specialized piece of **collateral material.** Its preparation requires careful thought. It is not simply a collection of good photos and some copy. It represents the "perception" (see five Ps) of your product or service often first seen by the prospective customer. It is not only an informational sales piece, but your product/service image. A successful, well-prepared promotional brochure for a product or service should contain the following key elements:

- Identification of the product/service, including its logo
- Descriptive facts about the product/service
- Directions on how to buy the product/service
- Online address
- Key telephone numbers
- Locations
- The person or individual to contact for more information (e.g., sales director, technical personnel, etc.)
- Special features
- Pricing information (if desired)

Including these elements will not necessarily guarantee that your brochure is successful. You must also consider the key points to preparing successful merchandise materials mentioned earlier and, of course, use professional photos, art, design layout, and copy to produce a quality final product. Following are some key points to keep in mind in reviewing your brochure or catalog before printing and distributing.

- Proof everything twice.
- Be extra careful about prices.
- Check and double-check your address, phone and fax numbers, telex number (if applicable), and online address, etc.
- Ask to review the final copy.
- Ask to review the actual distribution/mailing lists.
- If a photo of your product or service is used, be sure it is up to date, representative, and a sales tool; otherwise, do not use it.

Fact sheets/sell sheets are usually one page and are designed to assist in the sales process. These should be designed knowing that both your sales personnel and your customers will likely have access to the sheet. Therefore, it is a good idea to do a high-quality, professional production job. If the fact sheet is for highly repetitive use or for actual display, be sure it is laminated and cleaned regularly. Again, your image is directly reflected by the piece of material in the customers' view.

Flyers are announcements usually printed for quick distribution to stimulate interest in a special event or promotion. Flyers may be reminders or even an announcement of an event when time does not permit using another method. If you use flyers, take care that they have a professional appearance and are compatible with the other materials used to promote the event. Control their distribution to ensure that potential customers get the message. Flyers are an inexpensive way to reach the local market. Image concerns may make flyers an inappropriate delivery vehicle for some users or messages.

Banners are a highly visible merchandising tool and should be reflective of your desired image. Provide specific instructions on how, when, and where banners are to be displayed in your units.

Displays may be self-contained or set up at the location. A display is a three-dimensional visual which should entice the consumer to become a customer. Like all other merchandising, you should ensure that your displays are in keeping with your overall image. Remember that this also applies if you are using someone else's display in your unit.

Shelf talkers come in many types such as clip-on displays, electronic message displays, coupon dispensers, etc. Shelf talkers are very effective merchandising devices when instantaneous or spontaneous action is appropriate. When your products or services need to break through the clutter of many other products on the same shelf, a good shelf talker can win the merchandising battle for you.

Store kits are designed to support a promotion theme in a store. As inferred, a store kit provides visual merchandise/materials that change the store's overall static appearance into a dynamic sales environment. Store kits can contain ceiling hangers; wall and window posters; light filters; tabletop displays; tent cards; stand-alone displays, etc. Successful store kits include detailed but easy-to-follow instructions, precision timing with promotional launches, and motivational messages to employees. Remember to quickly remove the kits and store or dispose of them when the promotion is over.

Posters are a highly visible way to merchandise products, promotions, people, and services. Posters should adhere to the same image match rule as all other merchandising materials.

Video presentations are used by many businesses to present their sales messages. Video works well with younger generations who grew up with the medium. Videos should be tasteful, professional, and orchestrated/directed. Music selection (if desired) should also be appropriate and motivated toward purchasing. For sales presentations, videos should be as short as possible to convey the message. Remember that attention spans are brief. Be concise and visual with your message on video. Stay away from lengthy, rolling print or other distractions.

Clubs are yet another merchandising opportunity if your business or service lends itself to a VIP or frequent purchaser club concept. Whether your club is a physical facility (e.g., airline club) or an affinity group (e.g., frequent traveler/purchaser club) the same merchandising rules apply. Keep the image of the club, the supporting printed materials, membership cards, promotional offerings, etc., all in line with the **brand image** and positioning of your product/service.

Tent cards are another popular form of merchandising. Tent cards come in all shapes, sizes, and forms. Some practical considerations for using them are:

- Use all sides of the tent card.
- Design it in a practical manner to rest on a table or countertop.
- Make it look attractive.
- Avoid the temptation to use a "totally unique" tent card—it will usually be costly to produce, difficult to use, and constantly in need of replacement.
- Be sure that size and placement of the tent card are consistent with the purpose or message on the card.
- Monitor and measure the results of each tent card promotion to determine its real value to you.
- Avoid clutter or promotions that cheapen your overall product or service offering.

MERCHANDISING YOUR EMPLOYEES

Customers are often impressed when an establishment recognizes good employee performance. You can keep your customers informed and motivate your employees through a number of **in-house** merchandising methods. If you are in a labor-intensive industry, motivated employees with good service attitudes are very often the keys to a successful operation. Ensuring employee motivation is a very difficult task in the service business sector. In-house materials that help boost employee morale are important and have a direct impact on the sale of your product or service. Do not ignore strategies for improving employee motivation; such strategies are key marketing tools. Some examples are included in the following sections.

Employee-of-the-Month Programs

One of the most successful applications of motivational principles is the "employee-of-the-month" program. The visual aspect of this program is important; often, a photo poster is prominently displayed in a high-traffic employee area.

An even more meaningful—and potentially more beneficial—method is to establish a permanent display case for such a poster, thereby allowing your customers to also see this recognition award. This method provides even further recognition for the employee and fosters additional feelings of goodwill among both employees and customers. A successful employee-of-the-month program requires a well-planned program of support, frequently including external public relations and some form of reward for the recognized employees. Selection criteria, fairness in judgment, and the involvement of other employees as judges or award presenters are keys to success in making these employee-recognition programs work. Management's involvement in these programs and respect for the employees and their achievements are also critical factors.

Employee-Interest Promotions

Employee-interest promotions help motivate employees and increase the marketing exposures for your business. An employee-interest promotion begins by identifying an employee's hobby or a special interest. One example is a chef whose hobby was driving race cars. The hotel where he worked successfully placed a number of human-interest stories in the media about the "fastest chef in town." Management then displayed the news clippings and photos of the chef and his autos in a number of high-traffic employee areas within the property. Employee-interest promotion possibilities are limitless, but they should be used sparingly or their internal value may dissipate.

Employee Community Service Recognition

Another effective employee program is recognizing employees' efforts in their local communities. Many employees do volunteer work, make special efforts on behalf of charities, or make unique contributions to their communities. Identifying and providing public recognition for these employees and their service efforts benefits both your establishment and the employees. These are win-win promotions. Examples include employees who participate in walkathons for charities; employees who perform volunteer work for people who are sick, disabled, or elderly; and employees who help save lives as volunteer firefighters or rescue squad personnel. These activities all help to merchandise the quality of your business as expressed by your employees. Some key questions to review in the merchandising checklist follow.

MERCHANDISING CHECKLIST

___ Are the merchandise visuals compatible/supportive of the brand(s)/product(s)/service(s) image?

___ Is the merchandise effort part of an overall marketing strategy? Is it linked to other marketing weapons?

___ How will the merchandising effort be delivered?

___ Are point-of-purchase materials appropriate?

___ Where and when will the merchandising effort take place?

___ Are instructions and/or other critical communications included? Are there instructions for any setups or removal?

___ If consumer-oriented, does anyone in the trade need to be posted on site or vice versa?

___ Is the brand visible and consistent with brand identity guidelines?

___ Is there more than one way or one time in which this merchandise can be used?

___ Does the merchandising tie in to other creative looks, e.g., advertising?

___ Is there a check system in place to determine field/unit use and adherence to guidelines?

___ Will your merchandising material fit your retailer or outlet's needs? Do you need multiple-size store kits?

___ Have you developed a communications plan or incentive for the trade to use your merchandising offer?

Following is a recap of the merchandising tools discussed.

Merchandising Tools

- Brochures
- Fact/sell sheets
- Flyers
- Banners
- Displays
- Tent cards
- Shelf talkers
- Store kits
- Posters
- Video presentations
- Clubs
- Employee motivation programs

CASE EXAMPLE 1: ACCESSORIES AND GIFTS

In a number of industries, merchandising takes on the "value added," or, premium concept. For example, the Polo brand of fragrances (as well as many others in this category) do an exceptional job at merchandising. Not only are their in-store displays attractive, their merchandise value added offers are also real perception creators. As the tent card, wall poster, or ceiling hanger states: "Purchase this Polo fragrance and receive this carry-on bag (with the Polo logo) absolutely free" (okay, in some cases for only $5.00). The "perception" is that you are purchasing a small bottle of fragrance *and* getting a large bag—sometimes even filled with other cosmetic goodies. These value-added merchandise offers are supported by in-store point-of-purchase merchandise, by newspaper and/or magazine advertising, and by direct mail campaigns or bill stuffers from the department stores. This is a very effective use of merchandising and integration of multiple marketing weapons.

CASE EXAMPLE 2: COLOR THEMES

Perhaps the master of all merchandising is Victoria's Secret. This highly successful women's lingerie and apparel retailer designs their stores, including lighting, merchandise, and packaging, to be a composite merchandising opportunity. This complete color rethemeing conveys an entirely new look to the stores. Because visual perception is the dominant sense, Victoria's Secret takes full advantage. Their merchandising calendar may vary from year to year, but it is colorful and it transcends every aspect of the retail establishment. Winter white transforms into the February (Valentine's Day) reds. The reds turn to spring yellows or greens, etc. This not only occurs in the store, but in the look of the catalog, mailers, and Web site.

CASE EXAMPLE 3: PSYCHOLOGICAL MERCHANDISING

Studies have shown that the right motivational message at the point of purchase can influence behavior. For example, that large display at the end of the aisle in the supermarket with the handwritten sign that reads "SALE PRICE - $3.99" has been known to cause the item to be picked up and put into the cart—even though the regular price when the item is on the shelf may be $3.39.

The power of suggestion takes on many different shapes and forms when it comes to merchandising. One case example whose strength lies in the psychology of the message is the airport gift shop. For instance, on the gift shop window, there may be an oversized poster of two, small, sad-eyed children looking right at you, the busy traveler. The traveler who not only misses his or her children, but feels guilty about being away from home. The message on the poster, also in oversized print so you can read it from afar, simply says: "Did you remember me?" This is a powerful merchandising poster. It works and actually changes behavior, slowing the traveler and causing them to go into the gift shop and make a purchase.

One research project studied this actual poster/message and determined that the closer the children's items were to that poster and the entry of the store, the more likely they were to be purchased. Price was almost not a factor. In fact, the average markup of the merchandise in the test was 500 percent. This exemplifies the power of pushing the right buttons with your merchandising message.

Key Terms

- brochures/catalogs
- clutter avoidance
- displays
- fact sheets/sell sheets
- flyers
- merchandise
- point-of-purchase
- posters
- shelf talkers
- store kits
- tent cards

Chapter 8

Database Marketing

Communicating your sales or promotional message is challenging in today's crowded media marketplace. Getting your message directly to your target audience is what **database marketing** is all about. This chapter will discuss why database marketing has become increasingly popular, the components of a database system, and keys to selling through direct mail.

In 1884, Montgomery Ward mailed its first catalog. Soon, other retailers began using catalogs to reach customers. By 1902, Sears had produced over $50 million in catalog sales. America was experiencing an incredible explosion in direct mail sales.

No one in the early 1900s could have imagined what would occur in direct mail sales in the second half of the century. In the 1950s, a concept arrived that would further increase direct-mail sales and lead to the birth of database marketing: the credit card. As consumer acceptance and use of credit cards grew, so did the "data" to form a "base" list of prospective customers. Then, in the 1970s, came a technological development that really allowed database marketing to take off: the computer. By the 1990s, computer technology, optical and electrical scanning devices, and a multitude of software programs and other technological advances propelled database marketing to the forefront of many marketing plans. Today, database marketing is a multibillion dollar business influenced by many factors (see Exhibit 8.1).

More than technology has contributed to the success of database marketing. **Geographic segmentation** of the U.S. population (such as by zip code) and more sophisticated demographic information from the U.S. Census Bureau have helped shape the growth of database marketing. **Demographic** and **psychographic segmentation** have also played key roles in influencing the acceptance of this marketing tool. With the increasing demands placed on personal time, the weakening of the traditional television networks, and the overabundance of prod-

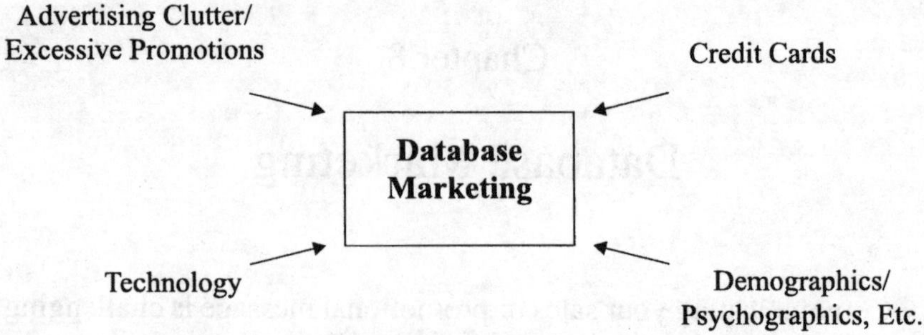

EXHIBIT 8.1. Influences on the Development and Popularity of Database Marketing

uct and service offerings, new ways to reach potential customers directly with marketing messages have become essential. Shifting and declining brand loyalty has highlighted the need for the personal and targeted approach of direct mail. Getting direct mail messages to consumers in a cost-effective manner and breaking through the advertising clutter with response-generating, creative direct mail pieces are some of the challenges facing database marketing today.

DATABASE SYSTEMS

To make a database system work, three key elements are needed: technology, accurate information, and prioritization.

Technology

Simply defined, database marketing technology is computer hardware and software capable of supporting database marketing. The degree of technological sophistication needed depends on the complexity of the marketing needs. The more mailing lists used, the more customer data stored, and the greater the frequency and measurement of responses, the greater the technological needs.

Accurate Information

A database is only as good as the integrity of the data it contains. Valid records, including correct addresses, correctly spelled names, most recent purchase activity, and so on, are all essential components of accurate database information. Clean lists (lists free of invalid or out-of-date information) increase response rates, reduce costs, and improve return on investment. When purchasing lists, always verify the last date the list was cleaned. Also **purge** (remove) duplicate records—few things turn off a prospect more than two personalized letters arriving on the same day that offer a "once-only" opportunity.

Prioritization

Having a conceptual understanding of which prospects and customers are likeliest to respond to your direct mail will help you improve return rates and increase revenues. In general, people who have recently purchased your product or service are most likely to remember you; they make great first-priority targets for a direct-mail piece urging them to make another purchase. The second likeliest response group would be those who have made multiple or frequent purchases. The third would be those who have spent the greatest amount of total revenue with you historically. The fourth likeliest group to respond is made up of those prospects that reside in areas or purchase from locations similar to those of your best customers. These priority categorizations will help you select likely responders to your direct mail and help you to develop realistic response expectations.

Group Priorities for Direct Mail

Group A—Recent Purchasers
Group B—Frequent Purchasers
Group C—Large Purchasers
Group D—Similar Purchasers

Keys to Successful Database Marketing

Like all other marketing methodologies, database marketing requires planning to be on target and successful. Following are ten keys to database marketing success.

1. *Preplan.* To successfully use any marketing tool, especially a very targeted one such as a database mailing, you need to pre-

plan. Preplanning not only includes developing objectives, return estimates, and a budget, it also includes determining where database marketing fits and what role it plays within your total marketing effort.

2. *Specify targets.* Unless you are very specific in lining up your target markets, your direct mail will be wasted. You'll need to specify your audience in terms of size, locale, and makeup (psychographic profile, **demographic profile,** benefits sought, needs, and so on). Once you have identified this target market, you're ready to take the next critical step.
3. *Select an appropriate message.* Selecting the correct message and presenting it in a manner that will entice your target market to respond will increase your chances of connecting with prospects. For example, if you are mailing to price-sensitive individuals, a strong financial incentive within your product/service offering will probably produce better results than one that offers no discount. On the other hand, if you mail a discounted offer to individuals who are more sensitive to ego and status issues, you may hurt your chances for success if your discount is viewed as cheapening the product or service. Selecting the right message to get the job done the first time is better than sending the wrong message and having to start all over again. For one thing, before you can get a corrected message out, someone else might connect with your prospect and eliminate you from the competition.
4. *Predetermine return on investment.* Ask yourself, how much return do I need to generate to cover my basic mailing costs? Then ask, how much more return do I need to achieve an adequate return on investment (ROI)? You should always try to predetermine your ROI and compare your direct-mail ROI with that of the other marketing tools you use.
5. *Maintain creative consistency.* Maintaining creative consistency with your direct-mail pieces provides multiple benefits. Some of these benefits include: clearly perceived brand identity, clearly perceived positioning, increased association/recognition from mailing to mailing (when multiple mailings occur), and carry-over brand awareness to other media.

6. *Integrate your mailings with your overall marketing program.* Multiple marketing methodologies working in concert and orchestrated within a total marketing program are much more likely to succeed than hit-or-miss, uncoordinated marketing efforts. Be sure to integrate your database marketing efforts with the overall marketing program for your product or service offering.
7. *Use clean lists.* Always use clean mailing lists. This is the best way to improve ROI and ***response rates.*** A clean list has a minimal number of duplicated, erroneous, or false addresses.
8. *Know when to mail.* The best way to decide when to mail is to determine when responses are needed. If you need business in December and you know that it takes six weeks to get results from a mailing, sending out your direct-mail pieces in December or January isn't going to help you. It is always good to prepare to mail sooner than you need to. Build in a "time cushion" to allow for correcting errors, fine tuning or redoing the direct-mail piece, and dealing with problems such as delays at the printer. Preparing early makes it more likely that you will be ready to go when your mailing date arrives.
9. *Repeat your message.* Use the power of repetition throughout each direct-mail package. The synergy of multiple messages and calls to action can only increase the chance that your prospects will see your message and respond. Use the outside of the envelope, front and back; use the response card or other reply vehicle; use every opportunity in the direct-mail piece to convey the message. Try to get your message out in like or identical form at least five times somewhere in each direct-mail package.
10. *Track the results.* How will you know how well or poorly a direct mailing did if you don't track the results? Tracking results will help you justify future mailings, compare direct mail to other marketing methods, evaluate the effectiveness of the direct-mail piece, etc.

Always remember to alert all of the departments within your business that will be affected by a direct-mail campaign. If you're mailing out a large promotional offer, be sure that staff members understand what the offer is, when they can expect customer responses, and what they are supposed to do to fulfill the offer.

SALES THROUGH DIRECT MAIL

If you were to look closely at all of the direct-mail pieces you receive in a week, you would see the results of great creative energies. Unless you look closely at your direct mail, you might not be aware of all of the things you "may" have won—from cashier's checks to cars, to lifetime memberships, to your own vacation home. Like most people, when you open your charge card or gasoline credit card bill, a handful of fantastic offers "too good to refuse" fall out of the envelope.

Keys to Direct Mail

Selling your products and services via direct mail presents special challenges and requires special knowledge. In direct mail sales, you do not have the chance to personally talk to your prospects, as you do in face-to-face or telephone sales. For direct mail to be successful, it must be sent to prospects that have needs that your product or service can meet. Therefore, starting with a good mailing list is vitally important. Then you must develop a good direct-mail piece—a communications vehicle that relates your product or service offering. It is also necessary to know when to mail and when to stop mailing. Last but not least, when prospects respond, you must fulfill your direct-mail offer promptly and accurately. In the following sections, each of these keys to direct-mail success will be discussed.

Good Lists

Knowing to whom your sales letter or other direct-mail piece is going is of primary importance. A simple thing such as the correct spelling of a manager's name means a lot if you want your letter read. Lists should constantly be purged of invalid or out-of-date information. Lists should be updated each time a new piece of information becomes available. Verify names, titles, and addresses from your most recent contact with each sales prospect. Constantly strive to be accurate.

The Direct-Mail Piece

You can develop checklist upon checklist of do's and don'ts for direct mail promotion literature. There is no single best approach. Sometimes a very personal approach is appropriate; at other times, a formal approach should be used. Some general rules for promotional literature are helpful, but if rules are strictly followed, they may inhibit an engaging personal touch. For example, when using a sales letter, one good guideline is to be sure to send an original—or at least have it appear to be an original. No one wants to read a "personal" letter that has been photocopied. Also, be sure to include the key to any direct-mail sales message—relate the prospective customer's needs directly to your product or service. If possible, place your message on one page. Time is important to everyone, and a personal, one-page letter has a much better chance of being read by Ms. Decision Maker than a multipage direct-mail package containing flashy but lengthy promotional pieces.

Knowing When to Mail

Knowing when to mail is important. Consider the example of a large publishing company that just came out with a terrific consumer-oriented book about saving money on federal income taxes. The publisher is excited because this is a super book—new ideas, right price, and so on. Why doesn't the publisher promote it in June and July when the press runs are complete? The answer is timing. People buy books about the federal income tax in October through March, not in June, July, and August. So, time of year is sometimes a consideration when you are deciding when to mail. Day of the week is also a consideration. If possible, when mailing to a business address, you should time your direct-mail piece to arrive on a Tuesday, Wednesday, or Thursday. You know what Mondays are like in a busy office. You also know that if your direct-mail piece arrives on Friday afternoon, it may not even make the reading file. Carefully consider when you need the business and when the best time is to send that letter.

Knowing When to Stop Mailing

Promotional materials and sales letters are expensive to create and send out. Thus, knowing when to stop mailing makes a lot of "cents." Many mailings may be sequential, with up to four or five pitches to the same mailing list. Be sure that you have a system that will eliminate the portion of the list that has already responded "yes" or "no" to an earlier mailing.

Timely Fulfillment

Once you get a positive response, be sure you are in a position to fulfill what you promised on a timely basis. If you fail to fulfill your offer, you may as well eliminate that customer from your "good" list, along with the names of their friends and neighbors—they won't be responding either. If you are mailing catalogs, be sure they are timed for arrival when you desire the purchasing to occur.

Strategic Marketing Applications

Database marketing/direct mail can be used for many purposes such as those listed.

- Customer retention programs
- Acquiring incremental business from existing customers
- Introductory/trial offers to prospective customers
- Establishing ongoing product/service dialogue
- Building marketing promotions
- Product/service information updates
- Changes in policy
- Announcements for events, new products/services
- Customer information gathering
- Customer feedback
- Test offers

When viewing the database checklist keep in mind what Peter Drucker once stated: "A database, no matter how copious, is not information . . . for information it must be organized for a task, directed toward specific performance, or applied to a decision."[1]

Database Checklist

- ___ Is your direct marketing program part of your total marketing strategy?
- ___ Are your mailings interlinked and supportive of your other marketing weapons?
- ___ Are your lists up to date and accurate?
- ___ Have you prioritized your mailings based on response patterns for optimum returns?
- ___ Does your direct mail reflect the positioning and image of your brand, product, or service?
- ___ Is your direct-mail campaign appropriate for the offer?
- ___ If you are using a purchased list or outside vendor have you checked the accuracy of the lists?
- ___ Is your direct mail being sent/delivered on a timely basis?
- ___ Have you calculated your return of investment/expected results?
- ___ Have you maintained creative consistency throughout your mailings?

CASE EXAMPLE 1: THE CHECK IS IN THE MAIL

Knowing the habits of your target market can be of immense value in database marketing. A problem many direct-mail marketers face is simply getting their message opened instead of thrown away. Many follow the practice of putting the message or a "teaser" on the outside of the envelope, and, to some extent, this helps. One case example of overcoming this problem is the travel agent. Travel agents, like many commissioned workers, rely on the payment check for their services. Many checks are sent by mail. Travel agents are inundated with all kinds of direct mail every day. Yet if one observes what happens to that mail upon delivery, one can learn the magic step to getting the envelope opened. Travel agency managers are experts at sorting their mail into two stacks. One goes directly to the wastebasket or floor for later action. The other stack goes directly in front of them and is opened immediately. The key is visual. "Pay to the order of" messages can be seen in window envelopes on checklike paper. These rise to the top of the stack and are opened immediately. The message is simple: know your target market's habits, know how to get their attention, and design your direct mail so that it gets immediate attention.

CASE EXAMPLE 2: BY INVITATION ONLY

Promotion pieces flood our mail every day, but invitations only come for special occasions. Sounds simple, but it works. People open invitations and discard promotional offers before they are opened. Think of the numerous credit card mailings you receive on a monthly (or even daily basis). Many of these never get opened because you already know it is a credit card solicitation with the teaser/trial period percentage printed in large type on the envelope. What you do open is the typed or handwritten envelope that looks like an invitation to a special event (wedding or social engagement). People like to receive invitations and/or are curious enough to open an envelope that appears like one. Designing your direct-mail piece to look or appear like an invitation, personal letter, or a check will help to ensure that your message/offer isn't trashed before it is opened.

Key Terms

clean list
database
direct mail
lists
merge
purge
response rates
ROI (return on investment)
time cushion

Chapter 9

Electronic Marketing

The electronic marketing weapon can have a number of looks. It can be telemarketing, visual (television shopping), or in written or digital form electronically transmitted via e-mail offers or by fax. It also includes advertising and promotions via the Internet, Web sites, etc. Web sites can include retail store sites, catalog sites, home shopping Internet sites, direct manufacturer wholesaler sites, customer service sites, and intermediary sites such as priceline.com or Travelocity.com.

In an age when value is being redefined to include speed and convenience, electronic marketing via the Internet is right on target in meeting a major consumer need. The utilization of the Internet as a marketing tool for your products/services may prove to be a valuable marketing strategy. The following section depicts the ways in which the Internet is used.

INTERNET USES

- Research
- Provide information
- Provide online buying and selling
- Provide online auctioning
- Provide online barter/trading/exchange
- Provide discussion forums
- Provide training
- Provide delivery of data (bits)
- Customer service communications

As with any of the marketing weapons, electronic marketing tools should be deployed as part of the total strategic marketing plan. Their design should be in concert with the image and positioning of your brands, products/services, and be interlinked to your other marketing strategy weaponry. Electronic marketing tools are ideal for building and actively managing and communicating with your customer base. Developing a clear concept of how to take advantage of the Internet is a must for most businesses today. Consider developing your own site, placing your banner on related Web sites, and having a strategy for easy access and quick response to customer calls.

Although database marketing has applicability to electronic marketing, each electronic marketing tool has its own nuances. Just as you would preplan your database marketing strategy, you should take the same approach with electronic marketing strategies. Irrespective of the electronic marketing tool selected, you will have to take into account the return on investment, measurement of the results, and overall benefits to the customers targeted. You will need to maintain creative consistency (site design, logo usage, etc.) to build awareness levels and familiarity with consumers. You will need to be sure you can fulfill your promotional offers and not undermine your pricing strategies. In addition, you will need to constantly monitor and track the results. You will have to remember that if you are on the Internet, you have removed geographic boundaries and must address this with respect to currency translation, pricing, delivery, languages, etc. View your Web site as you would a combination of your television/print advertising, your catalog, and your customer service/sales functions all rolled into one.

Some hints for Web site marketing include: make it easy to read (not too small/fine print and limited information per screen; use large visuals—small photos come out looking like postage stamps); select good contrast between your background and print/type colors; and always keep the user's perspective in mind. Remember, you may have had a professional technical genius design your Web site, but it may be used by someone (your customers or potential customers) whose knowledge of computers is very different from your designers/programmers, etc. A good idea is to pretest your site and response/order mechanisms/processes with average consumers. Listen, accept suggestions, and make changes. If your site has been up and running for a period of time, you might want to freshen the photos, look, etc. You may want to run a flag or banner indicating "new" or "update," etc.

Internet marketing should include a special focus on links to other sites. You should develop a comprehensive list and plan to achieve maximum cross-references, co-op links, and banners on other related sites. Be sure that you include your fax and phone numbers (800 number, etc.) for those who just need help to complete a transaction or have the need for information they cannot find on the site.

E-mail and fax offers should be presented to existing customers in a service-oriented manner. Customers should always be offered the option not to receive the message if they prefer. Remember to check the state laws where you plan to use faxes or telemarketing. Telemarketing should be scripted, not prerecorded messages, and should also follow strict guidelines and the letter of the law. Review these electronic marketing tools carefully before implementing them and consider if they will do more harm than good for your business. Remember that poorly executed or even flawlessly executed faxing, e-mail pitches, or telemarketing calls are viewed by many as annoying. The result could be a lost customer versus a potential sale. If you believe that these electronic marketing tools will work for you, train your personnel well and/or constantly monitor any organizations you contract with to provide the service.

Finally, keep in mind the uses of the Internet when developing your electronic marketing plan. Ask yourself if you can market your products or services in a way that provides information and offers a quick link to purchases, etc. Packaging and (site) presentations are two major keys to Internet marketing success. Your Web site is your image around the globe. Make it a good one. Review the questions in the electronic marketing checklist that follows.

ELECTRONIC MARKETING CHECKLIST

___ What role does electronic marketing play in your overall marketing strategy/plan?

___ What resources will be needed to execute this strategy? What will it cost? What will the return of investment be?

___ Should telemarketing be part of an overall marketing effort? Do faxes and e-mail play any role?

___ How does your Web site compare to the overall image and positioning of your business, brands, products, and services?

___ How does your Web site compare to your competitors'?
___ Is your site user (consumer) friendly?
___ How will you monitor any external vendors selected to handle your electronic marketing needs?
___ Where should your site be listed and links be built to and from?

CASE EXAMPLE 1: MAKING IT WORK FOR EVERYONE

One of the keys to electronic marketing is good links to other sites. This is especially important when you sell your products/services through other outlets. One case example is New Balance, an athletic shoe manufacturer. On a recent visit to their site, a customer was told that the local outlets did not have the shoes they requested in stock. The Web site then provided a list of links to other online retailers that carry New Balance products. The customer clicked on L.L. Bean and quickly discovered the same shoes in L.L. Bean's online catalog. L.L. Bean is one case example of an extraordinary, customer-driven organization. On L.L. Bean's Web site, the customer immediately noticed an 800 number to call for help or questions. Not sure of the size and style number of the shoes, the customer called the L.L. Bean 800 number, which was answered immediately by a well-trained customer service representative. The L.L. Bean system and customer service representative advised the customer to purchase the shoes one-half-size larger and that the style number was indeed different (a new style number). The order was promptly and professionally processed over the phone and the shoes arrived on the date promised. Good links, which listed an 800 number, and well-trained personnel, provided a successful sales experience.

CASE EXAMPLE 2: MAJOR MISTAKES

A customer attempted to purchase a designer fashion watch as a gift for Mother's Day. The watch was featured as a new item in a major women's magazine. The photo, wristband style, and $295.00 price were clearly visible on the magazine page. The customer went to a nearby store to buy the watch. In fact, he even brought the page from the magazine to be sure he purchased the exact watch desired. The store personnel, including the manager, stared at the magazine page and stated, "That must be a new item, we don't have it." No attempt was made to call their home office or another store in the area.

The customer returned home and called a number of other designer brand stores and retailers who carried the watch designer's products only to hear the same message, "We don't have it" or "It must be new." Undaunted, the customer logged on to the designer's Web site (something anyone in any of the stores could have done, but didn't). The customer "clicked" on watches and immediately saw the identical watch featured in the magazine. A small flag showed that the item was in stock but to be sure to call to verify express shipping if needed soon. (The customer thought this was a wise thing to do in view of the fact that Mother's Day was just a week away.) One problem immediately surfaced—the price on the Web site was $429.00. Another problem was that no 800 number was listed anywhere. Still wanting to purchase the watch, the customer located the designer's 800 number through information and asked to speak to customer service. The customer service representative stated that she didn't have access to the Web site because it was operated by someone else, and that she also did not have a computer terminal on which to access outside sites. The representative was well trained and told the customer that she would research both the magazine and Web sites and call back. The next day, she called back and said that she located the watch and could Federal Express it in time for Mother's Day. When the customer asked about the price, the service representative said it was $429.00. The customer stated that the magazine listed it for $295.00. The service representative then had the customer talk to a supervisor who stated: "Someone in merchandising or new products must have given the wrong price to the magazine. It's not our fault and the price is $429.00." The customer still purchased the watch and it was delivered as promised.

The customer then wrote to the president of the watch company and enclosed the magazine page and a printout of the Web site page. The letter outlined the customer's experience and also pointed out that the Web site and the magazine showed the identical watch at two very different prices. The customer also pointed out the fact that he was a loyal customer who had purchased numerous products over the years. Neither the president nor anyone from the organization ever responded. The customer (after six weeks) decided to call the company and was told that the customer service manager in the public relations area handled complaints. The call was transferred and the spokesperson stated: “We have had quite a few calls on that, and unfortunately it is the magazine’s fault” (did she really expect the customer to believe that the national women’s magazine ran a photo and price on their new watch without anyone from the company being involved?). The lesson here is multifold and simple. Be sure what you advertise on your Web site is the same price as in print. Be sure that your sales personnel and customer service personnel can readily access the same information as the customer. Finally, respond appropriately or lose a customer for life—as this company did.

Key Terms

currency translation
electronic marketing
e-mail
Internet
links
logo
Web site

Chapter 10

Packaging

In this chapter, packaging will be discussed from both a "products" perspective and "services" perspective. Products and services have both common aspects and differentiating factors. Packaging, be it for products or services, should be deployed as a marketing weapon within the context of your overall marketing strategy/plan. The packaging of your product or service should be consistent with your image and desired positioning. A number of valid definitions of packaging exist depending upon the industry sector and/or marketing application. For example, a traditional definition with universal and generic application might read: "packaging is the inside and outside environment that houses the product/service (look) and helps communicate the company's attributes and image."[1] An example would be a variety of products such as software, small appliances, etc. Another definition would state that packaging is the combination of two or more products or services offered to consumers for one price. An example would be a bundle of computer equipment, i.e., computer, printer, etc., or in the services sector, a travel package (i.e., airfare, hotel, rental car, etc.). Both definitions provide valid examples of packaging as a marketing weapon. Today, more than ever, consumers are buying packages of all types because packaging meets their needs and makes products/services more attractive. Multiple-item packages simplify the purchase (thus adding value through reducing time) and often save on a total price versus the cost of individual items. In addition, the marketer benefits by co-oping resources such as advertising dollars, etc. Although packaging employs many aspects of marketing such as advertising (creative design), promotions, pricing techniques, merchandising, etc., it is truly a marketing weapon in its own right.

The following lists some of the many potential benefits of packaging.

BENEFITS OF PACKAGING

- Awareness creation
- Attribute communications
- Positioning clarification
- Incremental sales
- Generation of trial
- Problem resolution
- Image enhancement
- Consumer convenience
- Increases product/service attractiveness
- Economics of scale
- Cooperative advertising
- Facilitate new product introduction
- New channels of distribution

One major benefit of packaging is that it provides some entirely new channels of distribution and methods to reach target markets. Packaging may also enhance image and positioning if you pair your product or service with another of even higher reputation awareness, and/or greater marketing capability. Just think what it would mean to sales if a Walmart became your packaging and distribution partner.

Packages of multiple products or services may be sold directly to consumers, retailers, wholesalers, distributors, etc. In selecting package partners, focus on the impact of the partners' (products, services, brands) overall image and reputation on your product/service/brand. Will it enhance your image or damage your reputation?

A package should convey a number of basics with respect to marketing. In packaging a single product, seek to create a package that: (1) attracts attention; (2) provides an exceptional visual appeal; (3) provides for the ease of dispensing and/or displaying the product; (4) allows for multiple location/placement; and (5) provides easy access. If you wish to really succeed, design or create a package that is unique and/or distinguishes your product/brand from all others in the category. Think of what the unique egg package design concept did for L'eggs pantyhose or what the golden arches did for McDonald's—instant awareness. Remember that awareness translates directly to sales, especially for new products/services.

If you are in a new business and just developing a product or service offering, consider developing a brand name which helps communicate positioning or creates awareness, and/or communicates (explains) what the product/service is all about, for example, AOL (America Online), Burger King, Citibank, etc. Choosing this brand strategy will enhance not only the packaging of your product or service, but will help to build awareness levels without spending dollars to explain what that nice-sounding acronym stands for.

When designing a package for physical products, take into consideration *everyone* who comes into contact with the package. Think of consumers who have to visually identify your product/brand, purchase it, carry it home, and possibly store it. Consider the shoppers, distributors, wholesalers, and retailers who may have to transport and place your product on shelves, in displays, etc. Take into account all other products of a category/competitive nature to assure that your product/brand distinguishes itself (unless you intentionally wish to "piggyback" on someone else's look or reputation—be careful legally). Finally, think about the use of your brand (logos, reputation, positioning, equity, etc.) if you plan to extend it to other products or services. Ask yourself, *will the brand extension help or hurt my existing product/services?*

One final caution on packaging involves the "level of expectation" concept. Be sure that your package and/or your inclusion in a multiproduct/service package doesn't overpromise. You may get trial business, but likely will have disappointed, nonreturning customers. You would be better off to seek trial through the use of a premium or other value-added offer or merchandising technique.

The following is a checklist of questions you should address with respect to packaging.

Packaging Checklist

___ What benefits will my business/product/service derive from packaging?

___ Does my product/brand package convey my desired image/positioning in the marketplace?

___ Will my awareness levels and sales benefit from inclusion in a multiproduct/service package?

- ___ If in a multiproduct/service package, is the image/reputation of my partner(s) equal to or better than mine?
- ___ Will I have enough control over my portion of the package?
- ___ Is there any negative aspect for my customers or intermediaries (agents/distributors, etc.) from my participation in a package offering?
- ___ Does my physical product/brand package create awareness, illicit response/action, and communicate attributes?
- ___ What incremental market segments will be targeted by the multiproduct/service package I participate in? Is there any risk of confusing my customer base?

CASE EXAMPLE 1: BEING DIFFERENT

Sometimes, a unique packaging concept can catapult awareness levels. Take the case of Apple Computer in the late 1990s. At that time, most computers came in one shape (a box), and in one of two colors, white (or some slight variation thereof) or black. When Apple decided to reintroduce its new iMac it also decided to be different. Apple recognized that consumers had become décor conscious both at home and in the office. They also recognized that not all homes or offices were black and white. Apple also understood that their potential customers were those either devoted to the original Macintosh computers and/or those who were antitraditional or what might be termed forerunners—ahead of the trend. For its new iMac, they created the nonbox, unique, curved shape computer in an array of bright colors. Not discounting the technical merits of the machine, Apple succeeded in standing out from the crowd and gained a whole new level of awareness. Apple made a fashion statement and succeeded by being different.

CASE EXAMPLE 2: RIDING A WAVE AND RIGHT NAME/RIGHT COLOR

For many years, one of the most successful new product launches was Lean Cuisine. Stouffer's rode the major market wave toward healthy foods and the trend toward quick preparation (convenience) and launched a real winner. Sales soared as Lean Cuisine not only hit the market on target, but also tasted great and had virtually no major competition. The trend toward lower calories, less fat, and healthy foods continued to grow with both the numerous warnings from various government studies and research from the medical community on the problem of being overweight. Combined with the growth in two-breadwinner households and singles on the move (both segments with less time), a continuation of a macro trend emerged. Whenever this occurs, look out for new competition.

The right name and right colored packaging example came in the form of the Healthy Choice brand in its very "healthy looking" green box. The new brand immediately took off and began to get its fair share of the market. The name Healthy Choice and its packaging also proved successful for brand extensions to other food products such as Healthy Choice deli meats, ice cream products, other frozen food products, etc.

Key Terms

brand name
bundle
packaging
piggyback
visual appeal
visual identity

Chapter 11

Branding

Branding is a key marketing weapon because it is the visible communicator of your positioning strategy. Marketing's role is to both lead the creative process and be the "keeper" of the brand (oversee its usage). Branding is complex and involves all elements in the marketing mix.

BRAND STRATEGY

Multiple components are involved in brand strategy. These include but are not limited to brand awareness; perceived quality; brand associations; other proprietary brand assets; measurements; selecting, creating, and maintaining associations; the name, symbol, and slogan; brand extensions; and the concept of revitalizing the brand.[1] It is important to understand each of these concepts because each plays a major role in an overall brand strategy (see Exhibit 11.1).

Before embarking on developing a brand or branding plan, it is essential to understand the components of brand strategy.

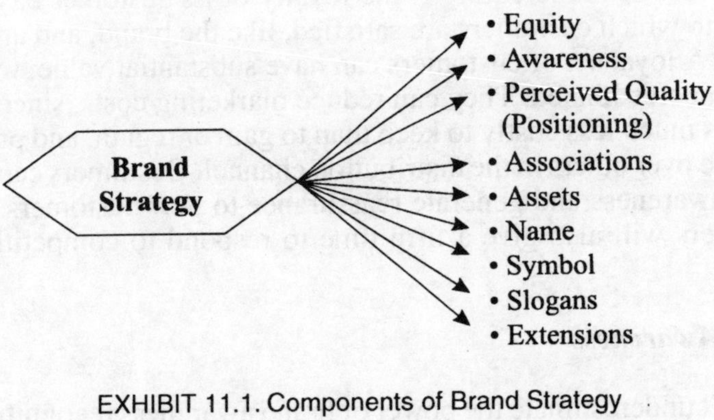

EXHIBIT 11.1. Components of Brand Strategy

Brand Equity

Brand equity is the net result of all of the positives and negatives linked to the brand, its name and symbols that add value to, or subtract value from, a product or service. These include **brand loyalty,** name awareness, perceived quality, and associations.

The short-term performance of a brand carries a considerable amount of pressure. These include the dictum that shareholder wealth is a primary goal of business, and the reality that stock prices are responsive to short-term performance measures. Short-term activities (such as price promotions) can show dramatic results, while brand-building activities (such as image advertising) may have little immediate impact. The challenge is to better understand the links between brand assets and future performance, so that brand-building activities can be justified.

Estimating the value of a brand can help to show that the underlying assets do have worth. The assessment of the value of brand equity can be based on the price premium that the name supports, the impact of the name on customer preference, the replacement cost of the brand, and the stock value minus the value of other assets. The most persuasive measure, however, may be a multiplier of the earning power of the brand. The multiplier would be based upon an analysis of the earning power of the brand assets.[2]

Brand Loyalty

The core of brand equity is the loyalty of its customer base—the degree to which customers are satisfied, like the brand, and are committed. A loyal set of customers can have substantial value, which is often underestimated. They can reduce marketing costs, since a customer is much less costly to keep than to gain or regain, and provides leverage over others in the distribution channel. Customers can create brand awareness and generate reassurance to new customers. Loyal customers will also give a firm time to respond to competitive advances.

Brand Awareness

Don't underestimate the power of brand awareness recognition, recall (your brand is recalled as being in a product class), and top-of-mind recall (the first recalled). People like the recognizable. Furthermore, recognition is a cue for presence, substance, and permanence. Recall can be a necessary condition to being considered, and can have a subtle influence on purchase decisions as well. It also provides the anchor to which other associations are linked.

Building awareness is much easier over a longer time period because learning works better with repetition and reinforcement. In fact, brands with the highest recall are generally older brands. Event sponsorship, publicity, symbol exposure, and the use of brand extensions can all improve awareness. However, developing recall requires a link between the brand and the product class. Name exposure alone will not necessarily create that link.

Perceived Quality

Perceived quality pays off. According to recent studies using data from thousands of businesses in the profit impact of market strategy (PIMS) database, perceived quality improves prices, market share, and ROI. In addition, it has been the top-named competitive advantage in a survey of managers of business units. It provides a reason to buy, a point of differentiation, a price premium option, channel interest, and a basis for brand extensions.

The keys to obtaining high perceived quality are delivering high quality, identifying those quality dimensions that are important, understanding what signals quality to the buyer, and communicating the quality message in a credible manner. Price becomes a quality cue, especially when a product is difficult to evaluate objectively or when status is involved. Other quality cues include the appearance of service people, public spaces, and other first visible impression areas.

Brand Associations

A brand association is anything mentally linked to the brand. The brand position is based upon associations and how they differ from competition. An association can affect the processing and recall of information, provide a point of differentiation, provide a reason to buy, create positive attitudes and feelings, and serve as the basis of extensions.

Positioning on the basis of an association with a key tangible product attribute is effective when the attribute can drive purchase decisions, but often it can also result in a specification shouting match. The use of intangible attributes such as overall quality, technological leadership, or health and vitality can sometimes be more enduring. The association with a customer benefit is another option. One study showed that the combination of a rational benefit and an emotional benefit was superior to a rational benefit alone.

Relative price position is often central to a brand. Is the brand to be premium, regular, or economy—and, further, is it to be at the top or bottom of the selected category? Among the other association types to consider are use applications, product users, celebrities, lifestyles and personalities, product class, competitors, and country or geographic area.

THE MEASUREMENT OF BRAND ASSOCIATIONS

Insights about what a brand means to people and what motivations it taps can often be obtained by using indirect methods of eliciting associations.[3] A customer, for example, can be asked to describe a brand user or use experience, to generate free associations with the brand, or to indicate how brands differ from one another. Another way to gain a rich profile of a brand is to ask people to consider the brand as a person (or animal, activity, magazine, etc.), and probe as to what type the brand would be.

A companion method would usually involve a representative sample of a customer segment which would scale the brand and its competitors with respect to such positioning dimensions as product attributes, customer benefits, user characteristics, use situations, or competitors. The result is a perceptual map that graphically identifies the important perceptual dimensions and shows the position of the brand for the customer sample.

Selecting, Creating, and Maintaining Associations

A successful brand position will usually follow three tenets: (1) Don't try to be something you are not. (2) Differentiate your brand from competitors. (3) Provide associations that add value and/or provide a reason to buy.

A key to creating associations is to identify and manage signals. A promotion can signal that nonprice attributes are not important unless it is structured so that it reinforces the desired image. To deliver an attribute and communicate that it exists may not be enough if the appropriate signals are not managed properly. Being consistent over time and over elements of the marketing program is crucial in maintaining associations.

Brand Name and Symbols

The name, symbol, and slogan are critical to brand equity and can be enormous assets because they serve as indicators of the brand and thus are central to brand recognition and brand associations.

A name should be selected by a systematic process involving the relation of a host of alternatives based upon desired associations and metaphors. The name should be easy to recall, suggest the product class, support a symbol or logo, suggest desired brand associations, not suggest undesirable associations, and be legally protectable. There usually are trade-offs to be made. For example, a name that suggests a product class might be strategically limiting when brand extensions are considered. A symbol can create associations and feelings. Symbols such as IBM or SONY that are based upon the name will have an edge in creating brand recognition. A symbol that includes the product class will help in brand recall when the link to the product class needs to be strong. A slogan can be tailored to a positioning strategy, and is far less limited than a name and symbol in the role it can play. A slogan can provide additional associations, or focus existing ones.

Brand Extensions

One way to exploit brand equity is to extend the name to different products. An extension will have the best chance when the brand's associations and/or perceived quality can provide a point of differentiation and advantage for the extension. Extensions rarely work when the brand name has nothing to offer beyond brand awareness.

An extension should fit the brand. There should be some link between the brand and the extension. The fit could be based upon a variety of linking elements, such as common-use contexts, functional benefits, links to prestige, user types, or symbols. Any incongruity could cause damage and result in the failure of desired transfer associations. In addition, there should not be any meaningful negative association created by the brand name. An extension could damage the core brand by weakening either its associations or its perceived quality. Probably the biggest risk of an extension is that the potential of a new brand name with unique associations may be lost.

Revitalizing Brands

One option for a brand which is old and tired is to pursue one of the seven routes to brand revitalization. First, attempt to increase usage by existing customers through reminder advertising or extending the distribution channels. This is both relatively easy and unlikely to precipitate competitive reaction. Second, find a new product use, which can be feasibly stimulated by the brand. A third way is to find new markets or to attack a neglected market. A fourth revitalization route is to reposition by changing associations or adding new associations. A fifth route is to augment the product or service by providing features or services that are not expected. A sixth route is to eliminate existing products with new-generation technologies. The seventh route is the extension option.

Revitalization is not always possible or economically justifiable, especially for a brand that lacks a strong position, is facing a declining market and is dominated by competitors, is not central to the long-range thrust of the firm, and lacks a revitalization strategy. One option is to divest or liquidate. Another option, "milking the brand," would be preferred when there is an enduring niche that remains loyal to the brand, the decline is orderly (with relatively stable prices), and the milking option seems feasible.

In a growing number of contexts, the brand name and what it means have, for many firms, combined to become the pivotal sustainable competitive advantage. Names have become pivotal because other bases of competition (such as product attributes) usually are relatively easy to match or exceed. Furthermore, customers often lack the ability or motivation to analyze the brand-choice decision at a sufficient depth to allow specifications to win the day.

Brand equity does not just happen. Its creation, maintenance, and protection need to be actively managed. It involves strategic as well as tactical programs and policies.

The components of a brand strategy need to be orchestrated so that all the parts work together to achieve the synergy required to market a brand. Planning requires that every detail, from the name, logo, and graphics treatment to the detailed marketing plan, be addressed. Before selecting a name, logo, etc., it is important to start with the "positioning objective" and then develop related strategies and tactics. In the case of launching a new brand, the "perceived quality" factor becomes a driving force. When creating an entirely new brand, clear positioning within the product category and in relationship to competitive products becomes a preeminent factor. Therefore, how the brand is portrayed—the actual name and look of the new brand—should take a preeminent position in the strategy. Equally important is the front-end planning. A plan needs to be in place to immediately establish a perceived brand equity. Positioning the new brand through its visual messages will create the perception.

In summary, the steps in implementing a brand strategy begin with the positioning objective and are followed by "linking" or creating the visual images that support that objective. These include name, logo, graphic treatment, and creative approach. Following these associations, is the next step, implementing a detailed marketing plan which includes but is not limited to the advertising strategy (creative and media plans); a promotional strategy (introductory promotion and retention promotion); the public relations plan (consumer and trade); the sales strategy for retention of existing business and capturing new business; the sales organizational approach; the direct mail/ database marketing program; the electronic marketing strategy; and the packaging.

Brand strategy is usually a "build" or phased activity. Phase I is the declaration or announcement phase; here you state your intention, positioning objective, and reveal your new look. Phase I is achieved through public relations and advertising. Phase II is the "work-in-progress" stage—the kickoff plus actions from the marketing plan which state "we are off the pad and ascending." Phase II draws upon all of the marketing weapons. Phase III begins the proclamation or statement of achievement—"we're meeting our goals"—delivering as promised. This phase is achieved through public relations and advertising. Phase IV usually employs all marketing weaponry and often is accompanied with some form of recognition, such as awards, milestones, etc.

New Brand

When introducing a new brand, critical steps need to be put in perspective with some key factors. First, timing—the brand needs to be ready to launch. The name, logo, and graphic treatment need to be service marked or registered. The brand identifiers should be ordered and ready to be put in place. These include the look/design of the brand and any collateral materials. Once the visual associations are ready to go, the brand marketing plan needs to be put into action. This begins with a communications plan, sometimes referred to as a memo or "letter number one."

Second, letter number one should outline the positioning so every employee in the organization can understand and explain what the new brand represents—how it is better than the old brand. This communiqué is usually accompanied with highlights from the overall marketing plan. It states when and where the new advertising will appear. It talks about the introductory promotions, new look, and all of the other positive momentum and esprit de corps building blocks.

Third, it is absolutely essential to have the "internal launch" take place prior to the "external launch."

Fourth, every business that adopts a new brand should consider a "new brand grand opening" event which reintroduces the business to key local contacts and the community.

Fifth, letters to existing customers should be developed and follow-up calls made to convey the new brand positioning. These letters should seek to excite and entice the customer to return or repeat purchase. An introductory incentive should be included if possible.

Sixth, special familiarization briefings should provide detailed information to all key intermediaries such as agents, distributors, wholesalers, retailers, etc.

Seventh, a comprehensive trade media public relations plan should be in operation at the time of the launch. Interviews with key executives and spokespersons, as well as trade advertisers delineating the brand positioning strategy should be ongoing at this juncture.

Eighth, consumer marketing plan steps also need to occur in sync with the launch. A new 800 number, Internet address, advertisements, promotions, photos, etc., need to be simultaneously lined up and ready to go. These marketing activities need to be executed with a grand-opening philosophy and a heavy, up-front expenditure level.

(Up front, meaning the first six months of the launch.) In essence, the largest portion of the annual budget should be spent in the months following the brand launch.

Ninth, every month, for the first three months, recommunicate in the form of an update—memo #1, then memo #2, and #3, etc.—to both your internal and external constituencies. Do this again at six months and at one year out.

Tenth, replace anyone who has not bought into the new brand positioning or is not communicating it with enthusiasm. This is poison to a new brand launch with both employees and customers.

In summary, it is critical to be ready with a detailed communications and marketing plan before the launch. It is essential to have the "association signals" designed, purchased, and in place at the outset of the conversion. Finally, make sure that all constituencies have been clearly and thoroughly briefed. The brand launch should have its own pert or critical path chart, with key dates and responsibilities clearly delineated. Regular progress briefings and meetings should also occur. A sound approach is to select the launch date (after planning) and then peg all of the critical dates/tasks which lead up to that day. Allow for delays with sign companies, suppliers, design issues, etc. Be sure that the "new brand" signs are within the square-foot limitations of the existing zoning regulations before you order signs, and be sure that you have taken and completed all legal steps such as registering your brand, slogans, etc.

The following is a checklist for **product branding.**

Checklist for Branding

- ___ Does the name reflect the positioning, product/service attributes or benefits?
- ___ Is the name appropriate to the product/service category?
- ___ Is the name globally acceptable (translates well)?
- ___ Is it simple, easy to remember and recognize?
- ___ Does it convey emotion or a positive mental image?
- ___ Is it easy to pronounce and visualize?
- ___ Does it relate to the product/service personality?
- ___ Does it lend itself to creative development both visually and in written copy?
- ___ Will it work on packages, signage, and reproduce (logo) in black and white and in small and large size?

___ Has it been protected legally (search completed also)?
___ Will it require any special treatment when used in color, print, or broadcast media?
___ How does it compare to your top three competitors?
___ Have you tested the name on your target market, employees, and other constituencies?
___ Is the introduction/launch plan developed and ready to go?

CASE EXAMPLE 1: THE CHARACTER OF A BRAND

The case example of the Disney brand and all of its associations and extensions could be called "from a theme park to a brand bonanza." Walt Disney created a brand that became synonymous with America, children, fun, entertainment, and quality product/service all in one. The proprietary assets of the Disney brand remain almost unmatched in today's marketplace. The theme parks, entertainment business/brand, the Disney stores in malls, and the hundreds of products from watches, toys, clothes, etc., are all linked to the Disney brand and the Disney characters. When it comes to brand extensions and brand associations, the Disney brands lead the parade down the main street of branding.

CASE EXAMPLE 2: NAME COMPATIBILITY

Launching a new product or service is always a challenging marketing task. One great asset to a successful launch is the actual name of the product or service. The name selected can require little or no explanation if it clearly describes the product or service. If it doesn't, it might require the use of valuable promotional and advertising resources just to explain what the name actually represents. Take the case of an entirely new service offering that truly picked an on-target name for its product/service offering—America Online or AOL. When the Internet revolution began to blossom along came a new Internet access service provider that wanted to capture the U.S. market (original objective). This market and service was new and the potential customers needed to understand what these new services were all about. A simple, straightforward brand name was selected, which, in a most succinct way, stated the market and the service AOL provided. Its name selection has further preempted others from claiming the unique "America" and online positioning. Its name is instantly remembered along with what it stands for in terms of what the brand is all about. Furthermore, the name selection has lent itself both to simple logo development and identification by initials, "AOL."

Key Terms

brand
brand assets
brand associations
brand awareness
brand equity
brand extensions
brand loyalty
branding
perceived quality
PIMS
product attributes
slogan

Chapter 12

Pricing

Pricing is the ultimate generator of revenues and profit. Although pricing strategies are somewhat different for products than services, be it price or rates or fares, the strategic marketing objective remains the same—maximize sales/revenue. In its simplest definition, pricing is the monetary value of a product or service. Pricing is directly reflective of your image, positioning statement, and perceived brand value. Many issues affect price. Certainly the cost of providing the product or service, competition, stage of the product life cycle, and market demand play major roles in determining a pricing strategy. In addition, the product type, seasonality, uniqueness of the product/service, trial or introductory offers, and new product/service improvements may influence pricing. With respect to demand, some products/services are referred to as either inelastic or elastic. A **price-inelastic product** or service is one for which demand will remain relatively the same when the price is raised or lowered. Many top-end luxury products/services fall under this category, e.g., Rolex watches, Mercedes-Benz autos, etc. Likewise, certain necessities such as water, needed medical supplies, etc., could be considered more inelastic than elastic. On the other hand, a **price-elastic product** or service is one for which the demand will increase or decrease in relationship to an increase or decrease in price. An example would be an increase in airfares, new housing, and related interest rates, etc. At the outset of determining your pricing strategies, you should view your product/service/brand category to determine its relative price elasticity.

Selecting a pricing strategy may involve many options. For example, you may wish to look at pricing on a geographic basis, or with respect to timing (e.g., where in the demand cycle or purchasing cycle are you launching your product). You may desire a lower, higher, or parity pricing strategy. You may view pricing differently in an excess capacity (supply) situation. This is sometimes referred to as a "short-run" pricing situation. In this instance, you would set your price to cover your variable costs and to make some contribution to fixed costs, overhead, etc. Your objective would be to recover some costs while reducing your excess supply. A "long-run" pricing strategy is generally viewed as pricing that covers all costs (fixed and variable) and results in a profit.[1] Most businesses desire the latter scenario. To determine how to price to break even or to generate a profit, a simple analysis called a **"break-even calculation"** can be done. To perform a break-even analysis (see Exhibit 12.1), you must first determine your **fixed costs.** Fixed costs are costs that do not change with fluctuating sales or promotions. These include costs such as rent, mortgage, lease, etc. **Variable costs** also must be calculated. Variable costs are costs that vary with the volume of production or sales. Examples might be utilities, transportation costs, labor, etc. To conduct a break-

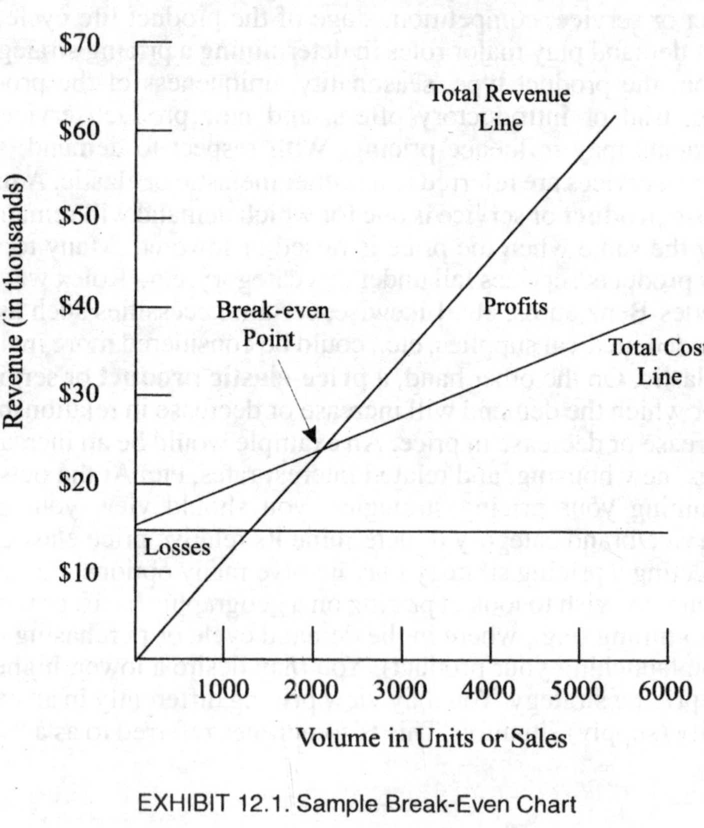

EXHIBIT 12.1. Sample Break-Even Chart

even analysis, you will also have to employ your intuitive judgment. As indicated, establishing the most effective price to charge for your product or service is based on many factors. The local market and competition will, in all likelihood, prove to be dominant factors in influencing a pricing decision. However, the local market conditions and your need to break even need not overly restrict your judgment or creativity in establishing a pricing strategy. Frequently, the most important factors in selecting the optimum rate or pricing strategy will come from your own intuitive judgment about what will work best for the product or service in view of the local market and competition.

Once the market has been analyzed and the competition profiled, a break-even analysis will assist in selecting the optimum pricing strategy. A break-even analysis looks at the relationship between total sales and total expenses for a product/service offering. Often depicted on a simple graph, the analysis demonstrates the effects of changing the levels of total sales in terms of dollars or volumes. The vertical (Y) axis represents revenue. The horizontal (X) axis represents volume in units sold, which can be expressed in whatever terminology is best for your business.[2]

In this analysis, total costs at the various levels of volume are plotted with a straight line that crosses the Y-axis at the level of fixed costs. In the simplest terms, total costs are a combination of fixed costs (costs that are incurred whether sales occur or not) and variable costs (costs that are incurred only when sales are made). Therefore, at zero sales, total costs equal fixed costs ($18,000 in Exhibit 12.1), at any level of sales beyond zero, total costs equal fixed costs plus the number of units sold times the variable cost per unit. Total revenue is also entered as a straight line starting at zero on both axes (revenue is only received as sales are made; that is, zero units sold means zero revenue). The point at which these lines cross represents the break-even point, or the point at which sales are adequate to cover costs. Any point above the total cost line represents profits; any point below the total cost line represents losses. In the sample chart shown in Exhibit 12.1, the break-even point can be stated either in dollar volume ($24,000) or in unit volume (2,400 units).

The break-even analysis formula is as follows:

$$PX = FC + VC(X)$$

Where:

P = Price
VC = Variable Cost
FC = Fixed Costs
X = Volume of units produced at break-even point (the number of units that must be sold)

Break-even charts are useful tools, although they are not always precise. Two mathematical equations can also be used to calculate the break-even points for units or sales.

The break-even point in units is determined by first subtracting the variable cost per unit from the selling price per unit. The result is then divided into the total fixed costs:

$$\text{Break-even point in units} = \frac{\text{Total fixed costs}}{\text{Selling price per unit} - \text{variable cost per unit}}$$

To determine the break-even point in sales, multiply the break-even point in units by the selling price:

$$\text{Break-even point in sales} = \text{Break-even point in units} \times \text{selling price}$$

With the basic break-even chart and the unit and sales equations, you can use the flexible break-even analysis to establish profit objectives and the required sales revenue to meet these objectives.

As indicated at the outset of this chapter, pricing strategies are influenced by many factors. First, the rationale behind selecting a low price strategy will be examined. Following are some reasons for selecting a low price strategy:

- To increase trial
- To preempt competition
- To expand market share
- To remain competitive
- To prevent competitive entry
- To introduce a new or improved product or service
- To increase demand and reduce inventory

Selecting a high price strategy may be an option for your product/service or brand. Following are some reasons to opt for a high price strategy:

- To substantiate a quality image/positioning (#1 box on the marketing strategy grid)
- A need for fast recovery of investment
- The product/service is inelastic
- The product/service has a short life span
- The market demand is rapidly increasing
- The product/service is unique or difficult to copy or reproduce
- Profits are the focal point rather than sales
- Dollars need to be accumulated for R & D costs

There are also many reasons one might select a parity pricing strategy for the product/service or brand:

- Better product/service or superior attributes compared to competition
- Better service and reputation
- Stronger guarantees/warranties
- Distribution advantage
- Newest design (look)

PRICING TECHNIQUES

In most businesses pricing can be used to maximize revenue and profit. Although not every one of these techniques may apply to your business (products/services), hopefully they will stimulate your pricing strategy thought process.

Technique 1: Offering a Price Range

A price range technique is most applicable for the service sector. It allows you to both "sell up" and "sell down." When demand forecasts are moving up, move up the price range. When demand forecasts are weak, move down the price range and take market share. Price ranges provide customers and prospective customers the opportunity to decide if they want additional services or fewer services. Price ranges also allow for discounting off the high end of the range.

Technique 2: Selling Up

Many customers and prospects are driven by different motivations. Some factors that support **selling up** include the size of the "ego," desire, prestige, uniqueness of the product/service, value-added offers, personalization, and customization.

Technique 3: Selling Down

Many customers and prospects are price/value seekers—always looking for the best deal or lowest price. **Selling down** allows you to meet price or rate resistance with a counter offer.

Technique 4: Value Added

Value added is simply including more for the same price. You may add 30 percent more product, provide an extra service, or include a premium or other value-added incentive to get your price.

Technique 5: Pay Later

"Pay later" is a concept that addresses the customers' or prospects' resistance to the price based on the rationale of not having sufficient funds for the product/service. Pay later pricing usually incorporates an interest or cost-of-cash amount factor in the stated price.

Technique 6: Up Front

Up-front pricing is a technique used to provide a perceived discount for an advance purchase. It is, in essence, a discount concept for paying at the time of order versus at delivery or usage.

Technique 7: Inflation Rate Plus Pricing

The **inflation rate plus** technique is more or less a simple rule of thumb—increase your prices at a minimum at the rate of inflation. This allows you to stay even. The "plus" factor simply means that you forecast how the inflation rate is impacting your costs and add some incremental price increase (cost plus) to ensure that your product/service profit margins remain intact.

Technique 8: Segmentation Pricing

Segmentation pricing is a technique that subdivides your market (be it geographically, psychographically, by competitive pressure, distributorships, etc.) and establishes different pricing for different segments.[3]

There are many other creative ways to price your product/service. The strategies may vary, but the objective is the same—sell all units/move all products and maximize yield/revenue (see pricing checklist).

Pricing Checklist

- ___ Is my pricing strategy appropriate for my positioning/image?
- ___ Does my product/service/brand deserve a premium price?
- ___ Should my prices be adjusted based on the demand forecast?
- ___ Should my prices be different based on my segmentation analysis?
- ___ How will I communicate pricing strategy to employees, customers, and intermediaries?
- ___ If I raise prices, will competition follow?
- ___ If I lower prices, will competition follow or undercut my price?
- ___ Will adding an incentive, value, or other incremental item/service allow me to retain price and build volume?
- ___ How elastic is my product or service?
- ___ Is there some way to differentiate my product/service and increase my prices?
- ___ Can I employ any of the right techniques to maximize revenue?
- ___ Will upcoming promotions affect my pricing strategies (my own and the competition's)?

CASE EXAMPLE 1: WINNING WITH THE SAME PRICE

In some instances, the same price may be charged for an item/ product or service but one provider may receive more business due to a competitive advantage. This advantage may be as straightforward as having a better product, or a combination of reasons. In this case example, we will look at a retailer who won with parity pricing (and sometimes even with a higher price) for many years as a result of a number of reasons.

In this case example, Sears, and specifically its appliance and hardware areas, will be examined. Sears has successfully defended its turf against the onslaught of appliance discounters, warehouse store concepts, etc. Some of the reasons for this involve Sears' success with parity pricing. First, Sears has an excellent reputation as a service provider after the sale. Customers know that if they buy a Sears brand or another brand at a Sears store, they will know who to call if a problem arises. This is not always the case with the competition. Second, Sears has a distribution/location advantage. Sears is just about everywhere. Third, brand recognition and reliability are trademarks of Sears' products and it stands behind its products. Sears' hardware is of high quality/durability and its store personnel know how to use the products. The personnel are trained.

Whenever you offer more convenience and more reliable service at the same price, you are likely to win. If you back up that price parity with a good reputation and trained point-of-encounter/customer contact employees, you will have even more competitive advantages and rationale to support your parity pricing.

CASE EXAMPLE 2: PAYING LATER ADDS VALUE AND MOVES PRODUCT

Often, when inventories are high and/or product models are due to be replaced, special pricing techniques are employed to "move product." One case example is the reduced pricing for computers at certain times during the year or during their life cycle. For example, a Compaq computer and printer (brand may vary) which regularly sell on a stand-alone basis for $999.00, but fall within the high inventory category can be priced as low as $499.00.* The * may read as follows: "The buyer is obligated to sign up with the Microsoft Network (MSN) for a time period equal to $400.00 at the time of purchase. A $100.00 manufacturer's rebate may be obtained from the printer company; allow up to 3 months for rebate."

In this case, the value added is the free printer. The "pay later" aspect of this offer is the contracted monthly fees to MSN. The offer represents a strong motivation to purchase a computer for half its regular price and receive a printer along with the deal. The mechanics of rebates and allowances between Compaq, the printer company, MSN, and retailer are invisible to the buyer.

Key Terms

break-even analysis
demand
elastic
fixed costs
high price strategy
inelastic
inflation rate plus
price range
pricing
selling down
selling up
value added
variable costs
volume

Chapter 13

Sales

Sales, like a number of other marketing weapons, has undergone many changes as a result of technology, competition, and customer/consumer demands. These changes have resulted in more strategy options, be it for direct sales to the end user of the product or service or intermediary sales. Technology and consumer trends have had an impact on personal selling in the retail and service sectors, on distribution systems, and on business-to-business sales. Although some key principles have remained intact, strategies, in general, have become more customized and the sales environment more competitive than ever. In this chapter, the focus is on sales strategy, understanding these changes, and providing tactical tools to both convert prospects to customers and obtain repeat business.

CHANGING STRATEGY

Overall sales strategies and philosophies have continued to evolve. In the 1950s, sales strategy first began to focus on customer needs and wants and on reflecting these in new products/services. Previous to the 1950s, a "manufacture the product and push it on the consumer" mentality prevailed. Consultative-style selling emerged in the late 1960s and early 1970s as an approach that emphasized identification of customer needs through effective communication between the salesperson and the customer. Strategic selling evolved in the 1980s and involved the preparation of a carefully conceived plan to accomplish sales objectives. In the 1990s, partnership selling (providing customers with a quality product *and* a quality, long-term relationship) emerged. In the new millennium, we have entered yet another era—"customization selling."[1] Today, products and services are tailored or customized to meet buyers' needs. Moreover, selling is also customized. Buyers expect sellers to provide them products and services designed to their exact wants and needs. Buyers expect to be able to purchase with speed, convenience, and at the best price in any number of ways. More and more, buyers are turning to self service—in essence, "selling themselves" based on the options offered on Internet sites. Sellers also are going to great lengths to facilitate customized purchasing.

Evolution of Sales Strategy

1950s—Manufacture it/push it
1960s-1970s—Consultative-style selling
1980s—Strategic selling
1990s—Partnership selling
2000s—Customization selling

The role of the traditional salesperson has evolved to what could be termed as a "techno-customer" service representative. Sales is customer service and customer service is a very important marketing weapon (more on this subject in Chapter 14). Sales is a direct, face-to-face or "screen-to-screen" contact marketing weapon. Human and/or electronic interaction takes place and has impacted both sales strategies and tactics. Interestingly enough, although the change has been dramatic (with respect to the process), some of the basic keys to successful selling are applicable in the new era of customization. The sales process and the keys to success have direct application in both face-to-face and screen-to-screen sales strategies. Personal sales and the sales success triad will be examined (see Exhibit 13.1).

PERSONAL SALES

A great deal of literature has been written on direct or personal sales—face-to-face sales calls. Some authors expound on the value of good grooming and a professional appearance, others go into sales psychology, and still others talk about such subjects as how to use biorhythms to make a sale. Many of these sales theories have merit and can help you sell.

However, the basics of successful personal selling can be stated quite simply. You must have thorough knowledge of your product or

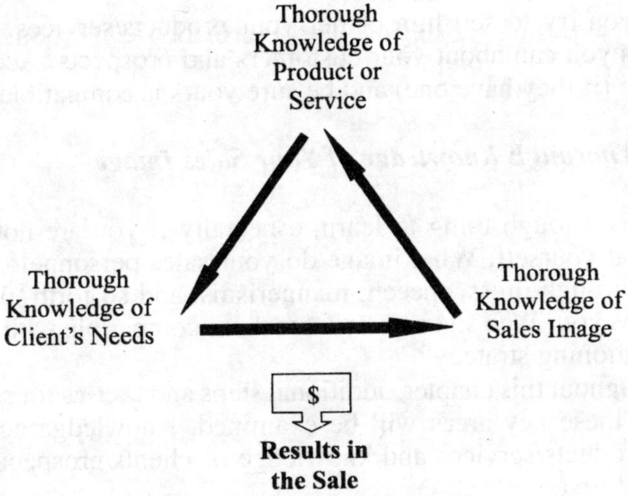

EXHIBIT 13.1. Sales Success Triad

service, thorough knowledge of your client's needs, and thorough knowledge of your sales image—that is, how you come across to clients. If you know your product or service and know how to identify your client's needs, oftentimes you can match your product/service to the needs of the client and make the sale.

Can it really be that simple? The theory is simple, but it takes careful study and a lot of hard work to put it into practice. Following is a closer look at three keys to personal sales, or the sales success triad.

Key 1: Thorough Knowledge of Your Product or Service

You don't possess thorough knowledge of your product or service until you know your product/service so well that you seldom, if ever, have to look up a fact or get back to a client. Your Web site should provide all the answers and a direct phone number to someone in your organization that has all the answers.

Key 2: Thorough Knowledge of Your Client's Needs

If you have thorough knowledge of your client's needs, then you've done your homework—you know the client's requirements before you try to sell him or her your products/services. Learn as much as you can about your customers and prospects. Access their Web site (if they have one) and be sure yours is compatible.

Key 3: Thorough Knowledge of Your Sales Image

This is a tough thing to learn, especially if you are not looking closely at yourself. What image do your sales personnel convey to clients through dress, speech, mannerisms, and so forth? What images does your Web site convey? Are these compatible with your image/positioning strategy?

Throughout this chapter, additional steps and **tactics** for success in each of these key areas will be examined. Knowledge acquisition about products/services and knowledge of clients/prospects will be reviewed first.

KNOWLEDGE ACQUISITION

A salesperson whose product knowledge is complete and accurate is better able to satisfy customers. This is the most important justification for becoming totally familiar with the products you sell. It is simply not possible to provide maximum assistance to potential customers without this information. Additional advantages to be gained from sales personnel knowing products/services include greater self-confidence, increased enthusiasm, improved ability to overcome objections, and development of stronger selling appeals.

A complete understanding of your company by your sales personnel will also yield many personal and professional benefits. The most important benefit, of course, is their ability to serve your customers most effectively. In many selling situations, customers inquire about the company's business practices. They want to know things about support personnel, product development, credit procedures, warranty plans, and product service after the sale. When salespeople are able to provide the necessary company information, they gain respect. They also close more sales.

Your sales personnel should also know your competition. It pays to study other companies that sell similar products to determine whether they have competitive advantages or disadvantages. Salespeople gather information from many sources. Company literature and sales training meetings are also important. Other sources include factory tours, customers, competition, publications, actual experience with the product/service offering, and Internet searches.

In sales presentations, knowledge of product features and your company's strengths must be presented in terms of the resulting benefits to the buyer. The information and benefits emphasized will depend on your sales personnel's assessment of customer needs and motivation. Exhibit 13.2 recaps potential sources of information.

In addition to these sources for knowledge acquisition, there are many other sources from which to develop prospects. These include: computerized databases/lists, friends and acquaintances, referrals, cold calling, directories, networking, and your competitors who "talk too much."

Sales Image

Understanding the relationship of your sales image with respect to your customers, prospects, and competitors can be vital for sales success. What image, positioning, and reputation does your company, products/services, sales personnel, and Internet site portray? How does this relate to your customers and prospects? Can you change anything to better position yourself in line with your customers/prospects? Let's examine a few areas where you might look to address this question of changing your sales image.

First, make a list of all points of encounter your customers or prospects have with your business. Include all visual, vocal, and elec-

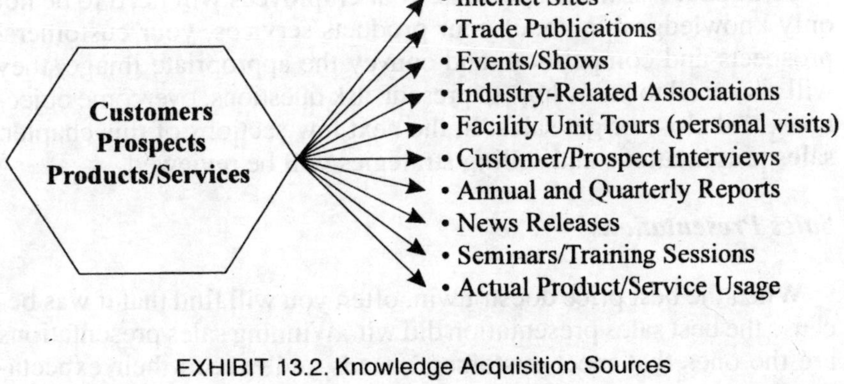

EXHIBIT 13.2. Knowledge Acquisition Sources

tronic points of encounter, e.g., sales personnel, phone operators (800 numbers), Internet sites, etc. Ask yourself if your sales personnel convey the image desired (dress, appearance, personality, style, etc.), not just for your business, but to be compatible with your major clients and prospects. In a business world made up of part formal business attire and part casual, this is increasingly important. If you have to err, do it on the side of being over-formal versus casual. What attitude or message is sent when your phone is answered or your sales personnel visit a client or prospect? Do they demonstrate a thorough knowledge of your product/services, competitive products/services? Are they prepared and sensitive to individual customer needs and nuances? Are they mature and motivated? Can they "read" customers? Can they sell? Now ask yourself similar questions about your Internet site. Most important of all, do not hesitate to fix or change any item or personnel that does not convey the desired image or is not compatible with your customer base.

Your knowledge acquisition should provide you with enough in-depth information to develop a customer strategy. Are your customers' buying motivations clearly identified? Are they methodically rational buyers? Do they purchase with a social motive or conscience? What role does emotion play? Do they prefer deals, bulk purchases, etc.? What are their payment preferences and delivery expectations? What role do they expect your business to play after the sale? The keys to finding the answers to these questions are: (1) analyze historic/past purchasing patterns; (2) listen, listen, listen; and (3) observe your customers/prospects and their relationships with other suppliers, look closely at their image/positioning and modus operandi.

To be successful salespersons, your employees will need to be not only knowledgeable about your products/services, your customers/prospects and competition, and convey the appropriate image, they will also need to know how to present, ask questions, overcome objections, and close or get sales. In the next few sections of this chapter, sales presentations and selling strategies will be reviewed.

Sales Presentations

When the best price doesn't win, often you will find that it was because the best sales presentation did win. Winning sales presentations are the ones that meet customers' needs and exceed their expectations. In general, the overall quality or "slick appearance" of the presentation does count (except when the customer profile indicates a bias against such presentations). Six keys to a successful/winning sales presentation follow.

Key 1: Preplanning

Preplanning is ascertaining what the customer's needs and expectations are and developing a detailed script. The script should include identification of type, depth, and flow of the sales presentation. The script should be a detailed outline and checklist of every item to be covered, the logical (from the customer's perspective) order in which each item is covered, and a listing of anticipated questions and related answers.

Key 2: Approach

Approach means setting up the presentation appointment through customer contact. It is important to listen carefully at this juncture for any additional clues the prospect or client provides. This can alter any number of items in the script, such as length of time, presentation flow/format, etc.

Key 3: Presentation

Presentation is the execution of the script. There are a number of types of presentations, and selecting the appropriate one is a key part of preplanning. Three of the major types of presentations that may be deployed are (1) informative, (2) persuasive, and (3) reminder. An informative presentation is designed/scripted to inform customers about new products, major changes (e.g., improvements) to existing products, or on unique products. Purchase per se will most likely not occur. Informative presentations should cover all major/new product/service features, benefits, and detail how the product/service differs from others. A persuasive presentation is what most people believe sales presentations are all about. Persuasive presentations are scripted to produce a sale (close). They are designed to relate to the customer/prospect on a customized basis. Focus is on the needs, beliefs, motivation, and behavior of the customer/prospect. Persuasive presentations often involve demonstrations, options to select from or fall back on, and converting that consumer to a customer or repeat buyer. A reminder presentation can serve multiple purposes. It can be used to keep awareness levels up (awareness levels correlate directly with sales possibility/chance), to reestablish relationships, and to remind the client about your products and/or services. In addition, reminder presentations provide an excellent occasion to identify any problems or new opportunities. Should any of your presentations actually involve product/service trials or demonstrations, be sure to prepare for this also. Make sure the product works and is timed appropriately.

Key 4: Negotiation

Most clients don't sign on the dotted line without some discussion. This interchange is known as negotiation. Buyer resistance and/or a desire to "get a better deal" is a natural reaction and part of the total sales process. Anticipation and appropriate response are keys to negotiation success. Major reasons for resistance include: the presentation/presenter; not meeting the prospect's/customer's needs; the product/service offering itself; price; time; or external reasons, e.g., the company's reputation. Any type of sales resistance should always be met with a positive/proper attitude and prepared response.

Key 5: Closing

Closing is an art to be learned and mastered. Often, there are different points in the presentation/negotiation phases where an astute salesperson can and should "go for the close." Rehearse the script and note the points. More importantly, listen to the customer/prospect for signals that they are ready for your close. These may be verbal signals such as: "That sounds good to me" or the more subtle "You've given me a lot of useful information," etc. Signals may also be nonverbal and more difficult to recognize such as the lifting of a pen or pencil from a table. In all likelihood, you will misread a signal, so prepare several different closes.

Key 6: After the Sale

This aspect involves everything from the "thank you" process (verbal and written) to the follow-up calls, billing, etc. The after-the-sale key is the most important with respect to developing repeat business, referrals, and keeping competition from succeeding. We will look more closely at the customer services marketing weapon in the next chapter. Exhibit 13.3 recaps the six keys to successful sales.

One additional method to assure that your after-the-sale step is well performed (which may possibly lead to additional sales) is to take notes and/or record comments. Analyzing this information will lead to product/service improvements, new processes/procedures, and to repeat/future business. The sales presentation process is sometimes not enough to win the sale, despite best efforts. In the next section, we will look at some additional selling insights, strategies, and tactics to help your business succeed in deployment of the sales weapon.

SELLING STRATEGIES

Numerous books, theories, and stories abound about sales strategies and techniques. In this section, some overall strategies for your business will be presented. At the outset, it is important to recognize that flexibility is important, as no one strategy will work for every customer or prospect. In fact, in all likelihood, multiple strategies will have to be employed with the same customer/prospect over time. Sales strategy selection is dependent upon many different circumstances. For example, are you dealing with a "reactive" or "proactive" sale? A reactive sale is when the buyer initiates the contact. In this scenario you move almost directly to overcome any objections and close the sale. If the seller (you or your representatives) initiates the contact, you are in a proactive sale. In proactive sales, you will use the

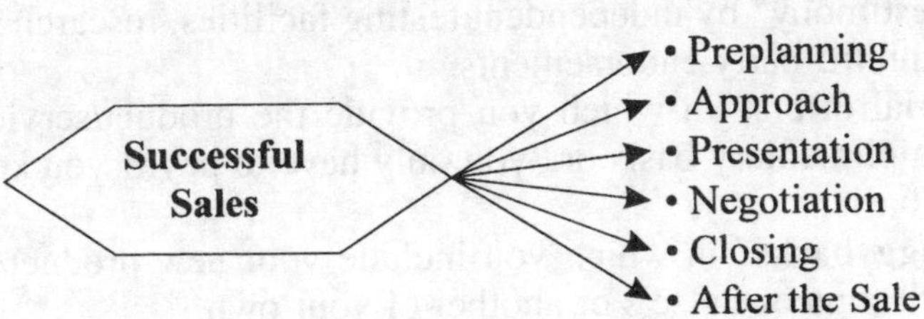

EXHIBIT 13.3. Six Keys to Successful Sales

six keys to successful sales previously delineated in this chapter. Both situations require you to ask "closed" and "open" questions. A closed question requires the respondent to only answer "yes" and "no." A closed question helps the salesperson control the conversation. An open question requires a more extensive response and is best used to let the customer talk or develop a dialogue. The ultimate goal is the same, making a sale or closing.

Making a sale for a new product or service requires a different strategy and tactics than making a sale for an existing/established product/service. Sales strategies may also vary based on the "customer type" you are dealing with, the type of resistance you meet, and the nature of the product/service itself. Some overall sales strategies follow.

- An established product/service selling strategy focuses on the brand's attributes, the company's reputation, the unique features of product/service, incremental sales, and extraordinary customer service.
- A new product/service selling strategy focuses on changing habits, developing interest, creating a new level of expectation, pointing out new, higher standards/benchmarks, building desire for the product, and creating a new customer base or market itself.

The script is going to be different from preplanning to closing. In fact, in the case of the new product, you may have to revert to a few other strategies to get to the close. These include:

- "Testimony" by independent testing facilities, research reports, and third-party endorsements.
- "Trial offers" in which you provide the product/service on a complimentary basis or "you only have to pay if you keep/like it" basis.
- "Piggybacks" in which you include your new product/service with someone else's or another of your own.
- "Samples" are one of the oldest methods to get acceptance of a new product/service offering.

For established products/services and in dealing with existing customers you may find that these strategies help to persuade a customer who is about to switch. Other strategies to keep existing customers buying your established products or services include:

- Presale contact reminders, thank you notes, and phone calls.
- Special additional product/service offering on the next purchase.
- Updates on what's new and improved.
- Trade ups, offering to take back a previous purchase as partial payment for a new or more expensive product line.
- Free product/services occasionally bestowed upon your existing customers (including merchandise, and other small, legal, tokens of appreciation).
- Upgrades are always appreciated, especially when there is a real perceived difference in the product or service.
- Surprises. Everyone loves a bonus or surprise, so remember to provide a few to your established customers.
- Extra care/attention means going beyond expectations such as being available when you wouldn't be expected to, e.g., delivery time.
- "In their favors" are simply bending your policies in favor of the customer whenever possible. Extending payments, advancing delivery dates, waiving requirements, etc., are all examples.
- "Conveniences" means accommodating your customer whenever and wherever possible. Drop shipping to multiple locations, splitting orders into multiple packs, and sequencing delivery times, etc., are a few convenience examples.
- "Special envelopes" are simply incentives or demonstrations of appreciation provided to your established customers in the form of an envelope whose contents contain an invitation, special offer to repeat purchase or return to use your service again, special discount, complimentary next purchase, etc.
- "Almost theirs" involves establishing a strong incentive (e.g., free upgrade, cases of product, etc.) if the customer makes just one more purchase, etc.

Selling strategies must be flexible, preplanned, and creatively designed to address what your research/knowledge acquisition data has told you will most likely please your established customers or new prospects. Always keep in mind that there is no profit or income until a sale is made. Up to that point all you have generated is expense.

Telephone Sales

Many times, a product or service is sold without the opportunity for a direct, face-to-face sales call. Obtaining business by telephone is an art in itself. There are a few golden rules to **telephone sales** that will help you achieve success. The first three are identical to the three keys we discussed in the previous section—thorough knowledge of your product or service, thorough knowledge of your client's needs, and thorough knowledge of your sales image.

First, just as in personal sales, you should know your product or service thoroughly. You don't want to hesitate or be forced to say, "I'll have to get back to you with those dimensions." Second, know about your prospect by doing research before you call, not while you're talking to him or her. Third, make sure your sales image is professional and positive—your sales image can be transmitted and detected over the telephone by your vocal expressions and telephone manners.[2]

The fourth key to telephone sales is perhaps the most important of all: Listen! Listen intently to prospects, and be ready with information about options and choices. Give the prospects a clear, accurate, and prompt response to every question. Phone sales should always include a recap, item by item, of all the details before reaching the fifth key. The fifth key to telephone sales is asking for the sale. The sixth key is to say "thank you."

Remember, when executing any sales strategy, whether it is personal, over the phone, or on your Web site, you should preplan, develop the script, and adhere to the keys to sales success.

Interdepartmental Communications

Sales not only depend upon the other marketing weapons (advertising, promotions, databases, pricing, etc.), but also upon all other functions responsible for getting the product/service offering to the customer when and as promised. Communications and follow up are essential with manufacturing, operations, transportation, and with whatever other functional areas that can potentially jeopardize your promises to the customer. Select your external vendors/partners carefully. They need to be as reliable and flexible as your internal functional departments if you are to keep your promise(s) to the customer. Customers do not like variations such as incorrect amount of product promised being delivered, wrong/delayed delivery dates, services not available, erroneous billing terms or calculations, dealing with call answering systems, etc. Communicate and eliminate problems before they happen. When you do find a problem, identify options/solutions that you believe will be acceptable to the customer *prior* to calling the customer. But, by all means, call the customer and be honest.

MEASURING AND REWARDING

Measuring

Measuring sales performance can be viewed in numerous ways. This section will provide many of those options. Choose the method that has the best applicability for your specific products/services. Be sure to take into account the type of selling environment. If the entire market (your market) is declining, be realistic and focus on taking market share or moving units/volume. Take into account the tenure (experience/capabilities) of your sales force. Factor in any seasonality or supply-related issues. Sales objectives, in general, represent the projected levels of goods (product) and/or services to be sold based on an accurate estimate of the market (growth trend) and the capacity of your organization to realize those opportunities. "Capacity" takes into account all of these factors plus the total marketing expenditures allocated. Sales objectives should be time-specific (start date/end date) and expressed in both dollars and units as targets to measure performance. Profits should also be part of any performance measurement.

Establishing sales objectives or benchmarks against which to assess performance can be accomplished using a variety of quantitative methods. You can focus on market share trends and set a market share percentage objective. You can assess your business/company's overall sales growth in comparison to your industry (or sector) sales growth rate. You can develop a composite or micro model of your closest competitors (assuming data will be available) and measure yourself against the composite growth index. You can assess your performance against your own previous performance rates and you can measure your sales performance against the growth rate of your target market.

Numerous qualitative factors influence sales performance measurements. These include overall economic conditions (interest rates, growth rates, etc.); competition (new, number of, strength, etc.); your product's life-cycle stage; the overall mission and personality of your business; and your marketing plan expectations/philosophy (e.g., have you intentionally set much higher than achievable/realistic goals).

In establishing your quantifiable overall sales/revenue objectives consider using multiple methodologies such as: (1) the **outside macro** approach, (2) the **inside macro approach,** and (3) the **expense plus approach.** Reconcile these results into a composite goal and then make adjustments based on your judgment and the influence of the qualitative factors previously discussed.[3]

- *Outside Macro Approach*—The outside macro approach involves establishing a quantifiable target for your sales percentage increase based on the trend in total market or category sales for the next three years. In essence, you are comparing the market growth trend for your product(s)/service(s) with your company product(s) service(s) projection (share).
- *Inside Macro Approach*—The inside macro approach method involves using your own sales history and projecting a three-year trend line using your judgment to exclude abnormal deviation from the history or factoring in any major known event (products/acquisitions, etc.) for future years.
- *Expense Plus Approach*—The expense plus approach involves estimating the sales levels required to cover expenses and make a projected profit (growth rates or increased expenditures need to be taken into account).

Each of these approaches will likely result in different sales objectives/percentage increases. Reconcile the differences by factoring in your qualitative factors/judgment to arrive at your overall sales objective to be measured against for performance purposes.

Sales data broadly include total sales; sales by product/brand or department; market share (your product's sales as a percent of the total market or categories sales); unit for unit (outlets, stores, properties, etc.) sales; seasonality of sales; geography of sales; target market segment sales; locations sales; product/service type sales; and sales by employee (usually sales force individuals). With respect to the latter, some industries or product/service categories maintain average ratios of sales ($/units) per employee (expenses). For example, in one product/service category the average ratio of sales per sales rep is fifteen times their cost (sales employee expense on average), while in another industry sector it could be thirty-five or ten. The sales per employee average is simply a guideline to help you establish a minimum threshold for your sales personnel to achieve. Measurements in general are utilized to measure efficiency (performance) and to form one basis for determining rewards (bonuses, raises, etc.). Other measurements include number of sales calls per dollar spent; percentage of market coverage per dollar spent; number of inquiries/leads per dollar spent; number, size, or value of orders per sales call; number of new customers per dollar spent; and average sales revenue per dollar of selling or distribution expense.[4] Finally, sales objectives for measurement purposes can be split between new versus established products/services and also by new versus established sales personnel.

Rewarding Performance

There are many different ways to reward sales personnel for achieving and exceeding their sales performance measurements/objectives. These broadly include, but are not limited to, basic compensation plans, **incentives** (tangibles and intangibles), and career advancement. Compensation plans usually involve direct monetary payments in the form of a salary and commissions. The mix of the two varies widely and in some cases, compensation may be purely salary or purely commissions. Many compensation plans also take into account customer satisfaction measures and overall company profit levels (thresholds). The major compensation plans usually utilized to reward sales performance from a monetary perspective are as follows.

- *Fixed salary plus bonus.* Salespeople functioning under this compensation plan tend to be more company centered and to have a fairly high degree of financial security if their salary is competitive. The bonus incentives help motivate people under this plan.
- *Straight salary.* Salespeople who work under this compensation plan are usually more company centered and have financial security.
- *Straight commission plan.* Under this plan, the only direct monetary compensation comes from sales. No sales, no income. Salespeople under this plan are very conscious of their sales. Lack of job security can be a strong inducement to produce results. However, these people may also concentrate more on immediate sales than on long-term customer development.
- *Commission plan with a draw provision or guaranteed salary.* This plan has about the same impact on salespeople as the straight commission plan. However, it gives them more financial security.
- *Commission with a draw or guaranteed salary plus a bonus.* This plan offers more direct financial security than the first two plans. Therefore, salespeople may adhere more to the company's objectives. The bonus may be based on sales or profits.

In addition to these more or less standard reward programs, some businesses use their own variations. Some modify a plan with rewards for new accounts, incremental commissions for certain items or time frames, etc.

Sales incentives include both intangibles and tangibles. Recognition programs are examples of an intangible (incentive or reward, salesperson of the year, new accounts leader, certificates of appreciation, etc.). Incentive rewards may take on a more tangible appearance such as automobiles (e.g., Mary Kay Cosmetics), merchandise, stock, travel, etc. Many times, incentive rewards are used to increase immediate and short-term performance, for instance, a one-month **sales contest** or a contest associated with a ninety-day new product launch. In the services sector, mystery shopper programs can include "instant" rewards for exceptional customer-related performance. In the next section, we will look more closely at customer service as a marketing weapon.

Sales Checklist

___ Is your overall sales strategy supported and interconnected to the other marketing weapons, e.g., advertising, promotions, etc.?

___ Have you developed specific sales objectives for repeat business?

___ Is your sales effort geared to the findings of your knowledge acquisition about your target market customers and prospects?

___ Is your sales force knowledgeable of your products/service offerings and trained to demonstrate the products?

___ Is the image conveyed by your sales personnel in line with and supportive of your overall business image and product/service positioning?

___ Are research and knowledge acquisition methodologies in place to provide your sales force thorough knowledge of your clients' needs and trends in the marketplace?

___ Is your sales force up to date on all competitive product/service offerings?

___ Do your Web site, phone response system (800#), and graphic presentations reflect the company image and positioning desired?

___ Are you developing individual (major) customer sales strategies?

___ Are your sales presentations scripted, rehearsed, and adhering to the six keys to successful sales?

___ Have your sales personnel received training in negotiations and technical support?

___ Do you have an after-the-sale plan/strategy in place?

___ Are your sales presentations and techniques appropriate for your new product introductions?

___ Have you developed a resource book of product/service testimonials for your sales force?

___ Is your sales force equipped to use "objection overcomers" and are they empowered to use them?

___ Are your telephone representatives scripted, trained to answer customer inquiries, and representative of your desired image/positioning?

___ Do you have an effective interdepartmental/intrafunctional written communications plan in place?
___ Are your sales personnel immediately notified of any product/service delivery changes or problems?
___ Do you have quantified and qualified sales objectives and measurements established that are appropriate and fair for your sales force?
___ Are your reward systems competitive, fair, fairly administered, and challenging but realistically achievable?

CASE EXAMPLE 1: THE TALE OF THE TWO INNS

Selling success is directly related to how well your personnel are trained to sell and how much they know about your products/services. In the case example that follows, we will see how two oceanfront New England inns handled the selling process.

The Inn at Ocean's Edge received a call from a potential customer who seemed hesitant about rates. The customer first asked the proprietor if rooms were available during a weeklong period in the busy season. The proprietor told the customer that there were still a few rooms available that week. The customer inquired about the rate. Sensing potential price resistance, the proprietor responded: "Have you stayed with us before?" The potential customer said no, he was not familiar with the inn and again asked, "What's the rate?" The proprietor then said, "Well, let me tell you a few things you should know prior to making a decision about staying at the Inn." What followed was an extremely informative and enthusiastic description of the oceanfront setting, designer rooms complete with whirlpool tubs, a fireplace, and a description of made-to-order breakfasts. The proprietor concluded by stating that the Inn was unique in the area because of its "4 Diamonds" rating by the American Automobile Association, and that he did expect all available rooms for that week to be gone once some of his previous guests called later in the month. The potential customer reserved a room and provided the appropriate deposit.

In this case, the proprietor knew how to sense resistance, knew he had to justify his rates, possessed the detailed knowledge of the product/service, and knew how to move the potential customer to action (close).

In another example, the potential customer called the Inn by the Sea in the same state with similar travel dates. The personnel at this inn used the top-down selling technique. First, they stated that they had a very nice suite/cottage available. The rate was just too high for the potential customer who didn't need a multibedroom cottage for two people. Sensing the response, the inn's personnel immediately dropped the rate to half for another room that they noticed "just became available." Now, the potential customer had previously stayed at this inn on a number of occasions (no one asked the question) and was aware of the fact that a few rooms were less than desirable in terms of location. When the customer asked, "Where is that (half-price room) located?" the inn's personnel said, "It is right off the lobby, close to the dining room." The customer knew that this was also next to the elevator, underneath the meeting room, and the noisiest room in the inn.

In this case, the inn's personnel had the right idea—go for the rate in season; however, they failed to "qualify or profile" the potential customer. The inn's personnel were selling without the knowledge that the customer knew the facility. Furthermore, no reasons were provided to justify the initial higher rated room/suite. Incidentally, this inn also had the prestigious AAA 4 Diamond award and the Mobil "4 Star" ranking.

CASE EXAMPLE 2: THE WORTHWHILE INVESTMENT

Many companies display their products for both training and customer familiarization. Very large companies with large product lines frequently train and display across the country throughout the year. Following is a case about one very large company and one hotel/resort chain.

The case begins with the step known as "knowledge acquisition." A large computer company periodically held training/display meetings at one or two locations of a hotel/resort. It was great business amounting to hundreds of thousands of dollars each year. In one after-the-sale session, the computer company manager casually stated that they had problems with all of the hotels/resorts they used for these training/display meetings. The alert sales executive for the hotel/

resort chain said, "Tell me about these problems." The computer firm manager replied, "Well, they are mostly technical/design problems. The ballrooms do not have enough electrical outlets, high enough ceilings, or adequate ventilation . . . we have wires taped down everywhere and the heat buildup is pretty tough to deal with." The sales executive knew that this computer company was one of four or five companies that held training/display meetings. The sales executive also knew that one company spent nearly $5 million dollars per year on such meetings.

It just so happened that this hotel/resort chain was planning to add another ballroom/exhibit to this resort and was also about to construct similar hotels/resorts in the middle and western part of the country. The sales executive asked the computer company client if he could meet with the head of all training and display shows at the chain, and go into detail about these needs. The meeting took place and it was determined that heavy duty electrical systems, "tracks" of outlets, ceilings four feet higher, and superior air conditioning and heat ventilation systems were needed to have the ideal meeting/display show space.

The hotel/resort chain told the client that they would build all of these needs into the previously referenced facilities at a considerable incremental cost. The computer company, in turn, signed a five-year contract for all of its meetings of this nature with the hotel/resort chain. The hotel/resort chain also signed other companies with similar needs. The end measurable result was $15 million in new revenue in excess of the investment to build the new facilities to meet the customers' needs.

In this case, customization might have been taken to the extreme, but the result was revenue, profit, and a long-term contract. The ability to listen to your customers' expressed needs, use of after-the-sale feedback, and taking subsequent action is part of what successful selling is all about.

Key Terms

approach
closing
cold calling
commission

consultative selling
customization selling
draw
expense plus approach
incentives
inside macro approach
negotiation
networking
outside macro approach
partnership selling
proactive selling
reactive selling
sales image
straight salary

Chapter 14

Customer Service

Customer service can be the most valuable marketing weapon for a number of reasons. Customer service plays a role in acquiring new customers, in retaining existing loyalty, and supports taking market share from competitors. Good customer service is most valuable considering that, at a minimum, it costs businesses five times as much to attract a new customer as it does to satisfy and retain an existing customer. A dissatisfied customer will sometimes tell more than ten other consumers/prospects about their unsatisfactory experience.[1] So, having a customer service strategy and plan are very important in deploying this valuable marketing weapon. Some companies fail to recognize customer service as a marketing weapon and underfund the function, or staff it with the lowest-paid (and sometimes least-trained) employees.

CUSTOMER SERVICE STRATEGIES

Customer service strategies need to be in place at every point that the customer comes into contact with your business or any representation thereof, be it personal, vocal, electronic, etc. These points are referred to as "points of encounter." Examine every potential point of encounter. These are the places/processes that your image and positioning are exposed to or being tested by.[2] In this section, the following will be reviewed: a ten-step process to customer service success, an examination of strategies and tactics, and the interrelationship of customer service with all the other marketing weapons.

Step 1: Recognition

The points at which your employees encounter the consumer are opportunities to win (or lose) the consumer. In the age of increasing customer dissatisfaction, the first step toward achieving service success is recognition. This is not the obvious recognition, after the fact, that service problems have caused sales to slip or that another company has taken more market share. Such problem recognition is reactive rather than proactive. For recognition to be proactive, observation and analysis of the points of encounter must occur. Quite simply, focus should be on the interaction of product or service with the consumer.

How often have you heard, "They really have a problem here. Too bad they haven't recognized and fixed it." "They" usually refers to top management, which has skipped the all-important thought process known as recognition. A decline in sales, employee turnover, consumer complaints—these are all reactive indicators.

True recognition in the proactive sense means knowing the points of encounter and assuming the customer's (also prospect's) perspective from presell to postsale.

Step 2: Identification of Problems

Recognition of points of encounter and customer problems is but one proactive step to customer service success. There are many ways to ensure preemptive recognition and prevent loss of market share or customers. Although there are a number of approaches, placing yourself in the role of the customer is one of the best. Ideally, it should be done incognito and often. It will make you aware of a service problem or at least give you a fresh look at the customer's perspective. Try to be observant and analytical. Always record the problems and think about possible solutions.

- Call the toll-free number of one of your establishments and analyze the response.
- Go incognito to your outlets, service centers, units, counters, or check-in desks and make notes of your observations (you may need a big notepad). Ask other customers about their experiences at the points of encounter.
- Go to one of your sales offices and read your literature (after all, your name or signature is likely to be on it).
- Observe your staff. Are they empathetic with your customers?

- After making these observations, go through the entire purchasing process and/or service experience and make a list of the direct points of encounter.

Review this list with the following objectives:

- Identification of the critical points at which the sale, loyalty, or purchase can be lost instantly if not handled properly
- Identification of the points that have to be corrected
- Identification of the points that present opportunities for making your service stand out above the competition

Here are some additional strategies and tactics with respect to recognizing problems/opportunities and identifying solutions.

- Use a shopper's service to check on your business.
- Talk to and, more importantly, listen to your customers.
- Observe and experience the offerings of your most successful competitors.
- Experience your own service as a customer.
- Personally review a random sample of complaint letters once per quarter.
- Solicit the opinions of your service offering from a focus research group every few years.
- List all points of encounter and have your management focus on one of these points each quarter.
- Check the current relevance of all points-of-encounter training materials and procedures. Update where appropriate.
- Spend at least as much time on the points of encounter as you do on the project/development aspects of your business.

Even if you are not in the service sector per se, adapt these steps to check on your sales force, retailers, wholesalers, distributors, agents, etc.

Step 3: Plan of Action

Having made your observations incognito, prepared lists, identified points of encounter, and come up with several ideas, you now need a plan of action. Before implementing it on a wide scale, test it to make sure it is executed properly. Not to do so can be disastrous. Test it, modify it, and implement it.

Step 4: Reallocation of Resources

Recognition, identification, and a plan of action are sometimes not enough to make the necessary change at a point of encounter. To remain competitive and successful, a reallocation of resources sometimes may be required. These resources may be financial, personnel, or equipment. Simple reallocations, such as hiring more phone operators to eliminate the interminable rings and busy signals, can set your company ahead of the competition. Probably half the callers hang up when the "next available service representative" recording comes on the line—that is, if they haven't been disconnected or forgotten who they called in the first place!

If your firm never puts a customer on "hold" or if the customer is always connected with a professional service representative, your chances of winning the customer are pretty good.

Step 5: Prioritization of Execution

The step least often taken and most often needed is the prioritization step. In a recent edition of *The New York Times,* I came across two very interesting help-wanted ads that may serve as examples. One fairly large block ad from Beth Israel Medical Center in New York sought a "Director of Guest Relations" (new position). The other ad, from a nationally recognized medical clinic read, "Wanted—Complaints Clerk." To me it was obvious that Beth Israel had (1) recognized that it was in a service business, (2) identified a point of encounter opportunity, (3) established a plan of action, (4) reallocated resources, and (5) prioritized the importance of a relationship with its patients. Note the difference in perspectives. Beth Israel views its patients as guests, and the person who relates to them is at a director's level. These are the obvious signs of a healthy, proactive service perspective. On the other hand, the medical clinic has the classical reactive mentality of looking for a "complaints" person and prioritizes this function with the label of "clerk." Which medical facility do you think will be perceived as better able to provide service? Following are some additional strategies and tactics to help prioritize and reallocate:

- In order of priority, list the points of encounter that need new or additional resources.
- In order of priority, list all projects (capital) dollars scheduled for allocation.
- Now prepare a new list, in order of priority, that blends the points of encounter items and projects items together.
- In identifying your project's capital needs, prioritize those that relate to your points of encounter.
- Review your non–point-of-encounter personnel count and payroll costs.
- Review your point-of-encounter personnel count and payroll costs.
- Allocate your resources to address the point-of-encounter personnel and related costs so that they can do their job right on a top-priority basis. (Can you imagine a firm that would spend a half-million dollars on a project and then deny point-of-encounter employees an increase of 50 cents per hour incentive pay or a $5,000 training program?) Review all of your firm's expenses; this could be called "current shock."

Step 6: Training of Personnel

Ask yourself if your business is suffering from human incompetence (also technological incompetence). The end product of a formal education process frequently needs to be retrained. Every one of your point-of-encounter employees needs to be trained or retrained. Also, check on your technology to see if it is functioning properly and to evaluate its ease of comprehension and use by the customer, prospect, and your employees. When your automated systems take over, do they work, that is, help with your customers? Or do they simply help you to lose the customer/prospect and help the competition? Reflect on your own customer experiences and you will quickly perceive the importance of assessing your automation.

Step 7: Recruiting the Right Personnel

To recruit and hire the appropriate personnel, you have to know the right questions to ask: What are the criteria for those who will be point-of-encounter employees? Do any of these employees sell, quote prices, or directly interface with the potential customer at the critical point of encounter—the actual purchase of your products/services? If so, what type of employee do you want to be responsible for bringing in revenue? Are these employees trainable; are they sufficiently intelligent to hold such positions or are they overqualified? If you can't answer most of these questions readily, your firm is either already in trouble or will be in trouble before very long.

Well-thought-out recruiting criteria can provide very great returns, and should be reviewed frequently. When did you last reevaluate job descriptions and hiring criteria for your point-of-encounter positions? If you believe that there is no need for such reviews because the products/services you offer have not changed, you are very wrong; your consumer is changing constantly. Some companies would advocate turning the organization chart upside down, while others would suggest that the pay scales be reversed. Obviously, there is no simple answer for all service-industry firms. However, all the steps must be taken into account: recognition, identification, plan of action, reallocation, prioritization, training, and recruiting.

Recruiting should be attempted only after a complete review of each point-of-encounter position. Complexity of job function as well as the types of consumers encountered on a daily basis should be thoroughly analyzed. Do you have (or want) minimum-wage clerks directly interfacing with $100,000-plus executives or large-volume purchasers?

Following are some additional strategies and tactics to facilitate and sharpen your recruiting:

- Have members of top management participate in at least one point-of-encounter position training session.
- Have members of top management work at least one eight-hour day (preferably an entire week) in one of the point-of-encounter positions.
- Review your training resources (people, procedures, and related budgets) annually to determine if they are adequate in preparing your personnel for service leadership.
- Ask customers to evaluate (via questionnaire or direct contact) how well they believe point-of-encounter employees are trained.
- Ask newly trained employees what else they believe should be taught.

- Ask the same question of your seasoned employees.
- Instruct all recruiters of point-of-encounter employees to ask themselves whether they would want to deal face-to-face with the person they are considering for the job.
- Personally participate in at least one interview session for a point-of-encounter employee.
- Consider upgrading your pay scale to attract seasoned pros away from the competition.
- Make sure your recruiters know exactly what you expect of them and then periodically check to see that they are doing exactly what you want.

Step 8: Communications

When it comes to communicating with the customer, no one is more important than the point-of-encounter employee. This employee is often the first to know when (and if) your service offering, price, policy, or procedural change is working. He or she is also a great source of information when you attempt to improve service. But, when it comes to communicating with these employees, corporate hierarchy in general does a less than stellar job. This, in tandem with the dissatisfied consumer, works to create the environment for disastrous customer service experience.

There are many examples of good and bad communication in the service industry. A case in point is CEO Bill Marriott Jr., who was renowned for his visits to virtually every hotel, restaurant, or in-flight kitchen in Marriott's multibillion dollar empire.[3] These were not your typical presidential appearances, but detailed inspections as well as walk-throughs to instill motivation. Mistakes were pointed out and employee suggestions were recorded and implemented on a broad scale if they were worthwhile.

Adherence to Standard Operating Procedures (SOPs) is mandatory at Marriott. It is therefore no coincidence that Marriott's operations and services are efficient and consistent. There are other examples, but the important point is the same in all situations—good communications. The conscientious CEO goes beyond motivation and inspection. The point-of-encounter employees are made aware of top management's interest in seeing not only how the job is being done, but also who is doing the job.

By definition, "communication" connotes a two-way flow—up and down. Small ideas turn into big winners if communication channels are open. For some reason, it is sometimes easier to inform one million customers of your offer than 1,000 point-of-encounter employees. One explanation for this is poor communication. An ad or service offer goes directly from the company to the consumer, but the memo describing that offer is often handed down from the vice president of marketing through the managers to the unit managers, to the department managers, to the shift managers and, finally, to the point-of-encounter employees. This process provides plenty of opportunity for a breakdown in communication. It happens all the time.

One thing is sure: Never assume that your detailed memo of instructions, the training video, and/or manual have been read, viewed, or understood by those who must use the information. The best way to find out is to put on the consumer's hat and try to get the service you have offered. Don't be surprised at what you find out. Any form of change may be difficult to communicate, and the difficulty can be compounded when the change involves behavior.

Step 9: Follow-up

In regard to follow-up, the previous example of Bill Marriott can be used. All of those walk-throughs would not have amounted to much unless there had been a positive form of follow up. During the Marriott follow-up process, a note was sent to the unit in question reaffirming the action to be taken or that the subject would be discussed upon the next visit. Granted, Bill Marriott had a phenomenal memory, but the key point is that because there was a follow-up, employees fixed what needed to be fixed.

Follow-up steps can assume a variety of forms. Some service establishments use shopper services, which essentially are professional shoppers/customers. They are hired to work as typical consumers, logging their experiences for management. Intelligent use of these findings, of course, is crucial. The results can be negative (employee dismissals), or positive (improved training programs, plans to improve performance and eliminate problem areas).

There are many effective follow-up techniques, and what is appropriate for your particular product/service offering may require special planning. But once a plan is devised, it must be implemented.

The procedure must be clearly communicated to those who will implement it, and then you must follow up to make sure it is done. Unless all of these steps are taken, the promises of your promotional ad will only lead to creating a more disappointed consumer.

Following are some strategies and tactics to improve communications and the follow-up process:

- Make a list of all point-of-encounter positions.
- Establish a personal communications calendar, scheduling specific, frequent dates to deliver your messages to these key people.
- Consider delivering these messages either in person, by video, or in writing (in that order).
- Make sure that all of your point-of-encounter employees clearly understand that their personal contact with customers represents the most critical element to conveying a good service impression.
- Listen. Listen. Listen.
- Communicate the right way by *showing* the employees—not merely telling them.
- Record and remember names and incidents, from your own employee encounters.
- "Retouch" those you can with a call or a note.
- Be sincere.
- Repeat all steps regularly. (Employee turnover is the most critical factor in diluting your message and communications in general.)

Step 10: Begin Again

For a number of reasons, this step is perhaps the most difficult. First, to some extent, having to repeat may imply that you have not been successful with the previous nine steps. Second, you need to go back to determine if, indeed, you did not succeed with any of the actions taken. If so, you will need to fix it or replace it.

Recap of the Ten Steps to Service Success

1. *Recognition*—knowing that there is a service opportunity and/or problem at the points of encounter.

2. *Identification*—determining what they are.
3. *Plan of Action*—developing the plan required to capitalize on an opportunity or deal with a problem.
4. *Reallocation*—finding the financial and/or human resources to execute the plan.
5. *Prioritization*—placing execution of the plan *at the top of the list*.
6. *Training*—preparation of those who are charged with taking action at points of encounter.
7. *Recruiting*—finding the very best persons for execution of the plan as well as for point-of-encounter positions.
8. *Communications*—conveying every aspect of your plan(s) accurately, thoroughly, and convincingly to all employees, with special focus on frontline personnel.
9. *Follow-up*—periodically review all the processes—beginning with the steps of recognition and identification.

Today's consumer is preconditioned and ready to challenge the product/service provider. Most surveys indicate that consumers in many product/service categories have reached a level of preconditioning that leaves them cynical toward the consumption experience.

Just as there are steps that your company (and management) must take, there are steps your employees must take to ensure customer satisfaction. No matter what type of service you provide, there are several keys to effective execution that will create recognition among consumers that your firm goes beyond the point of encounter.

- Expectations. Recognize that you must never deliver a service that falls short of what the customer or potential customer expects for the price they are paying. Meeting or exceeding customer expectations is what ultimately determines the level of customer satisfaction. Expectation levels in the mind of the consumer are influenced by the price you charge, their prior experience with your service offering, their prior experience with your competition, and what you promise in your advertising or sales message. Meeting customer expectations is absolutely critical to repeat business.
- Never blame the customer. Although some may argue with this categorical statement, you cannot lose by practicing it. The customer is always right, even if he or she is not! Simply stated: Let

the customer win. That doesn't mean you should allow the customer to take advantage of you. This means that your employees must understand that they have the flexibility and authority to bend policy when needed to satisfy a customer. Most surveys show that less than 5 percent of customers will actually take the time to complain about the service received. However, these same surveys show that almost 25 percent are less than satisfied with that service. This percentage grows dramatically when customers become increasingly cynical as a result of poor experiences with other companies offering the same type of service. When this occurs, two things can happen: (1) If you insist that your employees adhere so strictly to policy that customers are not allowed to feel they have won, you will lose 100 percent of those cynical customers. (2) If you have instilled in your employees the "let the customers feel they have won" philosophy, you will retain (and actually build) the loyalty of these customers.

- Clear communication with customers is essential to problem resolution at the point of encounter or purchase. Your employees must be able to tell customers precisely what they need and want to know or do. This is especially critical when you're involved in a promotional offer. After all, that is why the new customer has come to you in the first place. Make sure that everyone who has customer-contact responsibility and supervisors are thoroughly knowledgeable about all aspects of the promotion. If necessary, provide written communiqués and training videos. Augment these with in-person training sessions, and do so in a timely manner. Never start a promotion before all employees have received complete information and thorough instructions. Always provide a central resource for clarification should questions arise.
- Organize your procedures to reduce the time it takes to purchase your service offering. The number-one peeve of today's consumer is "standing in line." You must review and then revise your procedures to eliminate or at least shorten the time spent waiting in line. If the nature of your service precludes total elimination of waiting time, develop alternative plans to fill the time. This can be a customer service representative who preprocesses the customers or socializes with them. A video entertainment or informational display will also attract the customer and fill the waiting time.

- Undo what the customer has done to himself or herself. When customers discover that they are in the wrong, always avoid embarrassing them. The employee must be polite, empathetic, and tactful so that your customers save face.
- Never use business jargon that is unfamiliar to your customer. You cannot assume that even those who are in similar businesses use the same terminology as you.
- Trade-off time management is essential in personal contact situations. Each point of encounter must be analyzed and a determination made as to whether the strategy should be to go for optimum speed or special personal attention.
- Employee job performance criteria for all those in point-of-encounter positions, be they face-to-face, or over the phone, should clearly focus on execution of service with efficiency and politeness. This is what it's all about, and point-of-encounter employees must know that performing their job properly is what they are being paid for!
- Reduce time where service is expected to be fast. Fast and efficient service leads to satisfaction, especially today. In essence, cynical consumers' negative conditioning has led them to expect long lines and/or slow, inefficient service. Beat that expectation! Provide faster service and you will convert the cynical consumer into one who is more than satisfied.
- Sincere appreciation should be expressed at virtually all points of encounter, not just at the time of purchase. This must be instilled in every contact-point employee. This will ensure reinforcement of the perception that the customer is truly valued.

Following is a recap of these customer relation strategies and tactics.

Strategies and Tactics for Customer Service Success

1. **E**xpectations must be met
2. **N**ever blame the customer
3. **C**lear communications
4. **O**rganize to reduce time
5. **U**ndo what the customer has done to himself/herself
6. **N**ever embarrass the customer
7. **T**rade-off time management is essential

8. **E**mployee job performance criteria
9. **R**educe service time
10. **S**incere appreciation expressed

There are numerous other ways to let your customers win and let you retain their loyalty. Many of these were discussed within the chapters involving promotions and sales weaponry (Chapters 6 and 13). Successful enterprises have point-of-encounter plans and policies in place and widely communicated. Other firms demonstrate this through lower cost of sales (expenses), higher repeat customer levels, and brand loyalty.

Do not hesitate to use what is called "suggestive sales" with your customers. Suggestive selling is an important form of customer service. This is the process of suggesting merchandise or services that are related to the main item sold to the customer.[4] The suggestion is made when, in the salesperson's judgment, the added item will provide the customer with additional satisfaction.

The salesperson who is genuinely interested in helping customers solve their problems can enhance the relationship with suggestive selling. Some of the best ways to engage in suggestion selling follow. Having studied numerous successful companies and award winners at customer service, a number of common characteristics emerge.

- Leadership
- Formalized process or plan
- Focus on understanding customer needs
- Customer and employee feedback systems
- Responding with action on feedback
- Sales and service synergy
- Customer-retention motivational and promotional programs
- Reading the marketplace and competition and responding appropriately
- Practicing innovation through research and development and suggestion implementation
- Prominent recognition of the importance of point-of-encounter employees and giving them full support

Customer service strategies and tactics may vary for different types of customers or be tailored based on the developmental stage (see Exhibit 14.1).

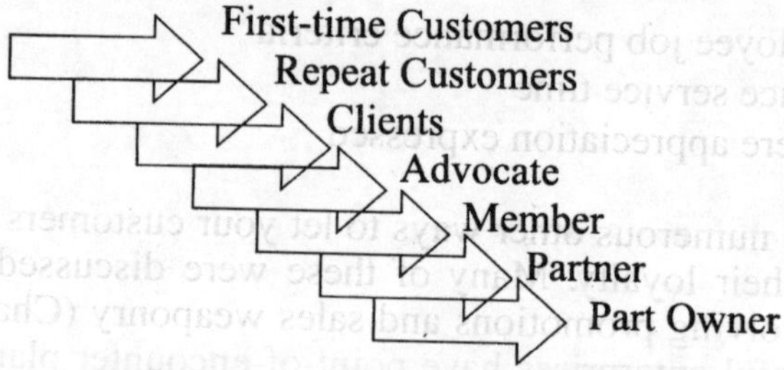

EXHIBIT 14.1. Customer Development Stages

There are hundreds of customer service tactics and ideas for every size and type of product/service business. The key to successful customer service as a marketing weapon can be summarized as follows: (1) recognize the points of encounter; (2) have a plan for customer service success; (3) empower your point-of-encounter employees with an armory of "let the customer win" tactics; (4) have a "check" system to see that customer service policies are being adhered to; and (5) make sure that your employee evaluations and compensation are directly tied to your CSI (customer satisfaction index). The following is a checklist of key items for customer service.

Customer Service Checklist

- ___ Is there a customer service plan/strategy in place?
- ___ Is it adequately supported with both human and financial resources?
- ___ Are you doing everything possible to thoroughly train and support your point-of-encounter employees?
- ___ Do you have an empowerment policy and do all customer contact personnel understand it?
- ___ Is there a customer and employee (point-of-encounter) feedback system?
- ___ Do all your personnel, vocal, and electronic points of encounter represent the image and positioning of your company appropriately?
- ___ Are you performing CPAs (customer perception audits) either internally or with shopper services?

___ Is customer satisfaction measurement an integral part of your employee evaluation and reward systems?

___ Are your recruiting guidelines appropriate for each of your point-of-encounter positions? Is your level of compensation appropriate?

___ Is customer service viewed as a marketing weapon of the highest value?

___ Do you have recognition programs in place for point-of-encounter employees who provide extraordinary service?

___ Does your sales organization understand the concept of suggestive selling and that it is indeed a valid customer service strategy?

___ Is the leadership of your organization actively involved as a champion of customer service excellence?

___ Is this message clearly communicated throughout the organization?

CASE EXAMPLE 1: REALLY TAILORED CUSTOMER SERVICE

Exceed customers' expectations and you will succeed. Knowing these expectations must come first before you go into action. This case is about the Davis Frame Company in Claremont, New Hampshire, a company that involves the customer in the entire fulfillment process and tailors the product to the exact needs of the customer.

After working with timber frame companies for more than a decade, master craftsman Jeff Davis and custom builder Rick Bascomb formed the Davis Frame Company with a simple objective: "to build the best post and beam homes by handcrafting each post and beam to perfection." To achieve this objective, the Davis Frame Company has taken some extraordinary steps and done some unique things.

The company employs artisans whose ancestors taught them the unique skills of timber cutting, finishing, and joining. They carefully handcraft each post and beam home. Not only do they have the best employees, they give those employees the best materials to work with. New England has some magnificent forests, but Jeff Davis goes to Oregon to procure the finest grade Douglas fir, with straight grain, minimal knots, light in weight, and as strong as oak for the frames. He has the lumber trucked to his craftspeople in New Hampshire where each piece is then hand cut, planed, chamfered, and sealed. Why does Davis transport timber across the country when it is readily available literally in his backyard? Passion. Davis has a passion for quality that only true craftspeople can understand.

Every home is designed together with the owners to meet their desires and to reflect their personalities. Each house, therefore, has a unique character, which ensures that no two will ever be the same. Each home bears the name of the family who jointly designed it with the firm. The Davis Frame Company does not produce "a colonial" or "a contemporary," it creates, for example, "the Ricci home" or "the Fricke home." As Jeff Davis states, "Tucked away in the back of one's mind is a vision of their ideal home. Our goal is to make that vision a reality."

His marketing and sales process totally integrates the customer and seller into a single team, moving toward the common objective of total customer satisfaction. Early on, Davis invites prospective customers to inspect and visit other homes he has built, talk with owners, and meet the actual workers. The firm works with the customer from site selection to landscaping. The Davis team stays with the customer every step of the way. They invite the customer to join them when the timbers are selected and when the timbers arrive for finishing in New Hampshire; they suggest tone, grain, or any other appearance changes on site or anywhere along the process. Naturally, if anything needs to be changed, even after the home is completed, the team takes care of it.

The Davis Frame Company epitomizes personalized customer service, quality, employee involvement, uniqueness, and excellence in marketing and sales. It is an example that everyone, from employee to owner, can learn and benefit from. This company is an example of those goals all companies should strive for such as pride, understanding your customer's needs, motivation, fulfilling expectations, targeted and on-target marketing, sales techniques, packaging and merchandising approaches, customer feedback, and an obsession with quality and being the best. Word of mouth and customer testimonials are strengths in the sales and marketing strategy, but so too are customer involvement, flexibility, openness, and need fulfillment.

CASE EXAMPLE 2: A TOTAL CUSTOMER MENTALITY

Some of the most renowned examples of dedication to customer service involve leadership and a heritage of excellence. This case example is about L.L. Bean, a pioneer in customer service since 1912 when it first introduced a 100 percent satisfaction guarantee. It still offers it today. The current L.L. Bean company is a model of point-of-encounter experiences that are meticulously orchestrated to provide a harmonious experience for the customer. Whether the sale occurs in their Freeport, Maine store, by phone, or through a catalog purchase, L.L. Bean is also a model of sophisticated consumer research at work, analyzing, experimenting, collecting data, and constantly applying research findings to enhance its offers to the consumer.

L.L. Bean stores say "quality" with one look. The clean, directional signage, well-landscaped entry with brick stairs and walkways, and green signage and white facility look inviting from the outside. (The catalog and mailings also appeal visually to customers' expectations, regardless of character type or market segment.) The customer traffic flow is a composite of value and quality seekers from every market segment, age bracket, and corner of the globe. Upon entering the store, the extensive use of wood, light effects, and constantly rotating merchandise displays create an instant feeling of warmth. Immediately visible are customer opinion forms, order forms, store directories, and helpful personnel. As soon as you walk in, you know you are in a special store. The feel is comfortable—even with a plethora of shoppers around you.

L.L. Bean offers unusual, quality merchandise in a wide selection and ample supply. Pick up a pair of slacks, and you'll try them on in a meticulously clean fitting room with help standing by in case you'd like them hemmed while you wait by one of the on-premises tailors. That is what customer service is all about.

The employees, dressed in the green and white theme or contrasting khaki brown, form a visual extension of the L.L. Bean quality. Before the extra sturdy, extra large, high quality L.L. Bean shopping bag (with green letters on white background) gets too heavy, an employee offers to hold it for you while you finish shopping. You notice that your eyes have improved because you can not only find the tags, you can read them (large letters). If an item in the display doesn't feature your size or color, an employee is ready to bring it out to you right then and there or, if it's not in the store's inventory, they offer to send it to your home.

L.L. Bean's merchandise is all top quality. Naturally, returns and exchanges are "no questions asked." L.L. Bean attends to customers twenty-four hours a day—for that is their policy—"We're always open." Vacationing customers can have their purchases shipped back home.

Although every customer inquiry is responded to personally and competently, L.L. Bean also uses the most up-to-date technology that provides customer history and preferences, such as previous payment choices, shipping, and payment preferences. For example, there is an ongoing restocking process to assure that incoming merchandise arrives on the store floor promptly and constantly. Cash register personnel always check that customers have the latest catalog or are on the mailing list.

L.L. Bean puts it all together—they know what their customers' wants and needs are, as well as how to fulfill those needs in every way. They succeed because they are masters at both point-of-encounter marketing and direct mail sophistication. L.L. Bean prepares state-of-the-art customer profiles from its own data research, and from secondary sources such as credit card databases and list profiles. Its direct-mail offers, while highly targeted, are also always in keeping with the quality service and sales excellence standards it has set.

Does it work? L.L. Bean has one of the most loyal customer bases of any business in the world. Its repeat factors are very high and customer satisfaction ratings are at the top of not only the retail sector, but almost all businesses. Moreover, it works to perpetuate itself through extensive word of mouth advertising. L.L. Bean is big business at its best—small and personal to the customer.

Key Terms

communication
CSI (customer satisfaction index)
expectations
follow-up

job performance criteria
point of encounter
prioritization
reallocation
recognition
SOPs (standard operating procedures)
trade-off time management

Chapter 15

Crisis Management

Most marketing books do not even mention crisis management as a marketing weapon. Not all marketing strategies are offensive in nature. Crisis management, usually involving multiple functions within an organization, is vital to marketing. Marketing, as the generator of sales/revenue is usually the most injured when a crisis occurs. A management crisis is an immediate and unexpected event that threatens the investments of shareholders, the ability of the organization to function/survive, and potentially the loss of all revenue. Crisis management is the management of the operations during the actual crisis (in the midst of the event) and the management of the business/corporation before, during, and after the crisis.[1] Most crises require "outside-in" and "inside-out" management. The management of your business/organization needs to include even the perception of crisis as a major event to be managed. A situation that is left unaddressed jeopardizes the ability of a company to function and ultimately hurts the brand. A crisis can happen at anytime and to anyone. Organizations that have experienced a major crisis include: AT&T, Boeing, Exxon, Gerber, TWA, Pan Am, Johnson & Johnson, Union Carbide, Johns Manville, Coca-Cola, and even the United States government. Thousands more could be listed. What strategies should be ready and put in place when a crisis occurs? Who is in charge? What are the responses? Who is the spokesperson? All of these questions and more should be scripted and addressed in a crisis management plan. Following is a review of the major parts of a crisis management plan and the strategies in each.

Part 1: Mission/Approach

It is essential to be organized prior to any crisis. Because you have no prior knowledge as to what is likely to occur or what questions you might be expected to address, you need to organize critical data about your company/business. Included items/data are your mission statement, a statement on the company's philosophy, related behavior, and standards. You will need statements on your overriding values, objectives, and performance standards. Any key benchmarks and records should be identified and their location made known to those who will respond to the media/public, or authorities. Most important of all, you should determine what/who needs to be protected (e.g., patents, brand equity, CEO, CFO, etc.) and identify your crisis management team members. Clearly identify who is in charge, who is the backup, and who is the next backup. Who will address the media? How will all the team members be reached (twenty-four hours a day)?

Part 2: History and Potential Crisis

Develop and record any significant historic information on any type of crisis or problem that has previously occurred. List past and all future potential crises. Identify levels, categories, and related definitions for each type. Remember that the smallest crisis can be organizationally debilitating if mishandled. In fact, usually the mishandling results in a bigger crisis unto itself. Recognize that crises occur in stages. The time leading up to the crisis is referred to as "precrisis" and the actual occurrence is referred to as the "crisis" or "event." Then there is the "postcrisis" period, when damage control needs to be effective. If damage control fails or the crisis is mishandled, the next stage occurs, which is the "resultant new crisis."

Part 3: Strategy/First Steps

Immediately notify the crisis team leaders and members the instant a crisis or potential crisis is identified. Notify the CEO (chief executive officer), CFO (chief financial officer), and the board of directors. Pull the crisis team together and get into motion. The team leader should immediately establish a "gatekeeper" whose job is to control all people and inquiries in an organized and predetermined manner. The leader needs to restate each team member's responsibilities.[2] A crisis room should immediately be set up. This should be a gathering place for response control which eliminates searching for people/

data, etc., thereby containing the crisis and related data to one locale. The crisis room should have a complete array of communications materials such as phones, faxes, video equipment, TV, computer, printer, etc. Stock a "crisis kit." A crisis kit should include the items listed in Part 1 (mission/approach) and any current "official" statements. Do not hesitate to use outside advisors. Finally, check on other departments and keep them alert and appraised to the degree you deem necessary to control the crisis. It is extremely important to quickly establish a media center, usually a room you can readily control entry to and that limits the media's movement. Equip this room with everything the media needs and make them comfortable. You do not want them roaming around your facilities or catching employees and pressing them for comments. Collect all data on the crisis and control access to the data to those who need to know and to those who are designated spokespersons.

Part 4: Strategy/Audiences

Immediately define and identify all audiences, e.g., victims' families, impacted employees, the media, etc. Prioritize a key list of data for all severe crises for your stakeholders. Identify the best mechanisms to reach each audience, e.g., personal meetings/briefings, telephone, videoconference, etc. Know each audience well and anticipate any potential problem (individuals) as well as any potential ally. Know and follow government rules, regulations, procedures, and laws.

Part 5: Strategy/Media

Identify your corporate media policy and spokespeople. Be sure that your appointed gatekeeper for the media is in place ASAP. Have a media database ready at all times with any meaningful data/facts noted. Have data from any "third-party source" available which support the company brands, products, personnel, and processes. The spokesperson should understand all rules and regulations prior to meeting with the media. Establish a "media inquiry system" including lists of information available and lists of available/authorized spokespersons, control process for media questions, etc. You and/or your spokesperson will probably not be able to respond to every question. Therefore, have a "fact checking process" in place to quickly follow up with answers for those questions. Remember to control, limit access, and most of all, be honest with the media.

Part 6: Walk-Through

Simulate a crisis and conduct periodic walk-throughs or drills for your crisis management team. When it comes time to face the media, be sure to do another walk-through with all spokespersons. Be prepared, always anticipate, and don't create another issue or crisis.

Part 7: Evaluation

Establish an item-by-item postcrisis checklist and evaluate your team's performance on each item. Make notations and take corrective actions on any items you feel did not go well. Contact external sources to get their reading and survey your internal constituencies. Conduct a complete content analysis of all newspaper clippings, video, footage, etc., on the event. Make detailed notes of what was done correctly and what could have been done better. Express your appreciation to all those who helped handle the crisis and to the media who treated your organization fairly. Reevaluate your crisis plan and make any modifications. Remember to reward your employees who performed well during the precrisis, actual crisis/event, and postcrisis periods.

Every company/organization should develop a file on all potential crisis situations. These include but are not limited to: fires, crashes, murders, deaths, major accidents, poisonings, health hazards/occurrences, theft, violence, employees, electrical/mechanical, financial, etc. Keep information on your own business, your plan for handling each potential crisis, topical related information, key industry and trade association related data, competitive information, and potential external resources. These files can make the difference between timely response and late response or successful crisis management or failure. The following identifies five key steps in crisis management.

FIVE KEY STEPS IN CRISIS MANAGEMENT

1. Respond appropriately based on the type, severity, or degree of the crisis. Inform and provide only that information which is required.
2. The "pace" of urgency should be directly related to the type of crisis and relative situation/timing required.
3. Provide enough detail to dispel the inquiry/crisis.
4. Issue a statement of resolution (crisis has occurred and been resolved) or an assurance statement (crisis identified and being handled/addressed).
5. Remember to thank and recognize all who helped.

Following is a checklist for crisis management with some key questions and items.

Crisis Management Checklist

___ Who is in charge when a crisis occurs? Who is on the crisis management team? Who is the team leader and backups?
___ Who are the spokespersons?
___ Who needs to be involved in each potential type of crisis?
___ Where will the crisis management room (center) be set up?
___ Who will be the gatekeeper?
___ Where will the media room be located? Who will monitor/manage the media?
___ What is in our crisis management kit? What should be updated?
___ Do we have a monitoring and data collection system/procedure to obtain and record information or similar crises when they occur within our industry?
___ Do we have up-to-date contact information (phone numbers, etc.) for all key stakeholders, crisis management team members, board directors, and external resources?
___ Do we have an internal "need to know" crisis communications plan and policy in place?
___ Do we have a recovery plan in place, which addresses our customers, intermediaries, etc., concerns?
___ Is our internal and external counsel versed on all federal, state, and local laws, rules, regulations, and procedures related to the potential crisis?

CASE EXAMPLE 1: WHAT NOT TO DO

When a crisis occurs, decisions have to be made as to the best and most appropriate course of action to take at that time. If we reflect on some of the crises that have occurred in the United States and the reactions by some U.S. leadership, we can readily recognize "what not to do." One rule of good public relations is "tell the truth." Not telling the truth only sets the stage for the next and perhaps/usually greater crisis—lying to your customers/constituencies and then getting caught (especially in national television). If this occurs, admit you were wrong or that a mishap occurred and move immediately to the correct-and-control damage phase. The closer and more personal the crisis is, the more outside objective assistance will be needed to help resolve it.

CASE EXAMPLE 2: THE UNBREAKABLE THAT WASN'T

A crisis can occur to your product/service as a result of someone else's actions. Take the case of the eyeglass company that had a franchisee cause a massive crisis for the brand. In this case, the franchisee/optometrist sold a pair of eyeglasses to a young man who played field sports and hockey. The buyer asked for unbreakable lenses (more expensive) but received breakable (less expensive) lenses. A hockey-puck accident occurred and the lenses shattered, injuring the hockey player's eyes. The media was immediately made aware of it and ran an evening news item about the accident. The state's attorney general felt obligated to conduct a large-scale investigation. For the eyeglass company, this was extremely devastating as a very large percentage of its total sales came from this market.

This is a case of bad practice by a third party under a company brand umbrella/name causing a major crisis. Some of the steps this chain took to control the damage follow. First, it assembled its crisis management team. Next, it went to its files and immediately determined the status and background on that specific franchise. It continued assembling information and further determined it did not (neither the parent company nor its franchisees) carry the specific lenses in question. The company next went to another crisis file dealing with potential eye injuries and noted that all lenses in the franchisee's state were tested for breakage. Its external investigation revealed that the lenses were in fact purchased from an unauthorized purveyor. It further checked the entire history of its unbreakable lenses with the manufacturer and determined that this type of accident had never occurred.

Given these facts, the company spokesperson was able to: (1) reassure the public about its lenses' quality/integrity; (2) distance the overall brand from the actions of one individual; and (3) divert the state's attorney general into looking at a generic issue related to licensing of optometrists versus the in-depth probe of the industry and company. Also, based on a review of the individual franchisee files, it was determined that the franchisee had in fact been notified that he was about to be removed from the chain due to other reasons. The company's signs were removed from that franchise and the matter was resolved in the most reasonable amount of time possible.

In this case, the preplanning, file system, and crisis management team/process were in place. Despite the fact that the crisis was caused by someone else (other than an employee of the parent company), the company managed the crisis and prevented it from turning into another crisis.

Key Terms

audiences
benchmarks
crisis
crisis kit
crisis management
crisis room
evaluation
media center/room
spokesperson
walk-through

Chapter 16

Marketing and the Law

Volumes of laws at the national/federal, state, and local levels abound that have direct bearing on marketing weapons and strategies. Anyone involved in marketing should check the laws or better yet, consult their legal department. Be sure that your external agencies/ suppliers consult their legal department regarding materials, promotions, advertising, pricing data, mailings, etc. Also, remember to give legal reviewers an adequate amount of time to review your marketing offerings/strategies. Don't print it, post it, advertise it, or give it to anyone unless it has been cleared as legal.

Numerous laws govern virtually every aspect of marketing. For example, at the federal level, there are major laws and entities, such as the Federal Trade Commission, justice department, etc., which focus on marketing practices.

Following is a list of some laws that affect marketing.

- *The Sherman Antitrust Act*—The Sherman Act, in general, prohibits "every contract, combination, or conspiracy" in restraint of trade, or monopolizing (or attempting to monopolize) any part of trade or commerce.
- ***The Clayton Antitrust Act***—The Clayton Act contains three basic prohibitions against: (1) exclusive dealing agreements and tying agreements with dealers and customers; (2) corporate mergers and acquisitions which may have adverse competitive effects; and (3) individuals serving at the same time as directors of competing corporations.
- ***The Federal Trade Commission Act***—This is used to supplement the Sherman and Clayton Acts and prohibits "unfair methods of competition in or affecting commerce, and unfair deceptive acts or practices in or affecting commerce."

- *The Robinson-Patman Act* (Section II of the Clayton Act)—Generally prohibits discrimination in prices or services between two purchasers which injures competition. Buyers can also be held liable. In other words, you cannot offer a different price to one buyer than you do to another, if the two are purchasing substantially the same product or service, during the same period of time, in the same quantity. This does not prohibit you from meeting a competitive price.

The laws also are very specific about what you cannot do with respect to your competitors. You cannot denigrate your competitors' products or services. You cannot make fraudulent demands for samples. You cannot have friends call and clog the competitors' phone lines. You cannot sell your products/services at cost or below in an attempt to force your competitor out of business.

The greatest danger in antitrust law is "contact" with competitors. Any kind of agreement or understanding with a competitor, formal or informal, oral or written, expressed or implied, in regard to prices, terms, conditions of sale, volume of production, limitations of production, sales, or territories, allocations of customers or product markets, or limitation of quality, is illegal under one or more of these acts.[1]

Violations of these laws have severe penalties, both for the individual and the company. Individuals can be sent to federal prison. These acts/laws are only some of the laws your marketing strategies must adhere to. There are numerous state and local laws with respect to virtually every marketing strategy. Following are just a few of the areas governed by laws:

- Product liability (**fraud,** deceit, misrepresentation, design defect, breach of **warranty,** product safety, etc.). The latter is monitored by the Consumer Product Safety Commission.
- Packaging/labeling law—promotional strategy and compliance
- Warranty compliance
- **Patent** protection
- Your **trademark** as part of your package
- Antitrust issues related to the channels of distribution
- Laws with respect to physical handling
- Sales laws

- Direct marketing legal compliance (includes privacy, high-pressure tactics, telemarketing, **copyright,** obscenity, **infomercials,** etc.)
- Franchise legal compliance (includes disclosure statements, terminations, trademark licensing issues, antitrust issues, etc.)
- Tie-ins and co-ops and coercion
- Pricing policy (includes price fixing, competitors, price discrimination, etc.)
- Promotional policies (includes time frames, access, coupons, mail fraud, label and advertisement issues, etc.)
- Traditional advertising (includes copyright protection, photographs, releases, film, headline compliance, "sale," "new," inclusion/exclusion, **disclaimers,** conditions, rules, "trial," "examination," wording, use of **flags,** use of money/currency, demonstrations, claims, comparisons, endorsements, etc.)
- Personal promotions (includes door-to-door sales, product demonstrations, cancellations, multilevel marketing schemes, **pyramiding,** referral sales agreements, **bait and switch** advertising, etc.)
- Credit/financing (includes truth in lending, disclosure laws, security interest, late fees, credit card purchases, damages, **cash discounts,** billing, prescreening, discrimination, credit reporting/checking, clear wording/contract terms, electronic fund transfers, fraudulent use, etc.)
- Collecting debts (includes dunning, telephone practices, prohibited practices, methods, etc.)
- Contracts (includes contractual relationships, terms, clauses, trade secrets, signatures, computer hardware and software agreements, employment contracts, contracts related to confidentiality, product and character licensing agreements, character copyrights, computer fraud, etc.)

Laws change every day; some are amended, others are replaced, new laws are approved, and even new court interpretations of existing laws are made. Before you launch that marketing weapon be sure that you are not violating the law. Remember to run your marketing strategies through the legal review process. Also, be sure to use the laws to your benefit as a marketing weapon. Set up a monitoring system of your key competitors' activities and make sure that they are competing fairly and in compliance with the law.

Key Terms

- antitrust
- Clayton Antitrust Act
- contact
- denigrate
- Federal Trade Commission Act
- fraud
- liability
- Robinson-Patman Act
- Sherman Antitrust Act

Chapter 17

Marketing Budget

A marketing budget should quantify costs of strategies and present the weaponry and related expenses in the best possible manner. The budget should clarify your overall strategy and the role of each marketing weapon in the plan. A budget should be prepared in a number of different ways to provide a reality check on the overall budget plan. Following are some of the methods you can utilize.

PREPARATION METHODS

- *Percent of Sales, Industry Averages*—Most industry sectors have averages which are expressed as "percentage of sales." The average is the percent of sales for the total marketing budget; e.g., on average companies in the industry spend 15 percent on marketing. Also, in many industry sectors the same percent allocations may be available for some of the marketing weapons/categories such as advertising at 5 percent, sales 7 percent, etc. Use the percent of sales/industry averages method to compare with your own averages. If you are higher overall, or in your industry category, explain the reasons, e.g., new product introductions, desire to raise awareness levels, adding sales offices, etc. Analyze the overall percentage comparison excluding these exceptions and see if you are in line with the averages.
- *Task Method*—This approach analyzes the objectives (revenue/sales increases desired, etc.) and then factors in the cost of the tasks (marketing weaponry) to achieve success. For example: the new product launch will cost X, the incremental and existing sales effort will cost Y, etc. The sum of X and Y to accom-

plish all base level and incremental level tasks is the overall marketing budget.[1] (Note: compare this to the industry average to ascertain how aggressive your spending is in relationship to the norm.)

- *Competitive Method*—Select your closest leading competitors (those most like your company and/or the industry sector leaders) and compare your marketing budget to theirs, both individually and on an average/composite basis.
- *Zero-Based Method*—This is a broad concept that can help you prioritize where you want to spend your limited resources. In **zero-based budgeting,** no expenditure is justified just because it was made last year. Every expense is reanalyzed and justified annually to determine if it will yield better results than spending the same amount in another way.[2]

One note of caution: frequently, vital expenses must be maintained at certain minimum levels. For example, a sales force or reservation system must retain certain expenses that relate to those functions and should therefore use extreme caution in applying zero-based budgeting. Some marketers subdivide the marketing budget into a "vital core" of expenses and "all other" categories, and apply the concept only to the "all other" category. Some consider this a violation of the principle of zero-based budgeting, while to others it is simply common sense. You are the best qualified to determine which approach is more applicable for your company/business.

In all methods, always seek to analyze and calculate the payback or revenue generation attributable to the expense category. For example, if you are adding $100,000 in incremental sales personnel and your ratio (multiple of per sales person cost in sales [revenue] generation expected per person) is twenty, then you should be factoring in $2 million in incremental sales (revenue) into the overall budget. Normally, marketing programs should be judged in total only on their ability to cover variable expenses and contribute to fixed overhead. Other useful comparisons include indexing the budget to previous years and related company sales. This simply helps to determine a general efficiency factor. This comparison, however, can be misleading without detailing the various factors that impacted each year's (previous and current) marketing budgets.

PRESENTATION COMPONENTS

- *Marketing Objectives*—At the outset, delineate the overall key marketing objectives such as percent revenue/sales growth, market share expectations, customer retention goals, customer satisfaction index target, brand awareness objectives, etc. Also be sure to include a "mandated" new or incremental objective, e.g., six major new product launches. Divide the objectives in a logical (to the audience) format—**short-term objectives** and longer-term or immediate—one year, and next two years. Another method is to present existing marketing programs and new programs and build to the total. Irrespective of method, you must provide the rationale for all increases or decreases if comparing to prior years. Also, compare your marketing expenditure's "trend line" to that of the industry sector, closest competitors, and competitive average/composite.
- *Budget Overview*—This is normally a one-page summary of the major expenditure categories and/or **marketing mix** (weapons). This should be expressed both in dollars and percentages of the total budget. Included would be media (TV, newspaper, direct mail, electronic marketing, outdoor, radio, etc.); production expense for the media; sales (personal selling); promotions; merchandising; public relations; marketing research; branding/packaging-related expenses; agency fees/costs; overhead; and any extraordinary items related to a new endeavor, e.g., acquisition integration expenses, etc.
- *Marketing Calendar*—A **marketing calendar** is a reference tool that provides a visual summary of how and when media expenditures will take place week by week. Usually, it references media expenses by breaking them down geographically (national television, spot markets, etc.) and by media weights by week (GRPs/TRPs). Marketing calendars can also be used for promotions/events in the same manner. These are referred to as the promotions or events calendar (see Part C and Appendix 1).
- *Program Plan Summaries*—These are summations of the major program plans or marketing weapons desired that are highlighted in the overall presentation, such as creative new advertising, new electronic marketing site, new image/branding campaign, new distribution system, new call center, etc.

- *Comments/Notes*—Provide a bullet point commentary or note on items which have an impact on the marketing budget. These include sales office lease escalator clauses; changes in commission structures; media cost increases; inflation-specific items; union contract settlements, etc. This will help explain variances or abnormalities.

One final note on marketing budget presentations: always take into account your audience. Lenders may and usually do have a different perspective than your directors or management. Tailor your marketing budget presentation to each audience, be accurate, and be prepared. The following is a marketing budget checklist.

Marketing Budget Checklist

___ How does your ratio/percentage compare to the industry sector average percentage? How does it compare to your closest competitors?

___ What has been the historic trend in your spending ratio/percentage compared to the industry and your competitors?

___ Are your objectives quantified and linked to the budget allocations?

___ Have you considered preparing and submitting an incremental spending budget tied to incremental results?

___ Have you identified expense increases which appear abnormal (also decreases)?

___ Has the mix of expense allocations (by marketing weaponry/ functions) charged on a dollar and percent basis within your budget plan and why?

___ Is your budget plan summary presented with both dollar and percent changes?

___ Have you prepared appropriate summations for media, promotions, events (calendars), etc.?

___ How does your overall budget index compare to previous budgets? Can you readily delineate the rationale/reasons behind the changes?

___ Have you prepared separate documents for all major new programs and/or major changes?

Key Terms

budget overview
calendar
competitive method
payback
percent of sales—industry averages
program plan summaries
revenue operation
task method
zero-based budgeting

PART C: THE MARKETING PLAN AND THE MARKETING AUDIT

In Part A the focus was on the strategy selection process. The overall business strategy was defined and multiple research methodologies to assess focal points that set the stage and provide the rationale for actual strategy selection were discussed. Parameters for competitive and environmental research and key concepts such as positioning, brand strategy, and target markets were also defined.

In Part B the major marketing weapons (functions) were defined along with their role and suggested strategies and tactics. Advertising, public relations, promotions, merchandising, database marketing, electronic marketing, packaging, branding, pricing, sales, customer service, and crisis management were discussed. In addition, the importance of laws related to these various marketing weapons were reviewed at the end of the section.

In Part C the focus will be on the structure and content of the strategic marketing plan from an organizational perspective. When applicable, definitions and samples of each section or component of a strategic marketing plan will be provided. These examples will be generic (you can fill in your business or change the content to suit your individual case).

Chapter 18

The Strategic Marketing Plan

THE PREFACE

The first part of the **marketing plan** is the **preface,** which is an introductory statement that briefly delineates what the document is all about or what to expect.

Sample Preface

The strategic marketing plan contains many recommendations from a mission statement to specific tactics that provide both generators of revenue and product/positioning improvements. Its focus is strategic, covering the next one to three years with respect to the overall market, as well as tactical, in that it addresses more immediate action steps to increase returns in the current and subsequent fiscal years. The strategic and tactical elements should be viewed as interlinked and, to a large extent, they are by-products of each other.

Overall, the strategies and tactics, while seeking to generate revenue, are based on the premise of improving market share by selling more to existing customers and creating new demand. The environmental and competitive assessment highlights the strengths, weaknesses, opportunities, and threats of your business. The mission statement suggests an overall vision that, once agreed upon, should be the focal point upon which future actions are based.

Finally, this strategic marketing plan is realistic in its application of resources, focus, and recommended action steps. It suggests specific ways to achieve the goals and objectives either from an operation and manpower methodology or a resource allocation perspective. It strongly urges coordination, cooperation, and communication to support the achievement of the mission.

EXECUTIVE SUMMARY

Following the preface, the written plan should move on to the executive summary. This is the key to presenting, communicating, and convincing ownership, investors, shareholders, and stakeholders to pay attention and to read on. The executive summary should articulate the organization's mission statement, goals and objectives, strategies and tactics, as well as address issues and highlight the planning document's recommendations.

Sample Executive Summary

An environmental and competitive business assessment of the strengths, weaknesses, opportunities, and threats reveals a crossroad in terms of the market. The overall ingredients for success are based in the assets of the brands, yet the accumulation of weaknesses and threats can disrupt the status quo. A major downturn in sales and the incremental deterioration of the distribution infrastructure are potential and real threats.

In summary, we are at that 50 to 60 percent threshold where we can secure our position, change and rejuvenate the distribution system, or struggle to maintain the current status quo. The recommendations contained in this marketing plan focus on the former option.

At this point in time, and for the duration of the plan's three-year period, the following mission statement is appropriate: "To become the industry leader known for product innovation, extraordinary customer service, and the best value in the marketplace."

Strategic marketing, infrastructure improvements, and new product development need to be targeted to offset pending market and related economic declines. A reasonable goal to strive for is a 7 to 10 percent annual growth, measured in revenues, during the planning period.

Five objectives have been identified to address this goal:

1. Enhance the overall product/offering, both quantitatively and perceptually.
2. Develop the infrastructure (including a new distribution system) to be customer friendly and to increase repeat purchases.

3. Broaden the customer base while providing for new revenues.
4. Maximize resources for strategic marketing.
5. Improve communications to all audiences, including current customers, suppliers, distributors, investors, and employees.

In order to achieve these objectives, three primary driving forces need to be addressed in the focal points of the strategy:

1. Enhance the perceptions of our existing brands.
2. Identify and select new pricing strategies and cooperative selling opportunities.
3. Accelerate the number of new products developed and shorten the development cycle.

To address these driving forces, this plan suggests the full use of all marketing weaponry—promotions, advertising, cooperatives, sales, events, and public relations—to work in synergy with the overall goal of revenue generation. Related strategies and tactics for each category of weaponry are suggested within the plan.

Furthermore, the objectives are supported with over forty specific recommendations; some require immediate attention, and others are to be implemented during the planning period. Also presented are the budget planning approaches. Highlights from these recommendations include:

- Selecting a vision or theme for the future (two are suggested for selection)
- Optional packaging concepts to immediately improve the first impression for all brands
- Potential development concepts to provide additional attractive new brands, while broadening the customer base
- Infrastructure improvements to increase the movement of products to the market
- Utilization of a full-service advertising and public relations agency
- A promotions and events calendar
- A public relations and communications strategy
- A specific cooperative opportunity

This marketing plan strongly urges development of a new image through the selection and communication of a vision or theme. Two such themes and appropriate supporting slogans are presented for discussion.

Six primary issues emerge for decision making:

1. The need for a full-time marketing function or an advertising and public relations agency
2. The selection of a new vision or theme
3. The need for new product development
4. An immediate plan for infrastructure and product-to-market delivery improvements
5. Changing visual perceptions and improving communications
6. Consideration of a 7 percent versus a 5 percent budget increase

Acting on the recommendations, reallocating budget expenditures, and the resolution of the previous issues should result in a measurable increase in revenues of 7 to 10 percent on an annual basis.

COMPETITIVE AND ENVIRONMENTAL ASSESSMENT

Another section usually located in the beginning of the planning document is the competitive and environmental assessment. This section provides a realistic assessment of the business's strengths and weaknesses, its surrounding opportunities and threats (commonly referred to as the SWOT analysis), and its competition. A strength is an asset or a resource that can be used to improve competitive position, such as strong brand equity, a new product, or a strong distribution system. A weakness is just the opposite—a deteriorating resource or lack of capability that may cause your business to have a less-competitive position, which can adversely affect market share. For instance, an antiquated distribution system or lack of a major market are categorized as weaknesses. Opportunities are developed from business or brand strengths, or positive circumstances, and can include superior products, high awareness levels, or the opportunity for unique products within your category. Threats are viewed as problems that focus on your weaknesses which can create a potentially negative situation.

Depressed wholesaler activity or a new competitor with substantial financial resources are examples of threats.

Your business/brand marketing plan strategies should be based on a realistic assessment of your operating environment and competitive position. This assessment should include a factual SWOT analysis that is both objective and subjective in nature. The perspective should also include an analysis of your competition, the business itself, and the next one to three years.

Sample Competitive and Environmental Assessment

Strengths

- Excellent brand equity/reputation
- Market-share leadership
- Breadth of product line
- Retailer relationships
- Superior sales force

Weaknesses

- Major brands losing share
- Competitors increasing with each new product
- Generic products undercutting margins
- Distribution system too slow/cumbersome

Opportunities

- Capitalize on retailer relationships to launch new product
- Give sales force more product lines to sell
- Develop state-of-the-art distribution system or acquire competitor with one
- Retake market share through short-term, aggressive, lowest-price strategy

Threat

- Projected major economic downturn
- External distribution system deteriorating
- New, costly, proposed government regulations
- Acquisitions of major competitor by cash-rich corporation
- New products with superior qualities

Summary/Assessment

Our brands and reputation provide us with a base of strength and an opportunity to take greater market share by pricing and new product introductions. Replacing the distribution system is critical to remaining competitive.

THE MISSION STATEMENT

The core of the actual marketing plan document begins with the mission statement, which is a concise, narrative statement summarizing an organization's objectives and ultimate goals. It provides a clear direction for everyone working in the organization, serves as a basis for communication, asserts a philosophy for doing business, and provides a basis for evaluating the organization.[1] In essence, a mission statement outlines why you are in business.

A mission statement represents the end result of your objectives as well as the achievement of your ultimate goals, while defining what your organization is all about. Once agreed upon, it becomes the benchmark against which all strategies and human and financial resource allocations are measured. Furthermore, a mission statement is a communications vehicle, whose purpose is to be clear, concise, and directional while focusing on the planning period, as well as the future. A mission statement is ultimately the end product of the leadership of your organization.

Sample Mission Statement

"To become the industry leader known for product innovation, extraordinary customer service, and the best value in the marketplace."

GOALS AND OBJECTIVES

The next step, which immediately follows the mission statement, is goals and objectives. Goals are both qualitative and quantitative, which means that they comprise both databased estimates and educated guesses, although realistic estimates are preferred. Objectives outline what needs to be accomplished during the time frame of the plan. They must be specific, measurable in a quantifiable manner, related to a specific time period, and focused on affecting the behavior of your market. Although the overall goal is the fulfillment of your mission statement, a very specific and quantifiable goal could be as follows:

Sample Goals and Objectives

To seek to offset pending economic declines (as a minimum target) with the achievement of actual growth through new product introduction, produce an annualized rate of (up to) 10 percent incremental revenue growth during the plan's duration.

Reaching this goal would be based upon the achievement of the following primary objectives:

1. Enhance the overall product offering both quantitatively and perceptually.
2. Broaden the customer base by providing new products.
3. Redevelop a new distribution infrastructure to be user friendly, and maximize marketing resources to facilitate repeat business.
4. Increase market share by 5 percent.
5. Improve communications to all audiences, including current customers, suppliers, distributors, investors, and employees.

Each of these primary objectives is supported with a set of strategies and tactics for their implementation in the strategy section of this plan.

DRIVING FORCES

There are three major driving forces, which are of such magnitude that they need to be discussed separately from the strategic issues. These driving forces, although interrelated to a large degree, should be viewed both individually and collectively as they support your objectives and strategies.[2]

Sample Driving Forces

Driving Force #1—Perception

We are clearly positioning as the current value leader in terms of quality product at a fair price. Our brands and sales force are perceived as the finest in the industry. Our overall perception by customers and competitors is one of leadership. We need to reinforce this perception or lose this advantage.

Driving Force #2—Pricing

Our pricing strategies have made us the most attractive company to deal with and provided us with great sales advantages. With support from our lower cost structure and quality product we have been able to take the number one market share position in most product/brand categories. We will need to capitalize on this and be even more aggressive to thwart new competition and maintain share in the coming economic downturn.

Driving Force #3—New Product Development

Our competitors and customers know us as the new product innovator. Our ability to develop and launch new products ahead of the competition is threatened by the many new specialty product upstarts and our deteriorating distribution system. We can protect this driving force by rapid implementation of the new/proposed distribution system and an accelerated schedule of new product launches.

STRATEGIES AND TACTICS

The next step of the strategic marketing plan focuses on how the goals and objectives as previously outlined will now be achieved. This section is called strategies and tactics. Strategies simply detail how the plan's objectives will be achieved. Tactics are the detailed items related to the strategies.

Sample Strategies and Tactics

Reference: Objective #1—Quantitatively and perceptually enhance overall product offering.

Supporting Strategies

- Launch all brand extensions in the next eighteen months.
- Introduce one new product per quarter.
- Implement the new package and signage designs over the next six months.

Tactics

- Begin brand extensions on West Coast first.
- Introduce first new product in New York City for media proximity and coverage.
- Unveil new signage designs at new unit opening in Chicago during franchise convention.

Reference: Objective #2—Develop a new distribution infrastructure to be user friendly and facilitate repeat purchases.

Supporting Strategies

- Design the new system to allow online customers access for order tracking.
- Increase the discount percentages for multiple-term contracts.
- Launch a new frequent purchaser incentive rewards program.

Tactics

- Provide major (category 1) customers with complimentary software at time of system implementation (co-op with vendor).
- Run sales contest when discounts are announced.
- Unveil at franchise/distributor show.

Reference: Objective #3—Broaden the customer base while providing for new revenues.

Supporting Strategies

- Expand the database list program and electronic marketing efforts.
- Launch new advertising campaign at twice the GRPs (gross rating points).
- Implement a new, more aggressive promotions calendar.
- Expand the sales coverage into Canada and Mexico.

Tactics

- Mail new prospects special introductory offers.
- Purchase incremental prime-time network television time.
- Increase the number of promotions and include a minimum of three trial offers during the cycle.
- Lease offices by December 1 and have them fully staffed by March 1.

Note that the sample strategies and tactics use different marketing weapons, e.g., brand strategies, packaging, public relations, database and electronic marketing, promotions, pricing, sales, co-ops, etc. Also, note how one objective is supported by multiple marketing weaponry working in concert.

PROGRAM PLANS

In some cases, an objective and related strategy may be of such magnitude or so extraordinary in nature that a separate, detailed program plan or **action plan** is delineated within the actual body of the strategic marketing plan, incorporated in the appendix, or provided as a separate document (even though it's summarized in the strategic marketing plan). In the generic examples presented, the "new distribution system" objective is an example of this type of treatment.

Certainly, it is appropriate to include items such as the media plan, the promotions calendar, new packaging, new pricing strategies, etc. These may also be included within the program plans section or in a tabled appendix.

RECOMMENDATIONS

Now that the strategic marketing plan detail has been outlined, it is time to provide specific recommendations for both a short- and longer-term perspective. Typically, these recommendations are related to the objectives previously detailed in the goals and objectives section of the plan. This interrelationship between the recommendations and objectives should permeate daily decisions and actions in a manner consistent with the long-term success of the overall strategy. Once the necessary decisions are made, specific action takes place.

Sample Recommendations

- To enhance the overall product offering we recommend the acquisition of a new line of products (brand X and/or company Y). This will also help us quickly broaden our customer base (supports Objectives #1 and #3).
- Immediate reallocation of an additional $5 million to expedite the implementation of the new distribution system (supports Objective #2).
- Retain our outside design expertise to refresh all packaging, brands, and corporate logo (supports Objectives #1 and #5).
- Establish a new communications function to oversee all communications functions and coordinate all efforts including the newly proposed "customer friendly" order/distribution system (supports objectives #1, #2, #4, and #5).

THE VISION

In many strategic marketing plans, a section outlining the company's vision is often included. The "Vision" is a statement that vividly describes the desired outcome of the overall strategic plan. Often, the section including the company's vision will present alternative scenarios for its future while providing both direction and purpose for its interim strategies and activities.

Sample Vision Statement

"To be viewed as the industry leader by customers, investors, employees, and shareholders as a result of our innovative products, service-oriented employees, and strong financial performance."

"To achieve preeminence as the industry leader through award-winning customer service, flawless product quality and delivery, and dedicated personnel worldwide."

SLOGANS

In many business or corporate strategic marketing plans, a company's mission, vision, goals, and objectives are reflected in the slogan. Slogans help build identity and can convey a company's position in the marketplace, such as: "Quality IS Job Number One" or "Innovation Through Investigation." Slogans can also be created and associated with marketing campaigns. Ultimately, a slogan becomes an image with which current and potential customers can identify.

Sample Slogans

- "Leadership Through Innovation"
- "The Quality/Value Leader"
- "Beyond Expectations"
- "Customer-Driven Product Excellence"
- "The Company of Tomorrow"

ISSUES

In the process of undertaking any strategic marketing plan, several issues will surface. These issues should be collected during the planning process and set aside for appropriate discussion at the end of the actual plan. Although some issues may resolve themselves during the planning process, others may divert the process or cause delays. Addressing the issues at the end of the plan enables the company to put them into perspective in relation to the plan in its entirety.

Sample Issues

- Twenty-five percent of brands (units, etc.) are in the decline phase of their life cycle and 35 percent are projected to be in decline in thirty-six months. Do we sell or rejuvenate?
- Top three leading brands/products are not doing well against biggest newly emerging market.
- Competitor's new products taking major market share.
- **"Underpenetrated"** (not enough stores/outlets) in three major markets and **"overpenetrated"** (too many stores/outlets) in three other markets.
- Lack of presence in Mexican and Canadian markets.
- Antiquated technology system in distribution hurting sales and customer relations.

MEASUREMENTS AND RESULTS

To ensure success, all of the activities within a strategic marketing plan need to be measurable. This can be achieved in two ways: (1) either the expected results are specific and quantifiable; or (2) they are related to key dates, milestones, or timetables. Likewise, qualitative accomplishments can be measured within time parameters or other established criteria, including polls, image assessments, or opinion surveys. Specifying these expectations is critical in determining which goals are being achieved and, as a result, whether strategies need to be modified.

Sample Key Measurements and Results

- Increase product/brand offerings by 20 percent during the planning period.
- Reverse the downtrend in the CSI (customer service index) and bring it back up to the 90 percent level by December 1.
- Have the new distribution system up and running (within budget) by June 1.
- Open the Mexico City, Toronto, and Vancouver sales centers by March 1.

- Consummate two cooperative product-marketing agreements—one by March 1 and the second by April 1.
- Review brand awareness levels after the new advertising campaign has run six weeks to ascertain if the 15 percent increase has been achieved against the target markets segment.

BUDGET

A key component of any plan is the budget plan, as it may often seem that there are never enough marketing dollars available for the execution of the plan. Although strategic marketing plans may offer a means for measuring various targets, such as increasing the revenue from 7 to 10 percent, the achievement of these goals is contingent upon budget allocations and meeting revenue goals to fund future objectives. Thus, it is first necessary to determine the plan's priorities and the costs associated with their execution. Then comes the balancing act—weighing what needs to be accomplished with what is affordable.

In a strategic context, numerous scenarios or options may be selected, and each can be interlinked with existing and new marketing strategies. For example, "If we exceed our revenue growth goal of 10 percent in year one, we will move to Option Two, increase the budget, and accelerate the new product development."

As indicated in Chapter 17, in the strategic marketing plan, the budget plan should be prepared by using a summation format and any desired (significant) calendars (promotions/events) and any special program plans. In this section, a sample overview of a marketing budget plan summation is presented with sample promotions and events calendars. All examples are theoretical/generic for exhibit purposes.

Sample Strategic Marketing Plan Budget Overview

This $31 million* budget is designed to achieve a 10 percent annualized growth in revenues during the planning period. The budget is premised upon the on-time introductions of all new products and the

---

*This represents an 8.5% increase over the previous year. However, it incorporates the six new product launches and new packaging costs.

projected slow downturn in economic conditions. Key objectives and strategies supported include the following:

- Achieving annualized revenue growth of 10 percent
- Adding 1.2 million purchases from new customers
- Increasing unaided brand awareness by 10 points
- The successful launch of six new products and the achievement of each of their year-one targeted revenue and sales objectives
- Launch of a new frequent buyer's promotion in conjunction with the launch of the new distribution system
- Development and implementation of an entirely new Internet site with links to the new, customer-oriented distribution system

The budget plan has taken into consideration the changes in pricing strategy, new packaging, and product introduction (Table 18.1).

TABLE 18.1. Sample Strategic Marketing Budget Plan Summation (Option #1,* Year 1)

Weapon/Tool	**$(M)**	**Percent of Total**	**Percent Change**
Advertising			
Media	10.0	32.3	10
Production	1.5	4.8	(2)
Promotions	7.5	24.2	5
Merchandising	1.0	3.3	—
Sales	5.0	16.0	8
Events	1.0	3.3	1
Direct Mail	1.5	4.8	5
Electronic	1.5	4.8	12
Packaging	.5	1.6	6
Research	.5	1.6	(12)
Miscellaneous	1.0	3.3	(15)
Total	**31.0**	**100.0**	**8.5**

*Incremental marketing expenditure options are contained in the appendix.

It is in line with industry sector and competitive spending ratios. We recommend that consideration be given to Option 2 presented in the appendix, which we believe would accelerate revenue growth by 10 percent annually with an incremental spending level of $2 million or 4 to 6 percent.

In many instances, it is helpful to present the promotions calendar (Exhibit 18.1) along with the budget. For some businesses, listing events and/or presenting them in a calendar format is also helpful (Exhibit 18.2).

THE APPENDIX

The final section of a strategic marketing plan is the appendix. Although appendixes are often included within the original document, relevant statistical data and research findings should be presented in an accompanying volume. This will ensure that the marketing plan it-

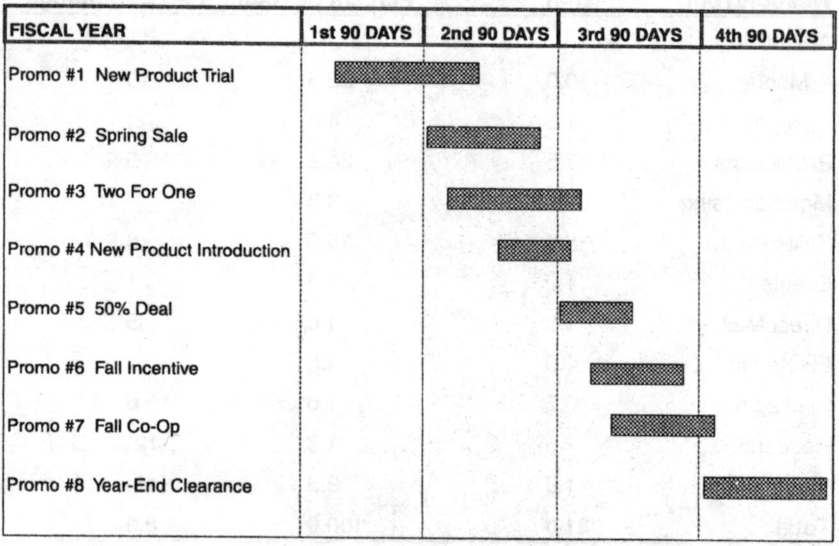

EXHIBIT 18.1. Sample Promotions Calendar

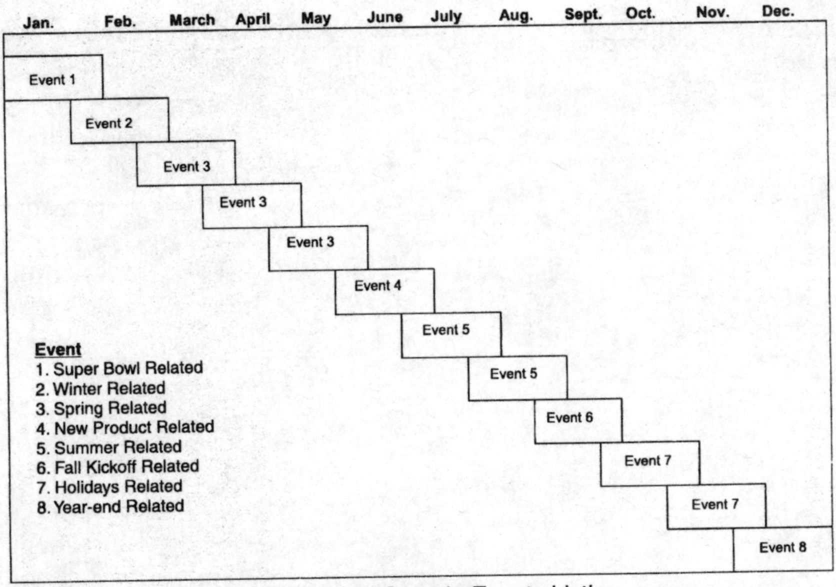

EXHIBIT 18.2. Sample Events Listing

self is not weighed down with excessive numbers and data. A sample of items that form an appendix are as follows.

Sample Appendix Table of Contents

1. Optional Budget Plans at Incremental and/or Reduced Levels
2. Marketing Budget Review Chart—Historical Trends
3. Research Findings Which Support or Negate Strategies
4. Distribution of Marketing Dollars by Weaponry
5. Detailed Promotional Calendar
6. Detailed Current Customer Trends
7. Information on Potential Co-op Partners
8. Other Data—New Logos, Package Designs, etc.

Chapter 19

The Complete Marketing Audit

When most people think of a marketing audit they usually focus on budget and organizational issues. Perhaps adherence to company procedures and policies comes into play, and/or even an agency review. With the exception of the agency review, most focal points of an audit of this scope are internal to the marketing operation itself. A complete marketing audit encompasses much more. Before looking at the scope of a complete audit, one should focus on the role and relationships that marketing is expected to play within the context of the total strategic and operational plans. This means going beyond the budget, organizational, or even operational focal points. The complete marketing audit should be targeted at three major areas and multiple focal points within each of these three areas (see Exhibit 19.1).

"Looking Ahead," or the environmental analysis, is the part of the marketing audit that focuses on the macroenvironment and the task environment. Both of these areas are external in nature and provide the overall parameters of the environment in which the marketing effort takes place and will take place.

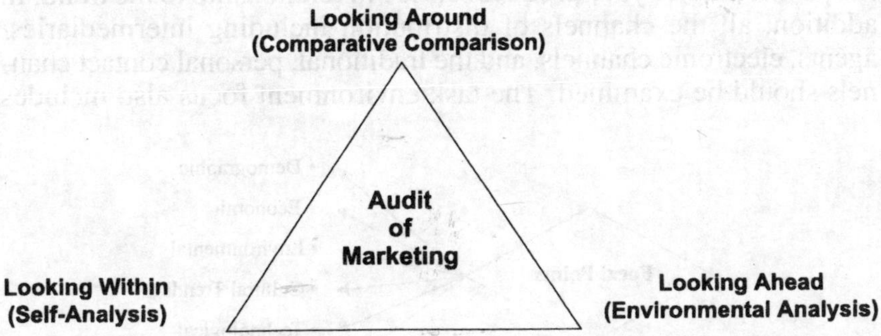

EXHIBIT 19.1. The Complete Marketing Audit Areas

The macroenvironment focal points encompass demographic, economic, environmental, technological, political, and cultural trends, which have a direct impact on current and planned (future) marketing activities (see Exhibit 19.2). Key questions need to be asked: What impact will changing demographics have on the company's products/services and what actions are being taken or are planned in response to these developments? What actions are in place or planned with respect to major economic developments such as income increases, prices, savings, credit rates, etc.? What is the impact and response to environmental trends such as rising energy costs (impact on pricing strategy and demand)? What is the company's record on environmental issues (pollution, waste management, etc.)? How do these affect the client base of existing customers and prospective customers? What major changes are occurring in technology that impact the distribution channels, presentation of product/service information, response times, replacement or threats to existing business and/or business processes? What changes in laws and regulations might impact current and future marketing strategies or change cost assumptions? What are constituencies' (investment community, customers, employees, franchisees, etc.) attitudes toward the company? What are the responses to changing customer lifestyles, values, and preferences?

Once the macroenvironmental assessment has taken place, it is time to evaluate the task environment (see Exhibit 19.3). This involves focusing on specific market trends and segments and analyzing changes in customer needs and buying processes, including price and the positioning of your product/service in relationship to the trend. In addition, all the channels of distribution including intermediaries/agents, electronic channels, and the traditional, personal contact channels should be examined. The task environment focus also includes

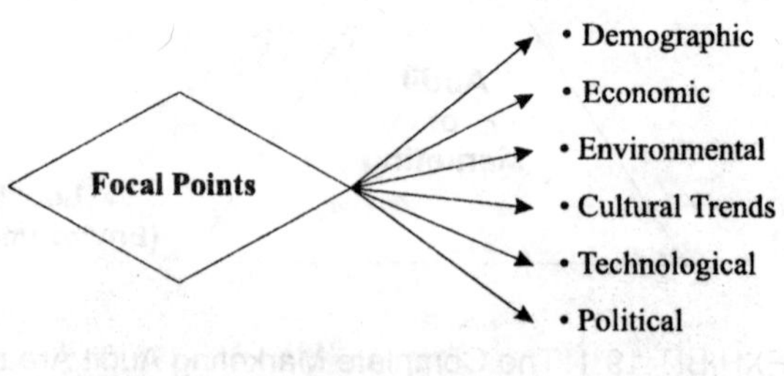

EXHIBIT 19.2. Macroenvironment Focal Points

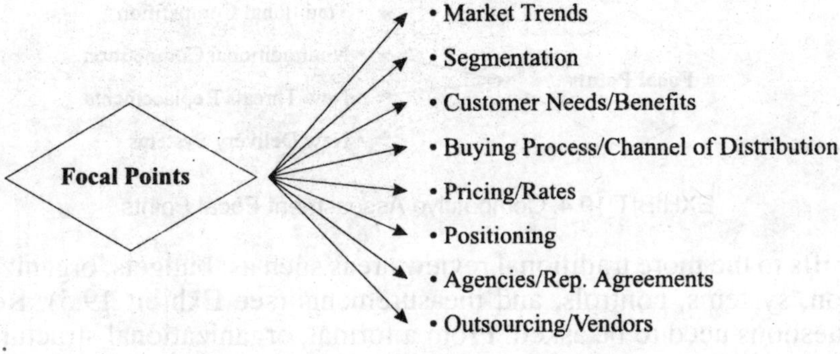

EXHIBIT 19.3. Task Environment Focal Points

assessing suppliers and any outsourcing, representation agreements, agencies, and **vendors.** These assessments should also consider which market segments and constituencies represent particular opportunities or pose new or emerging threats.

After assessing the task environment, a fairly accurate scenario will emerge that provides a picture of the present to near-term (and potentially intermediate-term) future external environment for marketing activities.

The next area for examination is "looking around" at competition (see Exhibit 19.4). This involves assessing both traditional competition and potentially new forms of competition. A review of who are the current and likely future competitors should be undertaken. For each, an evaluation of their objectives, strategies, strengths, weaknesses, financial clout (budget/expenditures), human resource capability (sales force, etc.), should be done. Who are their partners? What strategic alliances have they forged? What are they doing better than we are, and what is our response? How are we performing in relationship to market share, segment preferences, etc.? Finally, this is also the part of the complete marketing audit when all forms of new competition should be examined. Who is likely to emerge as overall new competitors, or as new threats for key market segments? Are there new competitors coming from nontraditional sources such as technological developments, new delivery systems, etc.? What is our response? Are we allocating resources to combat the competition and threats appropriately?

This brings the audit to its third major area, "looking within," or, the self-analysis phase. At this point in the audit process, the focus

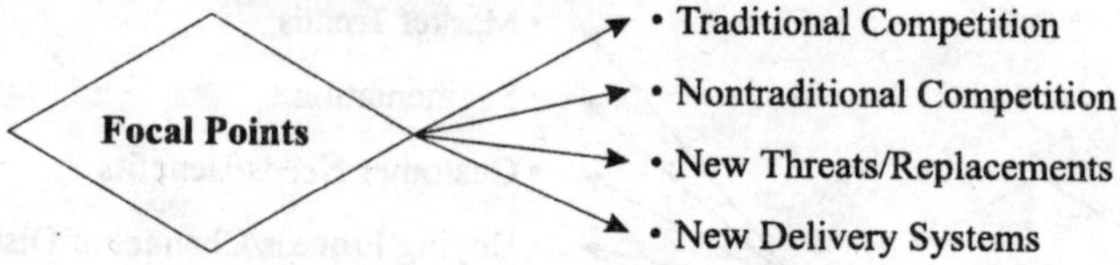

EXHIBIT 19.4. Competitive Assessment Focal Points

shifts to the more traditional review areas such as: budgets, organization, systems, controls, and measurements (see Exhibit 19.5). Key questions need to be asked: From a formal, organizational structure/perspective, does the chief marketing executive have the authority and responsibility to execute the charge—objectives, strategies, and expected outcomes? Are the marketing activities optimally structured along functional, products/services, brands, segments, end users, intermediaries, and geographic lines? Are there good intra- and interfunctional communications and working relationships? Are product/brand managers responsible for both planning profits and sales volume? What groups need more training, closer and more frequent evaluation, or more motivations/rewards? Are there interface inefficiencies such as problems between other organizational components and marketing? Are these problems being promptly and permanently resolved?

During this phase, overall strategies are reviewed, organizational structures reexamined, systems and procedures reviewed, functional areas assessed, and performance and productivity measures checked. Looking within involves reexamining the business mission, the marketing objectives and goals, and determining if these should remain or be revised. This self-analysis should focus on the breadth and depth of the marketing strategy. Are specific brand strategies adequate? Are product segmentation strategies and pricing strategies clearly delineated and understood by all? What strategies need to change due to the external environmental and competitive assessments? How will these be changed? Who will be responsible? When will results or outcomes be measured? Is the marketing mix in need of adjustment both from a financial and talent resource reallocation standpoint? Are there enough resources to accomplish the current and/or revised objectives and strategies?

The next focal point, "looking within," examines systems and procedures (see Exhibit 19.6). In looking at both focal points, a number of critical questions need to be answered. Are company decisions be-

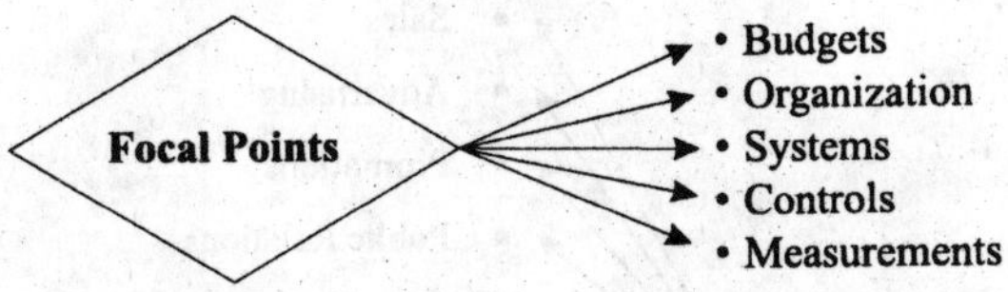

EXHIBIT 19.5. Traditional Review Focal Points

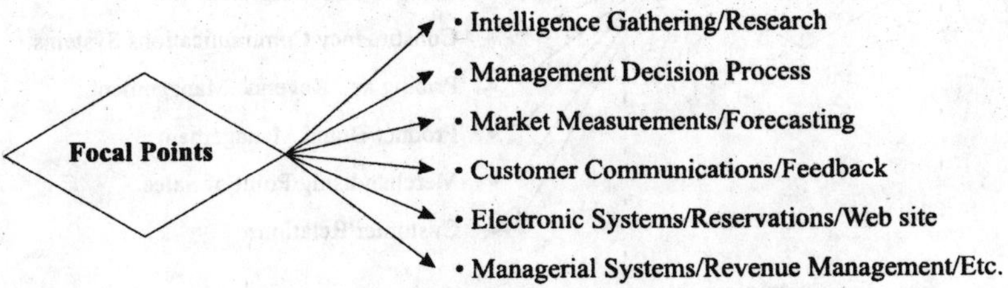

EXHIBIT 19.6. Systems and Procedures Focal Points

ing made on the basis of adequate marketing research? Are the data-gathering/intelligence systems providing timely and accurate information with respect to customers, competitors, distribution channels, prospects, suppliers, and all constituencies? Are the best and most objective quantitative and qualitative measurement and evaluation techniques being used for market measurements and forecasting? Is there a responsive marketing planning system in use which allows for rapid implementation of new strategies and reallocation of resources? How are prices/rates set, adjusted, managed, and measured? Are profitability and cost/payback analyses conducted for each major marketing effort, program, etc.? Do cost analyses and competitive intelligence comparisons reveal overspending or deficiencies? Are the strategies adequate to produce the desired results? Are sales targets and market share objectives realistic, achievable, and appropriately adjusted? Is the overall effort producing more with less, or producing less with more? Do any of the functional audits reveal problems or opportunities (see Exhibit 19.7)?

One method to ascertain how the total marketing strategy, organization, and plan is performing, is to develop a weighted measure. This "scorecard" (see Exhibit 19.8) can provide an overall grade for the total effect.

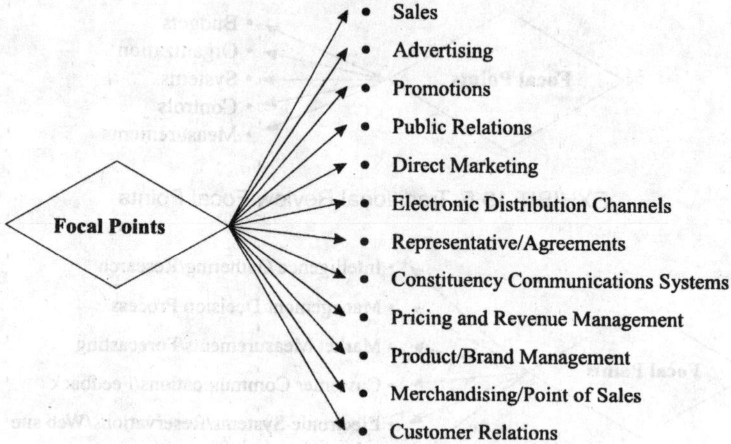

EXHIBIT 19.7. Functional Audit Focal Points

Factor/ Weight		1	2	3	4	5	6	7	8	9	10 BEST
	LOOKING AHEAD										
5	Macroeconomic Assessment	☐	☐	☐	☐	☐	☐	☐	☐	☐	☐
5	Task Environment Performance	☐	☐	☐	☐	☐	☐	☐	☐	☐	☐
10	Application/Adjustments	☐	☐	☐	☐	☐	☐	☐	☐	☐	☐
	LOOKING AROUND										
5	Competitive Intelligence	☐	☐	☐	☐	☐	☐	☐	☐	☐	☐
10	Application/Adjustments	☐	☐	☐	☐	☐	☐	☐	☐	☐	☐
	LOOKING WITHIN										
5	Budget Management	☐	☐	☐	☐	☐	☐	☐	☐	☐	☐
5	Control and Measurement	☐	☐	☐	☐	☐	☐	☐	☐	☐	☐
10	Research Responsiveness	☐	☐	☐	☐	☐	☐	☐	☐	☐	☐
10	Customer Responsiveness	☐	☐	☐	☐	☐	☐	☐	☐	☐	☐
10	Revenue/Pricing Management	☐	☐	☐	☐	☐	☐	☐	☐	☐	☐
15	Functional Effectiveness	☐	☐	☐	☐	☐	☐	☐	☐	☐	☐
10	Brand(s) Management	☐	☐	☐	☐	☐	☐	☐	☐	☐	☐

SCORING: Multiply the factor/weight × the ranking (1-10) = total points

OVERALL GRADE:

A+ = 970-1000 POINTS **B+ = 870-899 POINTS** **C+ = 770-799 POINTS**
A = 940-969 POINTS **B = 840-869 POINTS** **C = 740-769 POINTS**
A– = 900-939 POINTS **B– = 800-839 POINTS** **C– = 700-739 POINTS**
D+ = 670-699 POINTS
D = 640-669 POINTS **F = BELOW 600 POINTS**

EXHIBIT 19.8. The Scorecard

Appendix 1

Work Forms

WORK FORMS INDEX

FORM A: Target Markets
FORM B: Visual Perceptions
FORM C: Competitive Assessment
FORM D: Opportunities
FORM E: Mission Statement
FORM F: Objectives
FORM G: Strategies
FORM H: Promotions Plan
FORM I: Events Calendar
FORM J: Media Calendar
FORM K: Marketing Budget
FORM L: Brand Strategy Evaluator
FORM M: Press Release Format

FORM A: TARGET MARKETS

I. Consumer

A. Heavy User Profile ____________________

B. Geographic Profile ____________________

C. Demographic Profile ____________________

D. Lifestyle Profile ____________________

II. Business to Business

A. Industry Sectors

SIC Category(ies)

1. ________ 3. ________
2. ________ 4. ________

B. Revenue Potential

Rank Order

1. ________
2. ________
3. ________
4. ________
5. ________

III. Distribution

A. Direct Channels

1. ________ 3. ________
2. ________ 4. ________

B. Indirect Channels

1. ________ 3. ________
2. ________ 4. ________

FORM B: VISUAL PERCEPTIONS*

IDENTIFY THE TOP FIVE POSITIVE VISUAL PERCEPTIONS OF YOUR BUSINESS/BRANDS

1. ______________________________

2. ______________________________

3. ______________________________

4. ______________________________

5. ______________________________

IDENTIFY THE FIVE MOST NEGATIVE VISUAL PERCEPTIONS OF YOUR BUSINESS/BRANDS

1. ______________________________

2. ______________________________

3. ______________________________

4. ______________________________

5. ______________________________

*Use a customer's perspective, beginning with his or her point of encounter with your business/brand(s).

FORM C: COMPETITIVE ASSESSMENT*

LIST THE TOP FIVE STRENGTHS

Self		Competitor	
1.	______________	1.	______________
2.	______________	2.	______________
3.	______________	3.	______________
4.	______________	4.	______________
5.	______________	5.	______________

LIST THE TOP FIVE WEAKNESSES

Self		Competitor	
1.	______________	1.	______________
2.	______________	2.	______________
3.	______________	3.	______________
4.	______________	4.	______________
5.	______________	5.	______________

*Use the customer's/market's perspective, not your own.

FORM D: OPPORTUNITIES

LIST FIVE OPPORTUNITIES TO IMPROVE OR CREATE NEW PRODUCT OFFERING OR INFRASTRUCTURE IMPROVEMENTS

Product Offering	Infrastructure Improvements
1. ________	1. ________
2. ________	2. ________
3. ________	3. ________
4. ________	4. ________
5. ________	5. ________

IDENTIFY FIVE CO-OP PARTNERS OR TARGETS TO ENHANCE THE MARKETING AND DEVELOPMENT OF YOUR BUSINESS OR BRANDS

1. ________
2. ________
3. ________
4. ________
5. ________

FORM E: MISSION STATEMENT

MISSION STATEMENT

SLOGAN OR OTHER IDENTIFIER

FORM F: OBJECTIVES

QUALIFIED:

1. Increase current customer base by ______
2. Increase revenues by ______
3. Etc. ______
4. Etc. ______
5. Etc. ______

QUALITATIVE:

1. Improve ______
2. Enhance ______
3. Etc. ______
4. Etc. ______
5. Etc. ______

FORM G: STRATEGIES

1. ADVERTISING
   - Creative ______
   - Media ______
2. PROMOTIONS ______
3. CO-OPS ______
4. SALES ______
5. EVENTS ______
6. PUBLIC RELATIONS ______
7. DATABASE ______
8. INTERNET ______
9. OTHER ______

FORM H: PROMOTIONS PLAN

FISCAL YEAR	1ST 90 DAYS	2ND 90 DAYS	3RD 90 DAYS	4TH 90 DAYS
Promo #1 ______				
Promo #2 ______				
Promo #3 ______				
Promo #4 ______				
Promo #5 ______				
Promo #6 ______				
Promo #7 ______				
Promo #8 ______				

FORM I: EVENTS CALENDAR

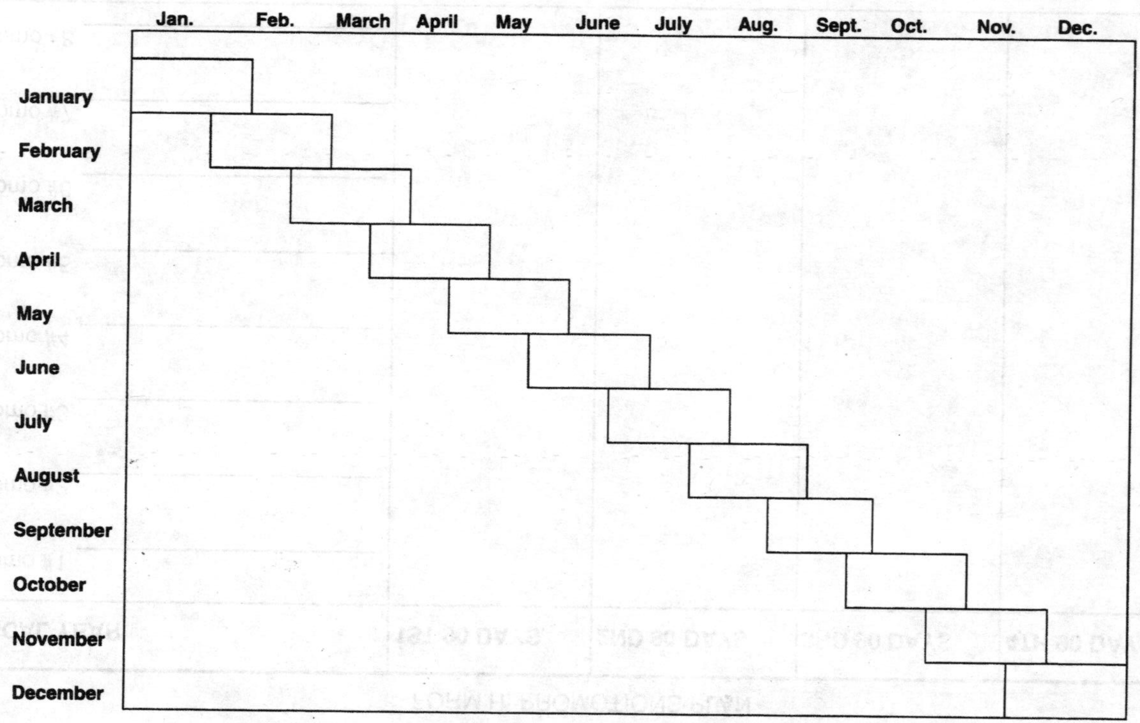

FORM J: MEDIA CALENDAR

Media Calendar

Year: ______

Broadcast Months (Week Beginning Monday)

Media	January	February	March	April	May	June	July	August	September	October	November	December

FORM K: MARKETING BUDGET

Mix/Weapon	$(000)	Percent	Target Market(s)
Advertising			
Media			
Production			
Promotions			
Sales			
Merchandising			
Direct Mail			
Electronic			
Public Relations			
Research			
Miscellaneous			
Agency Fees			
GRAND TOTAL			
Notes/Comments			

FORM L: BRAND STRATEGY EVALUATOR

Components	Brand Strategy Rating Poor 1	 Fair 2	 Average 3	 Good 4	 Outstanding 5
Loyalty (repeat favors)	○	○	○	○	○
Awareness	○	○	○	○	○
Perceived Quality/Value*	○	○	○	○	○
Positive Position Within Category	○	○	○	○	○
Differentiating Characteristics	○	○	○	○	○
Name Recognition	○	○	○	○	○
Brand Symbol	○	○	○	○	○
Recognizable Slogan	○	○	○	○	○
Marketing Programs Compatibility	○	○	○	○	○
Price Premium/Leader	○	○	○	○	○

*Relative to your competitive segment

Add up the score and multiply by two to see how your brand performs on a 100 percent scale.

FORM M: PRESS RELEASE FORMAT

News Release

For Immediate Release
Date Here

Company Name Here
Logo Here

HEADLINE HERE

City - (Summary of key points – paragraph 1)

____

(Other pertinent information – paragraph 2, etc.)

____

# # #

CONTACT:
(Contact person's name)
(Phone/fax numbers)
(E-mail address)

Appendix 2

Marketing Intelligence Information Sources

The sources listed as follows can provide a variety of secondary research information. You should obviously search the Internet and also contact the appropriate U.S. Government Web site. There are numerous publications issued by virtually every branch of the government on a regular basis. The U.S. Department of Commerce has numerous field offices, as does the Small Business Administration. Also, check the Government Printing Office publications center in Washington, DC. You can order publications directly from this source. Specific types of marketing and consumer-related information is also available from the U.S. Bureau of the Census. Also, media representatives and trade and consumer publications (e.g., *American demographics*) are excellent sources of data. In addition, there are a number of non-government-related sources that provide a variety of marketing information services.

Source	**Provides**
AC Nielsen Company 299 Park Ave. New York, NY 10171 212-707-7500	Demographics, retail sales, and media information for each DMA (designated market area) in the United States (i.e., television audience data, retail purchases, etc.)
Arbitron 142 West 57th St. New York, NY 10019 212-887-1300	Local market demographic/product usage profiles and media usage reports with target audience profiles, etc.
The Circulation Book P.O. Box 994 22619 Pacific Coast Highway Malibu, CA 90265	Circulation and penetration for all daily newspapers, Sunday papers, newspaper supplements, and magazines by metro area and TV viewers.

Claritas, Inc. 1525 Wilson Blvd., Suite 1000 Arlington, VA 22209-2411 1-800-234-5973	Offers PRIZM, a market segmentation system which divides the United States into numerous lifestyle clusters and social groups.
ClusterPlus 2000 Strategic Mapping, Inc. Corporate Headquarters 3135 Kifer Rd. Santa Clara, CA 95051-0827 1-800-472-6277	Demographic, media habits, and purchasing data on fifty plus classifications of American consumers in geographic targets down to the block level.
Dun's Marketing Services Offices nationwide 1-800-526-0651	Direct mail lists and geographical information on business.
Equifax National Decision Systems 1979 Lakeside Parkway Tucker, GA 30084-5847 770-496-7171	Provides Micro Vision, a service which classifies consumers into fifty plus segments down to the zip + 4 level.
Fairchild Fact Files Fairchild Books 7 West 34th Street New York, NY 10001 212-630-3880	Files on market trends, buying habits, advertising expenditures, sales and demographics profiles by product category.
Gale Research Company 835 Penobscot Building Detroit, MI 48226-4094 1-800-877-4523	The encylopedia of associations (U.S. and international), consultant directories, and the *Trade Show and Professional Exhibits Directory.* Also, management information guides and a variety of topical reports.
Leading National Advertisers (LNA) 11 West 42nd Street, 11th Floor New York, NY 10036 212-789-1400	Competitive spending information by medium, summary of national advertising expenditures by brand and industry category, etc.
Radio TV Reports, Inc. 317 Madison Ave. New York, NY 10017 212-309-1400	Source for copies of all competitive radio and television ads.

Rome Report 11 West 42nd Street, 11th Floor New York, NY 10036 212-789-1400	Contains business-to-business and trade advertising expenditures.
Simmons Market Research Bureau, Inc. (SMRB) 420 Lexington Ave. New York, NY 10170 212-916-8900	Products/services include MRI and SMRB which provide information on demographics, size, and media habits of the user/purchaser groups for various products/brands, etc.
SRI International 333 Ravenswood Ave. Menlo Park, CA 94025-3493 415-859-3032	Source of the VALS (values and lifestyles) program, which segments U.S. consumers into a number of distinct lifestyle groups for predicting consumer behavior.
Standard Rate and Data Service, (SRDS) 1700 West Higgins Road Des Plaines, IL 60018 708-375-5000	Newspaper rates and data service that provides population, expenditures for individual states, counties, etc., with household information. Also, provides numerous sourcebooks for mailing lists, media rate information, etc.
Viking and Penguin Books Viking Penguin, Inc. 375 Hudson Street New York, NY 10014 212-366-2000	Publishes *Information U.S.A.*, a reference guide for direct access to government experts, commerce data sources, census data sources, etc.
Yesawich, Pepperdine & Brown 1900 Summitt Tower Blvd., Ste. 600 Orlando, FL 32810 407-875-1111	Publishes *MONITOR*, an annual research tool that provides insight into social, behavioral, and travel-related trends among American consumers.

Appendix 3

Marketing-Related Associations

The marketing discipline is fortunate to have a number of outstanding professional associations that form yet another source for information sharing/intelligence. Following is a brief listing of some of these associations.

Association	**Focus**
Advertising Research Foundation (ARF) 641 Lexington Ave. New York, NY 10022 Telephone: 212-751-5656 Fax: 212-319-5265	Conducts/provides impartial and objective research on advertising effectiveness. Membership includes agencies, research firms, advertisers, media companies, and educational institutions.
American Association of Advertising Agencies (AAAA) 666 Third Ave. New York, NY 10017 Telephone: 212-682-2500 Fax: 212-953-5665	Provides counsel to ad agencies on operations and management and provides for professional development.
American Hotel & Motel Association (AH&MA) 1201 New York Ave., NW, Ste. 600 Washington, DC 20005-3931 Telephone: 202-289-3157 Fax: 202-289-3110 <www.ah&ma.org>	Provides a resource for statistical information and special studies for the lodging industry. Addresses governmental/legislative issues with potential impact on marketing.

American Marketing Association (AMA) 250 South Wacker Drive Chicago, IL 60606 Telephone: 312-648-0536 Fax: 312-993-7542	Assists in the professional development of the individual professional through a variety of educational programs and publications focused on marketing.
Association of Coupon Processors (ACP) 500 North Michigan Ave., Ste. 1400 Chicago, IL 60614 Telephone: 312-661-1700 Fax: 312-661-0769	Concentrates on improving the coupon industry from numerous perspectives, e.g., regulation, practices, etc.
Association of Incentive Marketing (AIM) 1600 Route 22 Union, NJ 07083 Telephone: 908-687-3090 Fax: 908-687-0977	Promotes education, quality, and ethical standards for those involved in incentive marketing.
Association of In-Store Marketing (AISM) 66 North Van Brunt Englewood, NJ 07631 Telephone: 201-894-8899 Fax: 201-894-0529	Promotes the awareness and use of in-store media/marketing programs. Offers guidelines/standards and a speakers bureau.
Association of National Advertisers (ANA) 155 East 44th Street New York, NY 10017 Telephone: 212-697-5950 Fax: 212-661-8057	Serves interests of corporations that advertise regionally and nationally (represents 80 percent + of all ad expenditures in United States).
Association of Retail Marketing Services (ARM) 3 Caro Court Red Bank, NJ 07001 Telephone: 908-842-5070 Fax: 908-219-1938	Represents suppliers of incentive services to retailers, provides educational research and information programs.

Council of Sales Promotion Agencies (CSPA)
750 Summer Street
Stamford, CT 06901
Telephone: 203-325-3911
Fax: 203-969-1499

An association for full-service promotion agencies that provides educational and informative information to its membership.

Direct Marketing Association (DMA)
11 West 42nd Street
New York, NY 10036-8096
Telephone: 212-768-7277
Fax: 212-768-4546

Provides conferences, meetings, publications on direct mail and represents its membership in government-related issues.

Food Marketing Institute (FMI)
800 Connecticut Ave., NW
Washington, DC 20006-2701
Telephone: 202-452- 8444
Fax: 202-429-4519

Provides research, education, and industry relations for its membership of food retailers and wholesalers.

Grocery Manufacturers of America (GMA)
1010 Wisconsin Ave., NW, Ste. 900
Washington, DC 20007
Telephone: 202-337-9400
Fax: 202-337-4508

Made up of manufacturers and processors of food and nonfood products sold to retail grocery stores and also provides public policy, trade relations, scientific and educational advocacy programs.

Hotel Sales and Marketing Association Intl. (HSMAI)
1300 L. Street NW, Ste. 1020
Washington, DC 20005
Telephone: 202-789-0089
Fax: 202-789-1725
<www.hsmai.org>

Provides educational seminars, certificate programs, publications, and local/national networking opportunities for those involved in selling meetings, group business, etc., to the hotel industry.

International Licensing Industry Merchandisers Association (LIMA)
350 Fifth Avenue, Ste. 6210
New York, NY 10118-0110
Telephone: 212-244-1944
Fax: 212-563-6552

Concentrates on those involved in the marketing of licensed properties and provides information, publications, seminars, and speakers.

National Association of Demonstration Companies (NADC) P.O. Box 1189 Bloomfield, NJ 07003-1189 Telephone: 800-338-NADC Fax: 201-338-1410	As a group of hundreds of organizations in the direct marketing area, its focus is to support the use, acceptance, and reputation of in-store demonstrations.
National Association for Information Services (NAIS) 1250 Connecticut Ave., NW, Ste. 600 Washington, DC 20036-2603 Telephone: 202-833-2545 Fax: 202-833-1234	Interest is in the interactive tele-media area as an advocate of the industry. Members include cable television, long-distance carriers, regional telephone companies, and publishing companies.
National Restaurant Association (NRA) 1200 Seventeenth Street, NW Washington, DC 20036-3097 Telephone: 202-331-5996 Fax: 202-331-2429	Provides readership on national issues related to the restaurant industry as well as major trade shows and associated educational programs through the foundation.
The Point-of-Purchase Advertising International (POPAI) 66 North Van Brunt Englewood, NJ 07631 Telephone: 201-894-8899 Fax: 201-894-0529	Serves all constituencies involved in/with POP (point-of-purchase) products and services. Acts to promote, protect, and advance issues for the industry.
Promotion Marketing Association of America (PMAA) 257 Park Ave. South New York, NY 10010 Telephone: 212-420-1100 Fax: 212-982-PMAA	As the largest organization in the promotions field, PMAA provides educational programs, information, and ad publications to its membership, with a focus on entertainment marketing, in-store marketing, product sampling, and small business.
Specialty Advertising Association International (SAAI) 3125 Skyway Circle North Irving, TX 75038-3526 Telephone: 214-252-0404 Fax: 214-258-0949	Provides leadership and information to those interested in the promotional products industry.

Travel Industry Association
of America (TIA)
1100 New York Ave., NW, Ste. 450
Washington, DC 20005-3934
Telephone: 202-408-8422
Fax: 202-408-1255
<www.tia.org>

As the largest association serving the broadest spectrum of the industry, TIA provides extensive marketing information, publications, seminars (including the Marketing Outlook Forum), and represents the industry on travel-related matters nationally and internationally.

Notes

Chapter 1

1. Yesawich, Peter (2000). Remarks: What exactly are we as we enter the new millennium? A look at the numbers and trends. Hotel Industry Investment Conference, January 24, Los Angeles, California.

2. Tregoe, Benjamin B. and Zimmerman, John W. (1980). *Top Management Strategy*. New York: Simon and Schuster, Inc.

Chapter 2

1. Hiebing, Roman G. Jr. and Cooper, Scott W. (1997). *The Successful Marketing Plan: A Disciplined and Comprehensive Approach,* Second Edition. Lincolnwood, IL: NTC Business Books.

2. Richey, Terry (1994). *The Marketer's Visual Tool Kit.* New York: AMACOM.

3. Nykiel, Ronald A. (1997). *Marketing in the Hospitality Industry,* Third Edition. East Lansing, MI: Educational Institute of the American Hotel and Motel Association.

Chapter 3

1. Reis, Al and Trout, Jack (1981). *Positioning: The Battle for Your Mind.* New York: McGraw-Hill Book Co.

2. Kotler, Philip (1999). *Kotler on Marketing*. Englewood Cliffs, NJ: Prentice-Hall.

3. Aaker, David A. (1991). *Managing Brand Equity.* New York: The Free Press.

4. Myers, James H. (1996). *Segmentation and Positioning for Strategic Marketing Decisions.* Chicago, IL: American Marketing Association.

5. McCarty, E. Jerome (1999). *Basic Marketing: A Managerial Approach,* Thirteenth Edition.

6. Lauterborn, Robert (1990). "New Marketing Litany: YPS Passe: C-Words Take Over," *Advertising Age,* October 1, p. 26.

Chapter 4

1. Bogart, Leo (1967). *Strategy in Advertising.* New York: Harcourt Brace Jovanovich.

2. Hiebing, Roman G. Jr. and Cooper, Scott W. (1997). *The Successful Marketing Plan: A Disciplined and Comprehensive Approach,* Second Edition. Lincolnwood, IL: NTC Business Books.

3. Nykiel, Ronald A. (1994). *You Can't Lose If The Customer Wins.* New York: Berkeley Business Books.

4. Hiebing and Cooper, *The Successful Marketing Plan.*

5. Buzzell, Robert D. (1991). Stouffer Hotels and Resorts: Competitive Strategy—Case Study N9-590-096. Cambridge, MA: Harvard Business School.

6. Dawson, Angela (1999). "Hitting the jackpot." *Adweek,* October 14, pp. 21-22.

Chapter 5

1. Nykiel, Ronald A. (1997). *Marketing in The Hospitality Industry,* Third Edition. East Lansing, MI: Educational Institute of the American Hotel and Motel Association.

Chapter 6

1. Hiebing, Roman G. Jr. and Cooper, Scott W. (1997). *The Successful Marketing Plan: A Disciplined and Comprehensive Approach,* Second Edition. Lincolnwood, IL: NTC Business Books.

2. Block, Tamara B. and Robinson, William A. (1994). *Sales Promotion Handbook,* Eighth Edition. Chicago, IL: Dartnell.

3. Hiebing and Cooper, *The Successful Marketing Plan.*

Chapter 8

1. Drucker, Peter (1974). *Management—Tasks, Responsibilities, Practices.* New York: Heineman.

Chapter 10

1. Block, Tamara B. and Robinson, William A. (1994). *Sales Promotion Handbook,* Eighth Edition. Chicago, IL: Dartnell.

Chapter 11

1. Aaker, David A. (1996). *Building Strong Brands.* New York: The Free Press.

2. Aaker, David A. (1997). *Driving Brand Value.* New York: McGraw-Hill.

3. Ibid.

Chapter 12

1. Hiebing, Roman G. Jr. and Cooper, Scott W. (1997). *The Successful Marketing Plan: A Disciplined and Comprehensive Approach,* Second Edition. Lincolnwood, IL: NTC Business Books.

2. Nykiel, Ronald A. (1997). *Marketing in the Hospitality Industry,* Third Edition. East Lansing, MI: Educational Institute of the American Hotel and Motel Association.

3. Berrigan, John and Finkbeiner, Carl (1992). *Segmentation Marketing: New Methods for Capturing Business Markets.* New York: Harper Business.

Chapter 13

1. Manning, Gerald L. and Reece, Barry L. (1998). *Selling Today.* Upper Saddle River, NJ: Prentice-Hall.
2. Nykiel, Ronald A. (1997). *Marketing in the Hospitality Industry,* Third Edition. East Lansing, MI: Educational Institute of the American Hotel and Motel Association.
3. Hiebing, Roman G. Jr. and Cooper, Scott W. (1997). *The Successful Marketing Plan: A Disciplined and Comprehensive Approach,* Second Edition. Lincolnwood, IL: NTC Business Books.
4. Manning and Reece, *Selling Today.*

Chapter 14

1. Varna, Terry G. (1992). *Aftermarketing.* Homewood, IL: Business One Irwin.
2. Nykiel, Ronald A. (1998). *Points of Encounter.* Kingston, NY: AMARCOR.
3. Brown, Kathi Ann and Marriott, J. W. Jr. (1997). New York: Harper Business.
4. Manning, Gerald L. and Reece, Barry L. (1998). *Selling Today.* Upper Saddle River, NJ: Prentice-Hall.

Chapter 15

1. Gottschalk, Jack A. (1993). *Crisis Response.* Detroit, MI: Visible Ink Press.
2. Ibid.

Chapter 16

1. Posch, Robert J. (1988). *Marketing and the Law.* Englewood Cliffs, NJ: Prentice-Hall.

Chapter 17

1. Hiebing, Roman G. Jr. and Cooper, Scott W. (1997). *The Successful Marketing Plan: A Disciplined and Comprehensive Approach,* Second Edition. Lincolnwood, IL: NTC Business Books.
2. Nykiel, Ronald A. (1997). *Marketing in the Hospitality Industry,* Third Edition. East Lansing, MI: Educational Institute of the American Hotel and Motel Association.

Chapter 18

1. Nykiel, Ronald A. and Jascolt, Elizabeth (1998). *Marketing Your City, U.S.A.* Binghamton, NY: The Haworth Press.
2. Tregoe, Benjamin B. and Zimmerman, John W. (1980). *Top Management Strategy.* New York: Simon and Schuster, Inc.

Glossary

action plan: A list of actions that must be taken to fulfill the marketing plan. It includes target dates, approved expenditures (as differentiated from unapproved estimated costs), and the person(s) responsible for implementing each action.

advertising: Any paid form of nonpersonal presentation made by an identified sponsor through a mass communication medium on behalf of goods, services, or ideas.

advertising media: The vehicles (newspapers, direct mail, etc.) used to carry the advertising message from the sender to the intended receiver.

agent: One authorized to transact business for another (principal) within the scope of a defined authority.

aided awareness: Awareness generated by asking individuals which brands, products, etc., they are familiar with after reading or reviewing a list.

bait and switch: A bait offer is an alluring but insincere offer to sell a product or service that the seller does not intend to sell. Its primary purpose is to switch consumers from the advertised bait product or service to sell something else, usually at a higher price or on a basis more advantageous to the seller. Its secondary purpose is to increase store traffic.

barter: The furnishing of products by an advertiser as full or partial payment for broadcasting time or free mentions on television or radio. Time so purchased is called barter time, and its purchase is usually arranged by a broker.

benchmarking: Comparision of your performance versus competitors.

brand: The name or symbol used to identify and differentiate a product or service from competing products or services.

brand development index: A measure of the concentration of a brand's consumption; typically, the units or dollars of a product consumed per thousand population in a year's time.

brand image: The pattern of feelings, associations, and ideas held by the public at large regarding a specific brand. Also brand personality.

brand loyalty: A measure of how loyal customers are over a period of time.

break-even calculation: A technique to determine the absolute or percent sales increase needed to pay for the cost of a promotion.

cash discount: A reduction in price granted to buyers who pay cash.

category development index: Determines a product category's strength on a market-by-market basis.

Clayton Antitrust Act: An act amending the Sherman Antitrust Act. It contains specific wording forbidding specific actions which lead to monopolies.

collateral materials: Print-based materials that assist in the marketing of products and services. Some examples include brochures, tent cards, posters, and promotional pieces.

competition: Any business concern, product, or concept that competes for customers in your market.

competitive research: Marketing research that compares your product or service to the products or services of competitors and tries to discover how consumers perceive and experience your product/service offering in relation to the competitors' products/services.

concentration: The percent within a given demographic target market segment that purchases the product, e.g., of all eighteen to twenty-four-year-olds, 80 percent are purchasers of the product.

consumer's perspective: The consumer's attitude toward a product or service that centers on the needs that it satisfies.

co-op advertising: Joining with others to advertise products, services, and/or a region or market.

cooperative promotion: A promotion involving two or more suppliers who join together in a common promotion for their mutual benefit.

copyright: A copyright gives its owner the exclusive right to reproduce ("copy"), sell, or adapt the work he or she has created for a limited time after the work has been fixed in a tangible medium.

coupon: A sales promotion certificate that entitles the holder to either a specified saving on a product or service, or a cash refund.

credit: Deferred time to pay debt. May involve finance charges and/or installment payments.

customer needs: What a customer really looks for or wants in a product or service.

customer perception: The ways in which the customer, in his or her own mind, looks at a product. This includes the customer's image of the product. Customer perception often differs from management's beliefs and perceptions.

customer satisfaction: Meeting the identified needs of each guest with a level of service and product quality that matches or exceeds the expectations created by your property's marketing message and related pricing.

database marketing: A sales and marketing methodology that sells and promotes by selective direct mail with the objective of increasing sales and profits.

delivery package: The essential tools, including required forms, copy, photos, fact sheets, and biographies, to ensure that you are ready to effectively execute public relations programs.

demographic profile: Demographic data describing characteristics of consumers related to specific products or services.

demographic segmentation: The division of a market by like characteristics such as sex, age, income, home ownership, martial status, occupation, and education.

direct mail: Promotional letters, advertising pieces, catalogs, or any other sales-oriented correspondence mailed to prospective customers.

disclaimer: Usually a statement in fine print that defines the conditions of an offer.

driving force: The core that really drives the business.

endorsement: A product recommendation given by a prominent celebrity (usually paid) or consumer targeted to the market segment(s) the advertiser is attempting to reach.

environmental research: Marketing research that focuses on external forces (economic, social, political, technological, etc.).

expense plus approach: Estimate of sales levels to cover expenses and make a projected profit.

exposure: The number of consumers actually hearing or seeing your advertising.

Federal Trade Commission Act: An act declaring that "unfair methods of competition in commerce are . . . illegal."

fixed costs: Costs that do not change with fluctuating sales or promotions.

flag: A "flag" on the front (and often on the sides) of a package refers to the graphic treatment (shape) and corresponding copy that calls attention to a promotional incentive.

flyer: A printed announcement of a special event or promotion, usually created for quick distribution by mailing it or leaving it at a location for passersby to pick up.

focus group: A marketing research technique that combines personal opinion solicitation in the form of group discussion with a structured set of questions.

franchise: In marketing, a contract right or license granted by a franchisor for compensation, usually to multiple franchisees, to do business under a certain name legally controlled by the franchisor and usually involving specific territorial, field-of-use, and product-quality traits. A contractual relationship establishing a means of marketing goods or services giving certain elements of control to the supplier (franchisor) in return for the right of the franchisee to use the supplier trade name or trademark, usually in a specific marketing area.

fraud: A deliberate misrepresentation or nondisclosure of a material fact, made with the intent that the other party will rely on it, and in fact the party to whom the statement is made does rely on it to his or her detriment.

frequency: The average number of times each household in the target population is exposed to a given ad message.

front-loading: Scheduling the use of the bulk of a budget for the first part of a planned promotion period; serves to assure that all of a budget is used for its originally designated ends.

geographic segmentation: The division of a market along geographic and demographic dimensions; for example, linking the number of people with similar characteristics (age, income, etc.) with specific geographic locations.

giveaway: (1) Merchandise or services given away for promotional purposes. (2) A television or radio show where merchandise is given away to contestants or to members of the audience.

gross rating point: A unit of measurement of audience size for television, radio, or outdoor advertising, equal to 1 percent of the total potential audience universe; measures the exposure of one or more programs or commercials without regard to multiple exposure of the same advertising to individuals. Also, the product of media reach times exposure frequency. Abbreviated GRP.

incentive: Cash, merchandise, or travel offered to consumers, salespeople, or dealers as a tangible reward for a purchase or sales performance. A premium.

inflation rate plus: A method for increasing prices that is based on the premise that increases should be at the inflation rate plus a percent target.

infomercial: A five- to fifteen-minute hybrid cable program having an informational and entertainment component similar to a typical television program but designed as an extended advertisement for a particular product.

in-house: A term used to describe a company that implements one or more services within the company as opposed to contracting with outside suppliers.

inside macro approach: Your own sales history review/projected three-year trend (with judgment).

intermediary: An individual or firm that facilitates transactions between consumers and suppliers. There are two types: Commercial (those earning commissions) and captive—those who facilitate transactions as part of their regular jobs and do not earn commissions.

introductory promotion: A promotion designed to introduce a new product or service to the market.

joint promotion: A mutually beneficial merchandising event with one or more outside companies promoting under a unifying theme or concept.

level of expectation: The quantity or quality of your product or service, as expected by your customers; a basic premise of advertising is that you never promise more than your product or service can actually fulfill.

logo: The artistic rendition of a brand name on a package. Also used in promotion materials.

mailing list: A collection of names and addresses maintained on a computer to generate mailings.

mapping: Use of multidimensional models based on quantitative and qualitative research to position products/brands/attributes against competitors in the marketplace.

market area: A geographical section of the United States that becomes a cohesive area for marketing. It tends to have the same distribution patterns, the same supply sources, and, frequently, political boundaries.

market potential: Sales volume for a product or service that is available to or desired by a supplier; influenced by category development and often expressed in terms of share of market.

market research: Marketing research that seeks to quantify and segment market demand.

market segment: A portion of the total market wherein all of those particular customers have something in common. There are many ways of segmenting a market; the most widely used is by demographics, e.g., sex, age, income, education, etc.

market share: A product's or service's piece of the total market for that product or service, usually expressed as a percentage or on a point scale.

marketing: The process of determining the target market, the market's needs and wants, and fulfilling these better than competition.

marketing calendar: A summary of a plan on a single page.

marketing mix: The levels and interplay of the constituent elements of a product's or service's marketing efforts, including product attributes, pricing, promotion, advertising, merchandising, distribution, and marketing spending, especially as decisions relating to these elements affect sales results.

marketing plan: (1) A strategy for marketing a product or service. (2) A comprehensive document containing background, rationale, and supportive detail regarding a marketer's objectives and strategies.

marketing strategy grid: A presentation/analytical marketing tool designed to help you select strategies to improve your market share and gain on the competition.

media: As used in promotion, all the different means by which advertising reaches its audience.

media mix: The different media to be used (magazines, radio, TV, etc.).

medium: Any vehicle used to convey an advertising message, such as television, magazines, newspapers, or direct mail. Also, the methods and tools used by an artist, such as a pen and ink, crayon, or photography.

medium use: Types, ad sizes, day part, length of commercials, etc.

merchandising: (1) Marketing activities, including sales and promotions, designed to make products available, attractive, and conspicuous in a retail store. (2) Solicitation of salespeople and retailer support for a marketing effort.

merge: A computer process whereby mailing lists may be "merged" together to facilitate zip code sequencing and testing segments.

metropolitan areas: A geographic segmentation technique that divides a market into areas within a large county or within a number of small counties; the core of such an area is usually a major city.

mission statement: A concise narrative statement summarizing a company's objectives and ultimate goals.

new product: A product that has been in distribution and available to the ultimate consumer for less than six months. Also, a product bearing a new brand name, or a newly introduced flanker item or line extension occasionally used loosely to refer to an improved product of an existing brand or a new size.

objectives: What needs to be accomplished during the planning period, expressed quantitatively and/or qualitatively.

on-pack: A premium, advertising matter, coupon, etc., attached to or part of the exterior of a product package.

outside macro approach: The trend in total market or category sales for the next three years.

overpenetrated: Too many stores/outlets in a trading area.

patent: Exclusive right (monopoly) to manufacture, sell, or otherwise use an invention for a limited period.

payout: A profit return on an investment of marketing expenditures, usually above the ongoing spending rate. Also payback.

placement: Where your advertising actually appears, be it a time slot on radio or television, an outdoor billboard near an airport, or a spot on a page in a specific issue of a magazine or newspaper.

platform: The item-by-item list of things that directly support your ad proposition.

positioning: The relationship of your product or service offering in relationship to all others.

preface: Introductory statement that briefly delineates what the document is all about or what to expect in the document.

press kit: A communications folder usually containing two pockets, the left is used for background information, the right is used for a press release.

press release: A formatted document, usually one to two pages, presenting concise and pertinent information on a topic/event deemed newsworthy.

price promotion: A promotion in which the incentive to purchase is based on price.

price-elastic product: A product for which the demand will increase or decrease in relationship to an increase or decrease in price.

price-inelastic product: A product for which the demand will remain relatively stable when the price is raised or lowered.

prize: Reward given to the winner in a contest, sweepstakes, or change promotion; also sometimes referred to as salespeople's incentive award, and official state lottery awards.

product attributes: Items of importance derived from the consumer's perception.

product branding: Labeling a product with a name by which it is marketed and identified.

product or service research: Marketing research that usually focuses on a product's or service's strengths and weaknesses in relation to the products/services of competitors.

product/service hybrid: A variation on a base product or service.

promotion: (1) A marketing tool that is a temporary effort to create extra interest in the purchase of a product or service by offering values in excess of those customarily afforded by such purchases; includes temporary discounts, allowances, premium offers, coupons, contests, sweepstakes, etc. Also sales promotion. (2) Loosely, any effort to encourage the purchase of a product or service.

proposition: The strongest factual statement you can make on behalf of your product or service.

psychographic segmentation: A method of subdividing a market based on like needs and psychological motivations of consumer groups.

public relations: A marketing tool that is the communications vehicle between your firm and current customers, potential customers, and the variety of other audiences in the marketplace.

publicity: One facet of public relations, it comprises the gratuitous mentions or exposures a company receives from announcements, events, and press releases.

purge: A computer process whereby mailing lists may be "purged" of duplicate names, pander names, and undesirable names that are to be saved for later mailings.

pyramiding: The concept of offering a variety of prices from which consumers may select; also includes the opportunity to sell up and sell down.

questionnaire: A data collection vehicle similar to a survey but usually briefer and less complex in content.

refund: (1) A promotion device that offers purchasers a return of some or all of an amount of money or coupons when they send proofs-of-purchase to the manufacturer. (2) To issue such a return.

region: A geographic subdivision within a country, often defined by natural borders such as mountains, major rivers, etc.

response rate: The percentage of the total audience that replies to a mailing.

sales contest: A competition open to a company's sales personnel or to prospects, structured to reward superior performance or unusually large purchases.

sales incentive: A reward in excess of salary or commission provided to a salesperson in return for achieving or exceeding a stated sales goal.

scheduling: When and at what levels advertising runs.

segmentation: The process of dividing the broad consuming market into manageable segments with common characteristics.

selling down: Lower your price or rate to meet the customer's need and overcome price resistance.

selling up: To seek to obtain a higher price for a product or service, sell a higher-profit-margin item, or obtain a premium price when demand favors the seller.

share: (1) The percentage of total retail purchases, in terms of dollars or units, for a given category of product that is enjoyed by any product or brand in that category. Also share of market, share of retail sales. (2) A rating survey of the percentage of the television or radio audience in a coverage area that is tuned to the program being rated.

shelf talker: A printed advertising message designed to hang over the edge of a retail store shelf.

short-term objectives: Immediate through the current year.

strategic marketing plan: A broad structure that guides the process of determining the target market, detailing the market's needs and wants and then fulfilling these needs and wants better than competitors.

strategy: How you plan to achieve the objectives you have set. For example: To increase business by 10 percent within the next twelve months: (1) increase outdoor advertising; and (2) shift some advertising to promotions.

survey: A structured research document designed to elicit consumer opinion, uncover facts, and gain insights on potential trends.

sweepstakes: A chance promotion involving the giveaway of products and services of value to a randomly selected group of those who have submitted qualified entries. To prevent infringement of lottery laws, such promotions do not require qualifying entrants to provide a monetary consideration, such as a purchase. The odds of winning depend on the number of entries received.

SWOT: An acronym for strengths, weaknesses, opportunities, and threats.

tactics: Specific items or steps to support the strategies.

target market: The most likely purchasers of your product.

telephone sales: A sales contact by telephone, whose primary purpose is to obtain a reservation for a room, a group commitment, or some other sale.

tent card: An internal promotion tool that rests on top of a table, desk, bureau, or other flat surface.

tie-in promotion: A single promotion event intended to encourage the sale of more than one product or brand.

trademark: A brand (work, name, symbol, or device or any combination thereof) adopted and used by its owner to identify its goods and distinguish them from those sold by others. Usually given legal protection so that its owner has exclusive rights to its use.

trade-out: An exchange of your product or service for advertising coverage.

trial: A purchase or use of a product or service by a consumer interested in personally evaluating its value, as a step preceding a subsequent purchase or regular use.

two-for-one: A promotion that offers consumers two units of product for the price of one.

unaided awareness: Considered more accurate, it involves consumers recalling specific brands, products, etc., without any assistance.

underpenetrated: Too few stores/outlets to take advantage of the market's potential.

variable costs: Costs that vary with the volume of production or sales.

vendor: Seller of property.

warranty: A subsidiary promise or collateral agreement, the breach of which entitles the buyer to make certain claims for damages, replacement, or repair against the warrantor. The warranty may be full or limited (depending on the express agreement) or implied by law.

zero-based budgeting: A budgeting concept that is premised on starting from zero and building up based on the resources required to achieve the plan objectives.

zip codes: Postal designations by which key demographic and purchasing information can be sorted/mailed.

Additional Key Terms

advanced premium: One given to a new customer in expectation that he/she will earn it by later purchases; a technique originated by the home service route firms.

advertising allowance: A payment or service by a manufacturer of goods to a merchant for advertising a product of the manufacturer.

advertising specialties: A form of direct advertising. Products that bear the name, address, and/or slogan of a business firm are given free by the advertiser to present or prospective customers. Sometimes called remembrance advertising.

agency of record: An agency that purchases media time or space for another agency or a group of agencies who happen to serve the same client. Abbreviated AOR.

allocation (in promotion): A preassigned quantity of merchandise to be made available or sold to an individually designated area or customer. *See also* ALLOTMENT.

allotment: Predetermined distribution of product for which the demand often exceeds the supply; for example, a special pack. Also, the total amount available of a particular special pack in a particular area or to a particular customer (e.g., a price pack allotment).

allowance: A temporary price reduction or discount offered to the retailer by the manufacturer. Sometimes given in the form of free goods.

Antitrust Improvements Act of 1976: Empowered attorneys general at the state level to bring suit on behalf of injured consumers in their states.

antitrust law: The general body of law that regulates or prohibits combinations, conspiracies, agreements, monopolies, and certain distribution practices that restrain free trade.

Antitrust Procedures and Penalties Act of 1974: An act increasing the fines for violation of Sherman Act provisions to $100,000 for individuals and to $10 million for corporations. It also made violation of the law a felony rather than a misdemeanor, with a maximum jail sentence of three years.

arbitration: A proceeding used as a substitute for the more formal trial. An arbitrator hears a dispute and decides which person should prevail.

automation: The computerization of manual functions.

bad faith: A person's actual intent to mislead or deceive another; an intent to take an unfair and unethical advantage of another.

banded pack: Two or more packages are banded together and sold at a reduced price. The packages can be the same or related products.

benefit and need segmentation: Divides a market into groups of consumers on the basis of the benefits they seek, the needs they expect to satisfy, and in some instances, the factors they hope to avoid.

bill allowance: A merchandising allowance in which the discount is not given to the retailer until he or she provides proof that he or she has complied with the merchandising requirements of the seller.

bill of sale: A written agreement by which one person assigns or transfers interests or rights in personal property to another.

blister pack: A package consisting of a card faced with a plastic casing enclosing the product. Also bubble card, skin pack.

bona fide prices: Under the Federal Trade Commission Act, these prices must represent the prices of actual purchases for a reasonable period of time in the same geographic area before they can be referred to in a sale that advertises price comparisons.

bonus pack: A specially packaged product designed to provide purchasers with an extra amount of product at the usual price.

borrowed interest promotion: A promotion that uses the recognition and/or impact of a well-known event or personality to capture the attention and interest of the target audience.

bottle hanger: A promotional or advertising collar designed to hang around the neck of a bottle.

bounce-back: A second promotion offer made to consumers to encourage additional purchases; e.g., a coupon for a second purchase placed within a product package, or a second offer of a different premium enclosed when the first premium is mailed.

box-top offer: An offer of a premium based on the return of the box top from a package or other appropriate proof-of-purchase.

boycott: An agreement or conspiracy to restrain or prevent the carrying on of a business by preventing or excluding potential competitors, suppliers, customers, or others from freely engaging in business or desired transactions with other businesses.

broadside: A giant folder, often sent as a self-mailer, used especially (but not exclusively) in direct-mail advertising to the trade.

business gift: A gift to a customer, stockholder, employee, or other business friend as an expression of appreciation. There is an upper dollar limit for purposes of a business tax deduction.

buying habits: The frequency and method of purchase.

cartel: An association of producers that attempts to control a market by limiting output and dividing market shares among its members.

cash refund offer: An offer by a manufacturer for a refund of money to a customer who mails in a label or a designated proof-of-purchase.

catalog showroom: A system of retailing in which stock is sold from a nearby warehouse and the retail store is used to display sample merchandise only.

caveat emptor: Means literally, "Let the buyer beware." The buyer purchases at his or her peril, and there are no warranties, either expressed or implied, made by the seller.

channel of distribution: The sequence of marketing agencies (such as wholesalers and retailers) through which a product passes on its way from the producer to the final user.

chronological work plan: A listing of action steps to be taken in date order, with identification of responsibility.

class action: A lawsuit or legal action brought on behalf of a large number of people with similar claims.

collection promotions: These promotions require multiple purchases to participate. Many also have some minor reward for a single purchase.

combination sale: A tie-in of a premium with the purchase of an item at a combination price, sometimes self-liquidation; often an on-pack.

commercial law: Rules governing business professionals

common carrier: A firm obligated by the terms of a government license to transport goods under stated conditions for all of the public who wish to employ its services.

comparative pricing: Pricing strategy that involves comparing the advertised low price with "normal" list prices in order to give the impression of overall discount prices.

conditional sale: The term is most frequently applied to a sale wherein the seller reserves the title to the goods, though the item is delivered to the buyer, until the purchase price is paid in full.

consideration: Bargained for benefit or detriment which, given in exchange for a promise, makes the promise enforceable.

consignment: A bailment for sale. Merchandise delivered or made available to an agent, with title or ownership to the goods remaining with the supplier. The cosignee does not undertake the obligation to sell or pay for the goods.

conspiracy: A criminal partnership in which two or more people combine formally or informally to accomplish an unlawful act. In a price-fixing situation, there must be express or circumstantial proof that a combination was formed for the purpose of fixing prices and that it caused them to be fixed or contributed to that result.

contest: A promotion device in which a prize is awarded to an entrant judged to have qualified by virtue of superior skill; entrants may be required to furnish a consideration (usually proof-of-purchase), without violating lottery laws in many states. (Any element of chance involved with the prize award would make the promotion an illegal lottery.)

continuity program: A continuing promotion offer with inducements to make additional purchases of the product (e.g., get one teaspoon for a label and $1.00, and the next spoon for a label and $1.00, etc.).

cost-plus theory: The recognition of the need to price or sell a product or service in periods of low demand by discounting the price beyond fixed and variable cost levels to stimulate sales.

deceit: A tort involving intentional misrepresentation or cheating by means of some device.

direct marketing: A system in which a seller builds and maintains its own database of customers and uses a variety of media to communicate directly with those customers.

direct-response list: A list of persons who answered a direct-response offer of another firm. This list may be purchased from the firm directly or through a broker for one-time promotion.

disparagement: A statement about a competitor's goods that is deceptive or otherwise untrue and is asserted to influence the public not to buy such goods.

distribution: The method of delivering the product to the customer—channels of distribution. Also, how and where the product is sold (geographic).

exclusive distribution: A strategy used to maintain prestige, image, and premium prices by granting exclusive rights to a wholesaler or retailer to sell in one geographic region.

expiration date: The last day on which a consumer can use a coupon or place an order for an offer.

express warranty: Actual statement made by the seller in reference to a material fact about the product.

face value: Actual cash discount value (for the consumer) of a coupon when redeemed at a retail outlet.

fair trade: A principle according to which retailers agree to sell an item at no less than the price agreed upon between the manufacturer and other retailers in the area. Until suspended, such practices were often enforced by state law (fair-trade law).

feature: (1) A retail item being given special sales attention, especially cooperative advertising of a price reduction. (2) An important characteristic of a product or service. (3) To give a retail item special sales promotion.

Federal Communications Commission: The regulatory body with jurisdiction over the radio, TV, telephone, and telegraph industries.

flanker: A new product that is marketed under an existing brand name, but is intended for use in a different (but usually related) product category. Also flanker item.

F.O.B.: An abbreviation for "free on board." A provision of the contract specifying at which point shipping costs are to be paid by the buyer.

Food and Drug Administration: The federal agency that has authority over the advertising, labeling, packaging, and branding of packaged foods and therapeutic devices.

forced distribution: Automatic distribution of a product by retailers as a consequence of anticipated or actual customer demand created by advertising or consumer promotion. In test markets, this is done by automatic placement of products in panels of cooperating stores.

free: A product or service that is an unconditional gift or, when a purchase is required, all the conditions to the receipt and retention of the product or service offered are clearly and conspicuously set forth in immediate conjunction with the first use of the word "free," leaving no reasonable probability that the terms of the offer will be misunderstood.

free mail-in (FMI): A premium that consumers may obtain in the mail without charge by sending in proofs-of-purchase.

free offer: An offer that does not cost any amount of money.

free-standing insert (FSI): A preprinted advertisement in single or multiple page form that is inserted into newspapers, particularly Sunday editions and supplements.

frequency discount: A reduction in advertising rates based on the number of insertions or commercials in a given time period.

FTC rules and guidelines: Refers to rules and guidelines adopted by the Federal Trade Commission. The terms "rules" and "guidelines" are not synonymous. Trade regulation rules define specifically which acts or practices are unfair or deceptive. Industry guides do not have the force of substantive law. However, the guides do advise the industry on how the FTC will interpret the law. A violation of a guide may lead the FTC to issue a complaint.

full warranty: The Magnuson-Moss Act requires that certain consumer products be labeled as having either a full or limited warranty. Products with a full warranty must meet certain requirements specified in the act.

full-service agency: An advertising agency that has a full range of services for research and development.

functional discounts: The means by which intermediaries are compensated for reselling to subsequent distributors in the distribution channel.

game: A promotional vehicle that includes a number of predetermined, preseeded winning tickets in the overall, fixed universe of pieces. Participants may learn immediately if they have won a particular prize category. Sometimes called instant winner sweepstakes.

generics: A category of unbranded products usually sold in a plain, one-color printed container by a retailer at substantial savings to the consumer as compared to national brand items.

group promotions: A promotion involving several brands from the same or different companies, usually integrated by a theme or mutually shared promotional overlay such as a sweepstakes or refund.

handbill: A circular that is intended for distribution by hand either to persons encountered on the street or to homes, offices, etc. Also throwaway, flyer.

heavy user: A recurrent consumer of a product or service who can be identified through demographics and other market segmentation techniques.

horizontal agreements: Agreements between competitors at the same level of market structure (for example, between two products or retail chains).

horizontal merger: The acquisition of one company by another company producing the same product and selling it in the same geographic market.

horizontal territorial division of markets: An agreement by which competitors on the same production or distribution level restrict their competitive activity to an agreed-on area.

image-related: Promotions that work to enhance a brand's name, use, or perceived quality.

impulse purchase: Purchase of consumer goods that had not been planned in advance.

in-ad coupon: A coupon placed in a store or chain's own retail advertisement, redeemable on the specified product only at the particular store or chain. Also, in-ad.

index preference scale: Plus or minus 10 from 100 (90–100–110).

in-pack coupon: A redeemable coupon enclosed in a product's package for potential later use by the product's buyer; may be redeemed on a subsequent purchase of the same product, or on a different product (cross coupon).

in-pack premium: A premium item enclosed inside a product's package, usually offered with a full measure of product at no extra charge.

insert: A special page printed by the advertiser and forwarded to a publisher who binds it in the publication. Also, an advertising tabloid placed inside a newspaper.

installment buyer: One who orders goods or services and pays for them in two or more periodic payments after delivery of the products or services.

instant redeemable coupon: A coupon placed on the outside surface of the package. The coupon can be removed easily without destroying the package and used as a price reduction on the current purchase.

instant winner promotion: A prize promotion in which the participant knows immediately if he or she has won a prize.

institutional advertising: Advertising whose purpose is to create goodwill for a company rather than to advertise goods or services.

interactive: A two-way information system whereby the information receiver can communicate directly with the information supplier.

interbrand competition: Competition among the manufacturers of the same generic product. This area, under certain federal court decisions, can be important in evaluating vertical territorial marketing plans.

internal data: Operational data on such items as sales, credit, and lists generated within the firm.

interstate: Operations crossing state lines or involving more than a single state. An important factor in many areas of law; whether you are selling interstate may determine whether you have antitrust exposure. For trademark registration, you must place your product in interstate commerce. Interstate telephone services come under the jurisdiction of the Federal Communications Commission.

Interstate Commerce Act of 1887: The first U.S. law to regulate business practices.

intrabrand competition: Competition between or among the distributors, wholesalers, or retailers of the product of a particular manufacturer of that product.

intrastate: Operations that remain within the boundaries of a specific state. Telephone services remaining intrastate are under the jurisdiction of the respective state's public service commission or board of public utilities.

investigative consumer report: Information about a person's credit history gathered by a company.

investment spending: Increased expenditures for advertising or promotion for a product or service, typically funded by temporary reductions in the profit contribution in the expectation of future increases in sales and profits.

island display: A retail store display that is accessible on all sides. Also, island.

joint venture: A company established for the cooperation of two or more companies in accomplishing a specific task.

keeper: A premium offered in direct-mail marketing for accepting a free trial of the sale merchandise which is kept by the consumer even if the sale merchandise is returned.

key account: (1) A major customer, from the viewpoint of a manufacturer or a distributor. (2) A major client of an advertising agency.

key code: To code an advertisement or coupon so that responses can be identified by carrier medium or distribution location. This usually involves putting a code number or letter in a coupon or in the advertiser's address so that the particular advertisement or medium producing an inquiry can be identified. Also sometimes called a key.

limited warranty: The Magnuson-Moss Act requires certain consumer products to be labeled as having either a full or limited warranty. Limited warranties are those that do not comply with the act's requirement for a full warranty.

line extension: A new product form, flavor, or formulation marketed under an existing brand name, intended for use in the same category as the "parent" brand's original product, or product line. Designed to draw new users to the brand's franchise from products competitive to the original product: e.g., "dry" and "oily" new shampoo products using the brand name of an existing shampoo are line extensions.

list price comparison: May be advertised as comparable to the advertised sales price of another only to the extent that it is the actual selling price currently charged in the market area where the claim is made and the comparable products are of at least like grade and quality, demonstrable by objective evidence.

list rental: An arrangement in which a list owner furnishes names and/or addresses on a list to a mailer, together with the privilege of using the list (unless specified) one time only. A list can be selected from a mass-compiled list on geographic, demographic, or psychographic bases, or it can be rented from a firm whose clientele closely resemble that desired (subject to the practice of many mailers and the Direct

Marketing Association to permit consumers to remove their names from unwanted lists). The list owner is paid a royalty by the mailer, usually a specific fee per name. The list owner will establish a specific date on which the user has the obligation to mail to a specific list.

location clause: A clause that limits the area in which the distributor may establish a sales outlet but does not limit the distributor to servicing customers who live within that area.

long-term objectives: One to three years.

loss leader: A retail item advertised at an attractively low price, often below cost, in order to attract customers to a store for the purchase of other, more profitable items.

lottery: A sales promotion device, illegal under most state and federal statutes (often ignored in the case of charitable or other nonprofit institutions), containing elements of chance, consideration, and prize.

mail-in offer: A promotion requiring the respondent to mail proofs-of-purchase, tear-off sheets, receipts, etc., to receive the item/money being offered.

make good: An advertisement run without charge by a medium as an adjustment for error usually because of omission or poor reproduction.

management contract: A contract to provide management for a facility for which fees are paid to the management company.

manufacturing representative: A sales representative of a manufacturer who may be either a salaried employee or a broker acting as an agent for several manufacturers on commission. Also manufacturer's agent.

market development index: The number of units or dollar value of all brands of a product or service category that have been sold per thousand population within an area in a stated period, usually a year. Also category development. Loosely, a product's, service's, or category's degree or rate of usage in markets and market segments to which it is available.

market planning: An arranged, structured process to determine the target market, its needs and wants, and their fulfillment.

market power: Ability of producers to expand their share of a prevailing competitive market. Factors to consider include current market share of firm, degree of concentration in the industry, the extent of product differentiation, and actual or potential government regulation.

marketing concept: A management philosophy that holds that the best means to satisfy corporate objectives is to focus all corporate efforts to find ways to permit customers to satisfy their desires.

markup: The increase in dollars or cents or a percentage, between cost and the selling price.

match-and-win sweepstakes: A form of sweepstakes in which consumers must take their symbol/number entry, which appears in print media, to the product or store display to determine if they have won a prize and what it is.

material statement: Any statement in a promotion that is capable of affecting the decision to purchase.

megatrend: A massive qualitative or quantitative trend that has a substantial impact on an enterprise or society.

member get a member: A phrase indicating a broad range of referral promotions by various firms whereby a current customer is offered free merchandise for soliciting other customers.

merchantable: Good quality and salable, but not necessarily the best.

misrepresentation: When a person, by words or acts, creates a false impression in the mind of another person.

monopoly: Individual action, joint acquisition, or maintenance by members of a conspiracy formed for the express purpose to control and dominate interstate trade and commerce in a commodity or service to such an extent that actual or potential competitors are excluded from the field; this action is accompanied by the intention and purpose to exercise such power.

motivation research: Research that attempts to relate behavior to underlying desires, emotions, and intentions, in contrast to research that enumerates behavior or describes a situation, it relies heavily on the use of techniques adapted from psychology and other social sciences.

multibuyer: A person who has purchased more than once from a firm on different occasions. May be called a repeat buyer.

near pack: A premium item offered for free or for a discounted price with the retail purchase of another product, and positioned near to (but not touching) this product at the point of sale. Also near-pack premium. A promotion making use of the near-pack premium. Also near-pack event. A container or receptacle used to hold and display near-pack premiums.

negative option: A buying plan in which a customer or club member agrees to accept and pay for merchandise announced in advance at regular intervals unless the individual formally notifies the company not to send the merchandise within the time period specified with the announcement.

nixie: A piece of mail that is undeliverable.

off label: A special reduced savings offer marked over the regular label of an item. Also, an inferior grade of a brand which is discount priced and specially labeled.

oligopoly: Market in which a few sellers control the supply of a product or service and, thus, its price or other terms of sale.

one-cent sale: A promotion offer where the consumer purchases one package at the normal price and the second package for one cent.

open: To begin the sale of a room category or rate.

out of stock: Merchandise that is not presently available but will be at some future date.

package insert: Advertising material packed with a shipment of a product, usually to advertise a different product.

packaged goods: Products wrapped or packaged by the manufacturer, normally of uniform sizes. Items are used broadly and frequently consumed; typically sold through food, drug, and mass merchandiser retail stores.

penetration: The total number of outlets/units a market will support.

per diem: The amount of money that individuals can recover from their organizations for expenses on a daily basis.

place utility: Value added to a product by making it available to consumers at a convenient location, such as their homes.

point-of-purchase advertising: A nonpersonal sales promotion implemented through window displays or counter setups in stores designed to provide the retailer with ready-made, professionally designed vehicles for selling more of the featured products.

position: In marketing strategy, the consumer perception of a product's or service's benefit or benefits, in comparison to its competition, which its manufacturer attempts to create and encourage via advertising, packaging, and/or promotion. Also positioning, as in product positioning, and near-product position. Also, the placement of an advertisement in a publication in terms of page number, side, etc., or of a commercial in a program. Also positioning.

premium: A product offered free or at less than its usual price to encourage the consumer to buy another product or make a commitment to a membership.

price discrimination: Generally, charging different prices to different customers.

price leader: A major producer in a given industry who tends to set the pace in establishing prices.

price segmentation: Identifies groups of consumers within a market whose purchase of products or services is within the limits of certain dollar amounts.

prima facie: At first sight; a fact that is presumed to be true unless disproved by contrary evidence.

product tiering: A variation in degree of a company's product quality or level of services.

promotion marketing: An element in the marketing mix designed to stimulate consumer actions and/or dealer effectiveness through various incentives.

promotion strategy: A statement of how a marketer plans to meet defined, measurable objectives or goals.

proof-of-purchase: Evidence that a consumer has purchased a product or service, such as a receipt, label, package, UPC (bar code), or portion thereof, etc.

prospect research: Marketing research aimed at providing a profile of present and future customers.

puffery: An expression of opinion (often exaggerated) by a seller, not made as a representation of fact.

quantity discount: A discount from list price for buying great quantities of merchandise.

redeem: To fulfill the requirements of a consumer promotional offer such as a coupon or trading stamps in a prescribed manner resulting in receipt of goods at a reduced price or free.

redemption: (1) The cashing in of coupons or trading stamps when merchandise is purchased in order to obtain discounts or premiums. (2) The percentage of coupons or trading stamps issued that are eventually cashed in. Also, redemption rate.

resale price maintenance program: A situation in which a seller of goods, such as a manufacturer, regulates the price at which the goods may be resold by the retailer. Presently illegal under the antitrust laws in most cases.

restrictions: Limitations and requirements that must be adhered to in order to qualify for an offer; for example, "Tickets must be purchased three days in advance."

retailing: The selling of a product or service directly to the consumer.

revenue maximization: Achieving the highest potential revenue through management of market mix, pricing strategies, and yield management.

royalty income: The fee paid to a franchisor by a franchisee for use of the brand name.

run-of-press: The status of an advertisement positioned at the publisher's discretion. Also, run-of-book, run-of-paper. Abbreviated ROP.

sale: A significant, temporary reduction from the usual and customary price of the product or service offered.

sales promotion: *See* PROMOTION MARKETING.

sampling: Delivery of a product to the consumer with the intent of encouraging trial of the product. The size of the sample will vary depending on consumer behavior and costs.

scratch-and-sniff: Trademark. A microencapsulation process used to convey a specific scent to readers of print media. Scents are released by scratching a properly treated area of paper or scratching tape affixed to the printed piece, which breaks the microscopic-sized plastic "scent bubbles" thus releasing the aroma.

seasonality index: A measurement that expresses the variation of sales of goods or services for a brand or category from an even distribution throughout the year as influenced by seasonal factors, e.g., suntan lotions have an extremely high summer seasonality index.

segment profitability: The profitability of a particular type of consumer or market segment, determined by analyzing the revenues generated through the sale of products and services to that type of consumer or segment.

self-liquidator: A premium having a cost fully covered by the purchase price for which it is offered. Also, a display unit provided to the manufacturer in return for payment by a retailer covering its cost. Self-liquidating.

share point: One percent of the total market or audience.

shelf card: A display card designed to be set up on a shelf in a retail store.

shipping and handling: Cost to seller of fulfilling and delivering orders. If an extra charge is required to make delivery of an advertised product, under FTC rules, that fact must be clearly and conspicuously stated in the offer.

slice of life: A type of commercial consisting of a short play that portrays a real-life situation in which the product is tried and becomes the solution to your buyer's need or problem.

slick: A proof printed on glossy (coated) paper, clean in appearance and suitable for reproduction. Also, enamel proof.

slippage: (1) Those people who purchase a product with the intent of claiming a promotion reward for such a purchase (e.g., send for a refund, a premium, or redeem a coupon), who fail to fulfill this intent. (2) The ratio between such purchases, and purchases by those people who claim such a reward; usually stated as a percentage of total purchases. Also, slippage rate.

slot: Describes a physical space in a trade warehouse that is used to store a product or price variation.

split run: In periodic printing, a press run that carries two or more different forms of an advertiser's message in different copies or issues to test the effectiveness of one advertisement against another or to appeal to regional or other specific markets.

standard metropolitan statistical area: A federally designated urban area consisting of counties that meet certain standards for population, urban character, and economic and social integration.

stock: The type of paper or material used for printed materials; usually defined by weight, grain, or texture.

Sunday supplement: Any of various nonnews sections included with a Sunday newspaper, such as comics, television schedules, FSIs, and, especially, general-interest magazine sections.

super saver: A popular term for a deeply discounted price.

swing buyers: Purchasers who will change their brands to take advantage of a promotion offer.

tear pads: These consist of several sheets in a pad, which are designed to communicate the details of a consumer offer at the point of purchase (usually affixed to a shelf or used in conjunction with a large piece of display material).

tear sheet: An unbound page from a periodical showing an article, advertisement, etc., as printed; used as a proof or as an extra copy.

test market: A limited geographical area in which a test of an alternate marketing plan variable or new product is conducted.

thirty-day rule: FTC rule which requires that mail-in offers for which the consumer has submitted payment must be shipped within the time promised or thirty days if a time is not stated. If shipment cannot be made within the required time, the supplier must notify the consumer of the delay and offer the opportunity to cancel the order.

tip-in: A preprinted advertising page or card inserted into a periodical whose regular page size is larger.

tip-on: A coupon, sample, or reply card glued by one edge to a page of advertising.

tort: An injury or wrong committed, either with or without force, to the person or property of another.

trade media: A group of publications and/or broadcast media that follow a specific industry.

trading area: The geographic territory where your customer lives.

trading stamp: Any of various stamps offered as premiums with merchandise purchases, the number given being a proportion to the total sale amount; such stamps, in specific numbers, are redeemable for specific types of merchandise.

trading up: An attempt to interest your customers in better, and usually more expensive, goods than they expected to buy.

traffic builder: A relatively low-cost premium offered free as an inducement to a consumer to visit a store for a demonstration.

travel incentive: A trip, either group or individual, offered to salespeople or dealers for meeting specific sales quotas. Often tied in with sales meetings at resort areas.

trend research: Identification of quantitative and qualitative preferences and attitudinal and behavioral directions in which the market or segments thereof are moving.

trial size: A product package of small size and low price, intended or serving to attract product trial.

twin pack: A promotion event wherein two product units are sold as one, at a discounted price; usually implemented by packaging that physically unites the two units and flags the savings offered.

unique selling proposition: Advertising claim about a product that is thought to be strong enough to cause customers to buy the product about which the claim is made rather than a rival product. To be unique, the proposition must be one that the competition either cannot or does not offer.

universal product code (UPC): A special code number and stripe on product packages used by optical scanners at checkout counters to automatically record the brand and its price.

vertical agreements: Agreements between distributors at different levels of the market structure to cooperate closely with one another in selling, pricing, promotions, and advertising.

vertical and horizontal integration: The interrelationship between two or more industry products or services performed or offered by the same firm.

vertical territorial restraint: Specified territorial area imposed by a manufacturer or supplier as a condition of doing business with a customer such as a distributor or retailer.

vision: A statement which vividly describes the desired outcome of the strategic marketing plan.

void: Null; of no legal effect.

volume merchandising allowance: An allowance offered to a retailer for the purchase of large volumes of goods; offered as an encouragement to the retailer to merchandise the goods aggressively. Abbreviated VMA.

wholesaling: The selling of products or services in volume to others, who, in turn, sell directly to consumers.

Bibliography

Aaker, David A. (1991). *Managing Brand Equity.* New York: The Free Press.

Aaker, David A. (1996). *Building Strong Brands.* New York: The Free Press.

Arnold, David (1992). *The Handbook of Brand Management.* Reading, MA: Addison Wesley.

Berrigan, John and Finkbeiner, Carl (1992). *Segmentation Marketing: New Methods for Capturing Business Markets.* New York: HarperBusiness.

Berry, Leonard L. and Parasuraman, A. (1991). *Marketing Services: Computing Through Quality.* New York: The Free Press.

Block, Tamara B. and Robinson, William A. (1994). *Sales Promotion Handbook,* Eighth Edition. Chicago, IL: Dartnell.

Bogart, Leo (1967). *Strategy in Advertising.* New York: Harcourt, Brace and World.

Clancy, Kevin J. and Shulman, Robert S. (1991). *The Marketing Revolution: A Radical Manifesto for Dominating the Marketplace.* New York: HarperBusiness.

Cravens, David W. (1987). *Strategic Marketing,* Second Edition. Homewood, IL: Richard D. Irwin.

Drucker, Peter (1974). *Management—Tasks, Responsibilities, Practices.* New York: Heineman.

Feig, Barry (1993). *The New Products Workshop: Hands-On Tools for Developing Winners.* New York: McGraw-Hill.

Gottschalk, Jack A. (1993). *Crisis Response.* Detroit, MI: The Visible Ink Press.

Hayden, Catherine (1986). *The Handbook of Strategic Expertise.* New York: The Free Press.

Holloway, Robert and Hancock, Robert (eds.) (1969). *The Environment of Marketing Behavior,* Second Edition. Lincolnwood, IL: NTC Business Books.

Kotler, Philip (1972). *Marketing Management.* Englewood Cliffs, NJ: Prentice-Hall.

Kotler, Philip (1999). *Kotler on Marketing.* Englewood Cliffs, NJ: Prentice-Hall.

Lele, Miland M. (1992). *Creating Strategic Leverage.* New York: Wiley.

Levitt, Theodore (1986). *The Marketing Imagination.* New York: The Free Press.

Magrath, Allen J. (1992). *The 6 Imperatives of Marketing: Lessons from the World's Best Companies.* New York: AMACOM.

Manning, Gerald L. and Reece, Barry L. (1998). *Selling Today.* Upper Saddle River, NJ: Prentice-Hall.

McKay, Edward S. (1993). *The Marketing Mystique,* Revised Edition. New York: AMACOM.

McNeill, Daniel and Freiberger, Paul (1993). *Fuzzy Logic: The Discovery of a Revolutionary Computer Technology and How It Is Changing Our World.* New York: Simon and Schuster.

Michalko, Michael (1991). *Tinkertoys: A Handbook of Business Creativity for the '90's.* Berkeley, CA: Ten Speed Press.

Myers, James H. and Tauber, Edward (1997). *Market Structure Analysis.* Chicago, IL: American Marketing Association.

Nykiel, Ronald A. (1992). *Keeping Customers in Good Times and Bad.* Stamford, CT: Longmeadow Press.

——— (1994). *You Can't Lose If the Customer Wins.* New York: Berkeley.

——— (1997). *Marketing in the Hospitality Industry,* Third Edition. East Lansing, MI: Educational Institute—AH&MA.

——— (1998). *Marketing Your City: U.S.A.* Binghamton, NY: The Haworth Press.

——— (1998). *Points of Encounter.* Kingston, NY: AMARCOR.

Parmerlee, David (1992). *Developing Successful Marketing Strategies.* Lincolnwood, IL: NTC Business Books.

Posch, Robert J. Jr. (1988). *Marketing and the Law.* Englewood Cliffs, NJ: Prentice-Hall.

Rapp, Stan and Collins, Tom (1988). *MaxiMarketing: The New Direction in Advertising, Promotion and Marketing Strategy.* New York: New American Library.

Ray, Michael and Myers, Rochelle (1986). *Creativity in Business.* Garden City, NJ: Doubleday.

Reis, Al and Trout, Jack (1981). *Positioning: The Battle for Your Mind.* New York: McGraw-Hill Book Co.

——— (1986). *Marketing Warfare.* New York: McGraw-Hill Book Co.

——— (1993). *The 22 Immutable Laws of Marketing: Violate Them at Your Own Risk!* New York: HarperBusiness.

Richey, Terry (1994). *The Marketer's Visual Tool Kit.* New York: AMACOM.

Schwartz, Peter (1991). *The Art of the Long View: Planning for the Future in an Uncertain World.* New York: Doubleday Currency.

Sherlock, Paul (1991). *Rethinking Business-to-Business Marketing.* New York: The Free Press.

Summer, J. R. (1985). *Improve Your Marketing Techniques: A Guide for Hotel Managers and Caterers.* London: Northwood Books.

Tregoe, Benjamin B. and Zimmerman, John W. (1980). *Management Strategy.* New York: Simon and Schuster.

U.S. Government Printing Office (1995). *Directory of National Trade Associations of Businessmen.* Washington, DC: Author.

Vavra, Terry G. (1992). *Aftermarketing: How to Keep Customers for Life Through Relationship Marketing.* Homewood, IL: Business One Irwin.

Wilson, Aubrey (1992). *New Directions in Marketing: Business-to-Business Strategies for the 1990's.* Lincolnwood, IL: NTC Business Books.

Yesawich, Peter (2000). Remarks at U.C.L.A. Investment Conference, January 24, Los Angeles, CA.

Index

Page numbers followed by the letter "f" indicate figures; those followed by the letter "i" indicate illustrations.